THE
EASY-CARE
GARDEN

THE
EASY-CARE GARDEN

A COMPLETE GUIDE
TO LOW-MAINTENANCE GARDENING

STEVEN WILLIAMS

Bloomsbury Books
London

First published in Great Britain in 1991 by
Webb & Bower (Publishers) Limited

Conceived, designed and edited by Thirlstone Editions,
7-9 King Street, Exeter, Devon EX1 1BQ
Text Copyright © 1991 Steven Williams

This edition published 1993 by
Bloomsbury Books an imprint of
The Godfrey Cave Group
42 Bloomsbury Street, London WC1B 3QJ
under license from Webb & Bower Ltd.
ISBN 1-85471-182-2

Typeset in Great Britain by P&M Typesetting Ltd, Exeter, Devon
Typeset in Plantin Light
Produced by Mandarin Offset Ltd
Printed and bound in Hong Kong

Contents

INTRODUCTION

Today more and more people seek the peace and relaxation that can be found in a well-kept and attractive garden, but many of us lack the inclination, time or, for a variety of reasons, the physical capability of maintaining it. When this happens and a garden demands more work than we can comfortably manage, far from being a source of pleasure, it can become a liability and its maintenance a time-consuming chore.

But is it possible to create a beautiful and fragrant garden that can be easily managed by the busy, reluctant or handicapped gardener? It is true that if no attention at all is given to any garden, this will eventually lead to trouble. Gardens are never static, and even in the best planned and well-planted gardens isolated weeds can germinate and plants can become too tall or require attention to ensure their well-being. However, as many well-designed, low-maintenance gardens have proved, it is possible to create a garden that will largely look after itself, demanding only a fraction of the attention needed by a conventional garden. The regular maintenance needed by such a garden becomes more in the nature of a routine 'potter' than the frequent and necessary hard toil often associated with conventional gardens.

The aim of this book is to show how, by planning, by the selection of suitable plants and by the application of labour-saving techniques, a minimal-maintenance garden can be created and managed. If the suggestions outlined on the pages that follow are adopted, even the busiest, the most reluctant or the handicapped gardener will become the master of his or her garden, not its slave, free to enjoy the garden and secure in the knowledge that any task not done today can safely be left until time is available or the weather is better without the danger of the garden's becoming, in the meantime, an uncontrollable, weed-infested wilderness.

Steven Williams

Part 1

1. THE IMPORTANCE OF DESIGN

There are several general principles of garden design that are common to the planning of all types of garden. Factors such as the uses to which the garden is to be put, your present and future needs, the size, advantages and disadvantages of the site, and the style of your house and its surroundings should all be considered when deciding on any planting scheme. When planning an easy-care garden there is the additional aim of reducing the work involved. This does not mean that all other considerations must be sacrificed to achieve this end. The recent revolution in gardening practice brought about by the introduction of hardier, more disease-resistant plant strains, slow-release fertilizers, safer and more effective herbicides and the availability of mature, container-grown plants has made the old image of the minimum-maintenance garden consisting largely of concrete a

Genista lydia and *Lonicera nitida* help to break up the hard edges of concrete steps.

thing of the past. It is now perfectly possible to include many of the traditional garden features in easy-care garden designs. This offers an exciting variety of choice to the easy-care gardener, allowing the creation of an almost infinite range of attractive, minimum-maintenance gardens.

A low-maintenance garden is most easily created from a new plot, when the garden can be treated as a whole and the overall planning and planting scheme carried out in one operation. The limitations of time rarely allow this, however, and although the overall garden plan should be finalized before any work starts, there is no reason why, providing the plan is adhered to, this work cannot be spread over several years and done in order of priority.

In many cases it will be necessary to alter to a more labour-saving design an existing garden that may have become too difficult to manage or that has been inherited from a previous owner. When you are presented with a tidy, established garden, it is important to assess what you already have and

which plants and features cause the most work. This will indicate what alterations are necessary and their priority. If the garden is unfamiliar to you, it is wise to live with it for a time before undertaking any major alterations. With some replanting and replanning, it may be possible to utilize some of the existing features in an easy-care design. These features may well include mature shrubs and trees. Some shrubs can be transplanted and included in the new layout. Trees are more permanent, but before designing a garden around an existing tree it is worth checking its health.

GENERAL PRINCIPLES OF GARDEN DESIGN

A garden is an extension of your living space, and it should, therefore, be both functional and attractive. The aim of good garden design is to make the most of your garden's potential so that the demands made on it by the members of the household are met.

Thoughtful design, rather than haphazard evolution over many years, not only saves time and money in the long run, but results in a much more practical, cohesive and flowing garden, which, in turn, gives greater scope for effective planting. The shape and positioning of plants and garden features, such as the beds, borders, lawns and terraces, can alter perspective in an awkwardly shaped or small garden, soften hard lines in a rigidly geometric or boxy garden, and accent attractive features and views or, conversely, mask ugly ones.

A garden is always more effective if the design is kept simple. Concentrate on providing only a few focal points. The inclusion of many small features will give the garden an enclosed, cluttered and 'busy' feel. Two or three well-shaped borders are far more pleasing and can be more easily managed than numerous small beds. Be bold when using shape and line. Long sweeping curves rather than hard, straight edges increase the sense of flow and greatly aid perspective.

Giving the garden an overall style also gives it a feeling of unity and harmony. The selection of a particular style for the garden is a matter of personal taste, but it is important that any chosen style be in keeping with the house and its natural surroundings. If the house has a definite character – a country cottage in a rural setting, for example, or a modern building situated in a town environment – this should be reflected in the garden. Introducing an alien style of garden into an unsympathetic environment or having a mixture of styles in any one garden rarely works. Although the way a garden is laid out influences the garden's eventual style and atmosphere, this is mostly affected by the type, colour and texture of the materials used in the construction of paths, patios, garden walls, fences, raised beds and garden furniture, and by the colour, form and habit of the plants grown.

FUNCTION

Before planning a new garden or altering an existing one, list what will be wanted from the garden and the purposes it is to serve. This will give an insight into the features that should be incorporated into the design and their relative sizes and priority.

In a purely ornamental, rather than a functional, garden more space can be allotted for the cultivation of suitable easy-care plants, with less emphasis on open areas for leisure activities. Extensive planting of the larger types of ground-cover roses, for instance, can make an attractive and easily maintained alternative to a lawn or area of paving.

If the garden has to be functional as well as decorative, open spaces such as terraces, patios and lawns provide space for recreational pursuits. A larger than normal terrace or patio, preferably adjoining the house or at least as near to it as possible, should be included if a great deal of eating out or entertaining in the garden is contemplated. Carefully situated walled patios can also act as sun-traps and provide pleasant, sheltered areas for sun-bathing. Lawns provide safe, soft play areas for children, where garden swings, slides and climbing frames can be erected or a sand pit built. Wherever possible, situate children's play areas so that they are visible from the house. If there is room, make a large lawn, perhaps at the expense of the borders or flower beds, for sports and games. Such games as badminton, croquet and soft-ball tennis can be scaled down so that, if planned for, they can be played in all but the smallest of gardens.

When listing your requirements, try to anticipate any foreseeable changes in lifestyle, abilities or situation that may occur in the future and allow for them in the design. The arrival of children, for example, can make extra demands on the garden, or a retired person may require a less-labour-intensive garden in the future than can be easily managed now. With foresight and careful planning, flexibility can be designed into the garden so that it can meet the changing demands of its owners throughout the years without requiring major alteration.

Once the types of features to be included and their priorities are known a scale plan of the site can be made and space allocated for them.

THE SITE

The advantages and disadvantages of your particular site will have a direct influence on the garden's eventual layout. Factors such as the garden's size and shape, its surroundings and outlook, the fixed structures or objects on the site – storage tanks or manhole covers, for instance – and the relationship to the direction of the sun and prevailing winds cannot be changed and must be allowed for in the overall design.

Large gardens present the designer with different problems from those posed by a small area. It is often easier to create a pleasing overall design in a large garden: an awkward shape can be more easily disguised by the planting of bold, irregular features, and the choice of trees and shrubs will not be limited by their eventual size. Nevertheless, a large garden presents a greater challenge to the low-maintenance designer. Generally, the larger a garden the more attention it will demand, and more careful consideration must be given to labour-saving aspects when designing for a large garden than would be necessary for a small one.

In a small garden it will be necessary to create a feeling of space artificially and design with the purpose of enlarging the available area visually. This can be achieved by utilizing any pleasant views and adopting a planting scheme that is in sympathy with the garden's surroundings. If the centre and area of the garden immediately behind the house are kept open, the garden will be led away from the house and, even in the smallest garden, a sense of perspective achieved. The feeling of space can also be enhanced by treating the house and garden as one integral unit, so that the garden becomes an extension of the house both visually and in function. It is particularly important in a small garden, therefore, to create a style that is sympathetic to that of the house and its surroundings. If you build walls or terraces, use materials that are similar in colour and texture to those of the house.

Although gardens come in a wide range of shapes, they are most commonly rectangular or L-shaped. Such regularly shaped gardens are the easiest to plan. All that may be necessary is some softening of the hard lines along the boundary walls or fences. Being already of balanced proportions, the situation and shape of patios, lawns and beds or borders will be far simpler than in awkwardly shaped gardens, where proportion and balance will have to be created artificially by thoughtful shaping and positioning of garden features to take account of perspective and line.

In awkwardly or irregularly shaped gardens, well-placed, gently curving beds can disguise a garden's boundaries, producing an informal, flowing effect, which will be far more pleasing to the eye than if the lines follow the garden's perimeters.

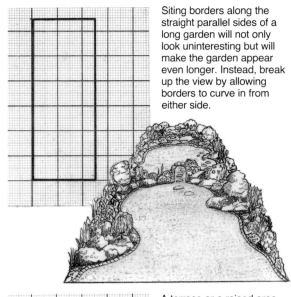

Siting borders along the straight parallel sides of a long garden will not only look uninteresting but will make the garden appear even longer. Instead, break up the view by allowing borders to curve in from either side.

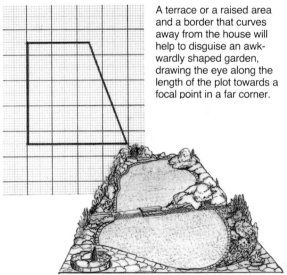

A terrace or a raised area and a border that curves away from the house will help to disguise an awk-wardly shaped garden, drawing the eye along the length of the plot towards a focal point in a far corner.

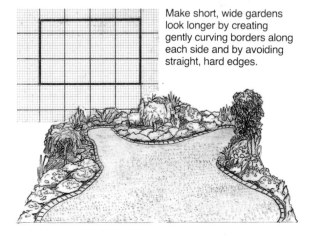

Make short, wide gardens look longer by creating gently curving borders along each side and by avoiding straight, hard edges.

The parallel sides of a long, narrow garden tend greatly to exaggerate its length. Make the side boundaries as inconspicuous as possible by choosing a low fence that will blend into the planting scheme on each side. Paling fences are ideal for this, becoming almost invisible behind clusters of shrubs or trees. Where this is not possible, disguise tall walls or high fences with suitable planting. Straight-edged side borders and long lawns tend to draw the eye along the length of the garden into the distance. To foreshorten the perspective, allow the side borders to curve into the garden at several points along their length. This will reduce the strong lengthening effect of the parallel sides. As an alternative or in addition to this, the end of the garden can be sectioned off by a low wall or by planting a sweeping line of well-positioned shrubs or trees.

If the garden is short but wide, it will be necessary to emphasize its length. Avoid any transverse features like beds or paths that cross the garden at right angles as these will dramatically foreshorten the perspective. Keep the centre of the garden open to give a feeling of space. Slanting the main axis of the garden diagonally so that an area of lawn or paving curves away to a far corner can increase the apparent length of a garden dramatically. The eye will be led along the axis to any focal points created at or near the garden's boundary or to the views beyond.

The use of colour can also greatly aid perspective in a garden. Strong, bright colours, especially bright reds, oranges and yellows, appear nearer to the eye than cooler, pastel colours, such as soft pinks, pale blues and light greens. Strong colour planted towards the end of a long garden will shorten the perspective; paler colours will visually lengthen short gardens.

Sloping sites can present a variety of difficulties to the gardener according to the direction and severity of the slope. Whenever possible, provide a flat terrace at house level. This maintains continuity between house and garden and provides a comfortable, easily accessible, sitting-out area from which the garden can be viewed. Gently sloping gardens can be planned and planted in a similar manner to level sites, bearing in mind that downward slopes have the effect of lengthening the perspective in a garden whereas rising ground foreshortens it.

In a very steeply sloping garden, ease of maintenance should be the main consideration and should greatly influence the choice of features to be included in the design. Mowing a steeply sloping lawn, for example, despite what some lawn-mower manufacturers would have us believe, is an arduous, difficult and possibly dangerous task, irrespective of which type of mower is used. Replace grass on steep slopes with non-attention-requiring ground-cover subjects, which will not only clothe the ground but will help to bind the soil together and prevent erosion. On sites that are particularly steep or difficult to reach, the whole garden can be planted in this way, the ground-covering subjects being punctuated by attractive, flowering, easily maintained shrubs such as olearias, potentillas and genistas to provide interest and to act as focal points in the garden.

Terracing several areas or all of the garden is an alternative means of dealing with a steep site, although this can involve a great deal of earth moving and is, consequently, hard work. If terracing is undertaken, try to blend the terraces and their retaining walls as naturally as possible with the rest of the garden. This can be achieved by allowing the terraces to curve and follow the contours of the land, by choosing the materials carefully and by planting suitable plants in the walls or letting plants cascade over the tops.

SCREENING

When designing any garden it is important to look beyond its boundaries. There may be a pleasing view from the house or garden that you do not wish to block; if so, you may decide to highlight this by adopting a planting scheme that leads the eye towards it. Experiment by isolating any desirable views from the house or garden by holding two books about 30cm (12in) apart in front of you and panning round, while looking between them.

On the other hand, your garden may be near to an unsightly or noisy feature such as pylons or a road, which would be best screened from view. The first reaction is often to plant a barrier along the site boundary. More effective screening can be achieved, however, by well-positioned foreground planting. Being closer to the eye, foreground planting can screen a wider area. The best way of ascertaining the optimum height and position of trees and shrubs for maximum screening effect is to employ a helper with a pole (a long fishing rod or several garden canes tied together can be used). Stand at the point in the house or garden from which you wish the unsightly feature to be hidden from view and ask your helper to stand in a direct line between you and the feature, as far away from you as the size of the garden will permit. You may find that in this position you would need a screen of such height that it would be impracticable for your garden. Have the helper walk slowly towards you

Allowed to grow informally, *Ilex* (holly) is an excellent choice of screening plant for the easy-care garden.

until the point is reached where the feature can be hidden by a screening plant of a suitable height. This method will enable you to identify possible positions for the larger shrubs and trees that should be included in your layout for screening purposes. Many gardeners only consider evergreens and conifers when screening against eyesores or noise. Well-grown, deciduous trees with fine twigs will be just as effective a screen against sound as evergreens and are preferable to evergreens in windy districts.

The immovable eyesores that so often have to be accommodated in domestic gardens – manhole covers, oil storage tanks, coal bunkers or sheds, for example – can also be camouflaged or screened from view. An inconveniently situated manhole cover is best disguised by incorporating it into a large bed or by creating around it a small, irregular bed of low-growing, spreading plants, such as *Cotoneaster horizontalis*, euonymus or *Thymus serpyllum*. Tubs can be used where this is not possible, but it is not wise to place a single tub directly on top of a manhole cover as this, far from disguising it, actually draws attention to it. Use a collection of

One of the easiest ways of working out the optimum height of a screening plant requires nothing more complicated than a pole made from a fishing rod or garden canes. Sit or stand in the house at the point from which the eyesore is most often seen and ask a friend to hold the pole and to stand in the garden between you and the object to be obscured. The nearer your friend is to you and the house, the lower the screen that will be required.

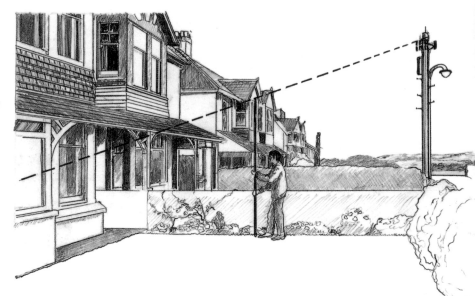

tubs with, if possible, some extra planting around them. If a single tub has to be used, it should be the same size and shape as the cover.

If the larger unattractive structures, such as oil-storage tanks or coal bunkers, are painted a dark colour, they can appear almost invisible in the dappled shade cast by carefully positioned tall plants grown nearby. Alternatively, these structures can be screened from view by the careful siting of shrubs or by the erection of a trellis supporting a slow-growing climber such as *Hedera helix* 'Buttercup'. The temptation to choose rapidly growing plants for screening purposes should be avoided; although they make an effective screen more quickly, they continue to grow and, from then on, may require regular attention to keep them under control.

ASPECT

When you apportion space for beds, borders, patios, terraces and other garden features, you should take the garden's aspect into account as this can have a decisive influence on their positions and on the garden's eventual overall layout. Identify which parts of the garden face north, south, east and west and endeavour to site the main features of the garden – patios, rose beds, herbaceous borders and so on – in the sunniest positions to exploit good aspects to the full. In the northern hemisphere a south-facing wall, fence or hedge can be of great value for growing plants, especially those of doubtful hardiness, and such an asset should not be wasted. Shady, northerly aspects, or those exposed to strong, cold winds, on the other hand, present a harsher environment for plants, and the choice of suitable subjects will be more limited.

In general, southwest- and southeast-facing aspects provide good environments for plants, but you must take care not to plan features that include early flowering plants or early soft fruit in a southeasterly aspect, especially if your garden is prone to late spring frosts. The blooms, buds, blossom or fruitlets of otherwise hardy plants can be severely damaged by the rapid and sudden thawing of frost when exposed to the early morning sun.

REDUCING WORK BY DESIGN

The more features there are in your garden, the more attention your garden will require. Before deciding on a layout, therefore, it is important to make a realistic assessment of the time that you wish to devote to, or that will be available for, tending the garden. Even with the best intentions, it is no good being over ambitious and creating a too complex design in the hope that the time for its management will somehow be found in the future. This will certainly lead to the garden becoming a burden and eventually getting out of control. When and how often this time for gardening is going to be available must also be considered, as this can have a direct influence on the choice of features to be included in the design. If a few hours can be managed on a regular weekly basis, those features that require small but frequent amounts of attention, such as a lawn, can be safely included. If, however, only a few weeks during the year are available, as would be the case with the gardens of holiday homes, the choice of features will be more limited.

When you are altering an existing garden, you may, from previous experience, already have an idea of which features demand the most attention.

These can be either eliminated altogether or reduced in number and size and replaced with more labour-efficient features.

HARD SURFACES

Hard surfaces demand the least attention and increasing their size in relation to planted areas can considerably reduce the amount of work involved in maintaining the garden. A large terrace created at the back of the house, for example, is both functional and attractive, as well as labour saving, and it can provide an ideal environment and setting for container-grown plants such as miniature roses or small shrubs.

Garden paths should be planned so that they provide direct access to the areas of the garden where the main activities or work take place. They should also be of sufficient width to allow the easy movement of garden implements, such as loaded wheelbarrows and mowers, without their becomimg entangled in the bordering plants. Sharp bends or corners in paths should be avoided as they not only make access difficult but can create areas that are difficult to plant and so become infested with weeds. Wherever possible keep paths straight. If curves are needed for going around an object or for interest, keep them gentle. Where changes of level make steps necessary, make these wide and shallow to allow planks to be used to facilitate the transport of wheeled garden equipment. Alternatively, sloping ramps can be built at the side of the steps.

If garden paths are subjected to a great deal of traffic or to general hard wear and tear, they should be covered with a suitable hard surface such as paving. This is particularly important for paths that lead around the house as this will provide easy, safe and dry access between the house and garden.

Carefully sited garden paths can also act as a barrier across which some of the more vigorous· spreading plants cannot transgress, and they can, therefore, be used to confine plants such as the more rampant ground coverers to their allotted spaces, effectively preventing their spread to, and subsequent invasion of, other planted areas.

Large expanses of hard surfaces, especially in big gardens, can look monotonous and give the garden a rather forbidding appearance. This can be overcome by using a variety of surfacing materials for different areas and functions throughout the garden. In general, hard surfaces close to the house are best covered with more formal surfacing materials such as paving stones or tiles, while those areas further away can be covered with materials like stone chippings or gravel. The difference in texture gives added interest and provides a range of decorative effects. When mixing materials, however, choose with care. It is easier to create a more natural effect if the colours of the different materials complement or harmonize well with each other and are sympathetic with those of the house and surroundings. Wet the materials before buying and examine the resulting colour change. Contrasting colours can be used to give a special effect, but too rich a mix can draw attention away from, or clash with, nearby planting or other garden features.

The effect of large areas of paving can be softened by introducing plants into the hard surface itself. Remove a paving stone or leave a gap between stones, fill the space with soil and plant with clump- or mound-forming plants such as *Dianthus gratianopolitanus*, *Phlox subulata* or *Thymus serpyllum*.

HARD SURFACING MATERIALS

As hard surfaces are the most permanent and expensive features of the garden, it is important that the right kind of material is chosen at the outset. There is a bewildering range available, and the choice will depend on the style of garden you wish to create, the size of area to be paved, the durability required of the material and the use to which it is to be put, the ease with which it can be laid and, of course, its cost.

When choosing paving units, such as stones, tiles or cobbles, make sure that the unit size fits well with, and is in proportion to, the size and shape of the area to be covered. Large paving units can look out of place in small areas, while small ones give a fussy look to a large space. Bricks, however, seem to suit any size of area. Keep the shape of patios and terraces simple, and choose a unit that will fit in well with the overall size and shape so that you do not have to cut and tailor slabs. Not only is this difficult but some of the cheaper materials tend to crumble when cut.

Paving

Formally cut, natural stone, such as York stone, is an ideal choice of surfacing material for more formal areas of the garden. It is relatively easy to lay, attractive and hard wearing, but it is expensive and can be difficult to obtain. Nevertheless, it should last a lifetime and is a great asset to any garden. Irregularly cut natural stone, suitable for crazy-paving, is a cheaper alternative but is more difficult to lay. Even cheaper are manufactured, simulated-stone paving slabs, which, being of regular size and thickness, are very easy to lay. These are available in a range of colours, shapes, sizes and textures. Smooth paving should be chosen for seating areas or terraces where you want to stand tables and chairs.

Textured or rough stone paving provides a better non-slip surface for sloping paths or for damp, shady situations where algae or frost can make surfaces slippery.

Tiles

Tiles are a useful and cheaper alternative to cut stone or paving for more formal hard areas of the garden. As there is a wide range of materials, colours and sizes, tiles should be chosen with particular care. Brightly coloured or patterned tiles may be quite appealing in the showroom, but they can look garish and clash with plants when laid in the garden. The best and most natural effect is often achieved by using baked clay tiles. If frost is a problem in your area, check that the tiles are frost-proof before purchasing, otherwise they may crack in icy weather. As most tiles will need to be grouted, the choice of a suitable grouting material is also important as this will contribute to the overall effect. A material that is a similar colour to, or that harmonizes well with, the tiles will be most satisfactory.

Bricks

As many houses are predominantly built of brick, using bricks of a similar colour and type for walls and hard surfaces in the garden is an ideal way of achieving continuity between the two. Although old or left-over building bricks are cheap and easy to obtain, their use cannot be recommended for covering any areas that are subject to hard wear, as eventually they will flake and become uneven. A weathered effect may be desirable in a period garden, but if a more practical, longer lasting brick surface is required, brick pavers should be used. These are more intensely fired during manufacture and are harder wearing and easier to lay than walling bricks, but they are more expensive. Bricks can be laid in a variety of patterns to provide added interest to the surface, but take care not to cover too large an area with too intricate a pattern. The richness of colour and the quantity of elements used can become overpowering. Grout between bricks with cement or mortar to prevent weeds growing.

Concrete

Poured concrete is a quick and cheap way of making a permanent hard surface. However, mixing and laying it is often an arduous task, although hiring a cement mixer or buying ready-mixed concrete can reduce the work involved. As large, unrelieved

Brick pavers can be laid in a variety of patterns to provide hard-wearing and attractive paths, which mellow with time and blend with most types of house.

areas of grey concrete can have a rather austere appearance, make concrete more attractive by adding to the mix one of the special weatherproof colourants that are now available. A textured, non-slip surface can be produced by brushing the surface of the concrete before it has dried.

Granite setts

Granite setts are available in brick or half-brick sizes, and they will make an extremely hard-wearing, if expensive, surfacing material. Their use should be considered with care, however, as grey granite is alien to many situations and will look out of place in most gardens. Where granite is unsuitable or a more refined effect is desired, concrete paving setts may be a useful substitute. Both surfaces can be difficult to walk on comfortably and are unsuitable for furniture or for children's play areas.

Cobbles

These rounded, pebble-like stones can be either laid loose or packed tightly together and set into concrete. Cobbles are cheap, they blend in well with planting, and they provide an excellent background for flowers and foliage. When individual stones are laid end on, they can be difficult to walk on, and they are, therefore, useful for filling in awkward areas or corners that would not otherwise be walked on. Smaller grade cobbles laid with the flatter sides uppermost and set into concrete make interesting paths.

Gravel and stone chippings

Cheap and easy to lay, gravel and stone chippings blend well with planting and are extremely easy on the eye. They give a far more informal and relaxed feel to the garden than some of the 'harder' surfacing materials. Large areas of gravel can be used where it is necessary to restrict planting to a minimum for extreme ease of maintenance or to create a scree garden, a type of garden that was popular in the 19th century and that is again becoming fashionable. To create a scree garden, dig over and level the ground, clear it of weeds and enrich the soil with fertilizer. Cover the whole area with heavy-duty black plastic sheeting. Make planting holes in the topsoil through the plastic in which plants can be grown. The plastic should then covered with a thick layer of gravel, shingle or stone chippings. Smaller gravelled areas of the garden can be treated in this way, or gravel can be spread on to a hard-core base. A retaining edge is necessary for paths to stop the gravel spreading about, and, until the gravel becomes well compacted, some weed

control will be required. However, once bedded down, gravel surfaces require little or no maintenance. There are many types, grades and colours of gravel, beach shingle and chipped stone available, and the choice will depend on availability, the surroundings and the type of materials already present in the garden. If natural stone paving has been used elsewhere in the garden, for example, it is particularly effective if chippings from the same type of stone are used for the less formal areas. This gives an interesting variety of texture while maintaining continuity of colour and material.

Coarse tree bark

Pulverized bark, often used as a mulching material, can also make a useful 'loose' surfacing material. It can be an unusual alternative to gravel, especially in a woodland setting, where it blends in well and gives a very natural effect. Such surfaces are easy to lay and need little maintenance except an occasional 'topping up' from time to time. Pulverized bark can also be used to create temporary paths for clean and dry access to all parts of the garden.

Laid to a depth of 5–7.5cm (2–3in), coarse tree bark is useful both as a weed suppressant and as an informal path.

Timber

Wood is an unusual surfacing material, which can be used for paths or terraces. Paths of stepping 'stones' made from cut logs can look very attractive, particularly when set into a coarse gravel surface. Wooden decking can be a visually pleasing alternative to stone for the construction of terraces, especially in the smaller gardens of modern homes where a raised masonry terrace would be too dominant. As a surface material, however, timber does have disadvantages: in areas of high rainfall and during long, damp winters it needs to be treated regularly with preservative and given a non-slip finish as it is prone to rot and can become slippery with algae and moss.

LAWNS

Despite their reputation for being labour intensive, lawns can be an attractive, functional and efficient way of covering large areas of the garden. And where cost is a consideration, they may be the only practical choice, especially if the garden is large. If well planned, a utility-grade lawn (see Chapter 6) can require less attention per unit area than either flower or shrub borders and will be a perfect foil for showing off other plants in the garden to their best advantage. Therefore, as long as your garden is relatively level and the regular weekly mowing required during the late spring and summer is not a problem because of physical incapacity or lack of time, laying down the greater part of the garden to lawn should be considered, for the larger the area of lawn, the less space will remain for other, often more costly and labour-intensive, garden features.

Much lawn maintenance can be eliminated or, at least, considerably reduced by thoughtful planning. Many garden lawns are allowed to run right up to flower beds, and while this may look attractive, it does create a great deal of work. The plants at the front of the border will need supporting or trimming back from time to time, otherwise mowing will be made difficult and bare patches will appear on the grass if plants are allowed to encroach or flop on to it. The lawn edges will also require frequent trimming by hand, a time-consuming and laborious task, which, if neglected, makes the whole lawn look untidy. There is also the ever-present danger that the grass will spread into the flower beds during any prolonged period of neglect. Unless the lawn is bounded by paths or paved areas, surround it with paving, edging stones or a double row of bricks to a width of 30–45cm (12–18in). Set these a little below the level of the lawn so that the mower blades are not damaged. This eliminates the need to edge and trim the lawn by hand as the mower can run on the paving beyond the lawn's boundary, allows space for any encroaching border plants and creates a containing barrier between the lawn and flower bed.

As mowing is the single most frequent task involved in maintaining the lawn, it should be made as easy as possible. Mowing with an efficient machine is not in itself a particularly arduous task – as a general guide, 84 sq m (100 sq yd) of lawn will take an average of six minutes when using a mower with a cutting width of 30cm (12in). What takes the time is manoeuvring the machine past shrubs and under trees and through narrow winding paths or into sharply angled corners. When planning a lawn, therefore, it is important to shape it to ease mowing. Use gently curved or rounded corners rather than right angles, and do not include awkwardly shaped island beds in the lawn. Always allow sufficient space for turning the mower, and avoid grassing over any inaccessible or steeply sloping areas of the garden to which transporting a heavy machine, as well as mowing, will be difficult.

If time does not permit very frequent mowing, it may be worth considering a meadow lawn, a type of lawn that is particularly suitable for informal or large gardens in rural settings. Meadow lawns require little attention as most of the grass is left rough, needing only occasional topping – to a height of about 10cm (4in) – once or twice a year with a rotary mower or hired power-scythe. Bulbs and other plants, especially wild flowers, should be naturalized in the long grass to provide interest and colour. If a small area of short grass is maintained near the house and one or two mown, winding paths lead off through the meadow lawn, the contrast between the rough and mown grass can give a pleasing effect.

A traditional lawn may be easily converted into a meadow lawn. Spike the lawn well after cutting and mix a selection of wild flower seed with an equal volume of damp sand. Broadcast this mixture over the lawn surface and rake in hard. The seeds will germinate and when mature, the more vigorous plants will seed themselves and colonize the area.

GROUND COVER

The use of ground-cover plants is now becoming well known, and they are increasingly used for providing a weed-suppressing covering for banks and borders or beneath trees and shrubs. However, as most ground-cover subjects require only the minimum of attention, they can also be used as a low-maintenance surface covering for large areas of the garden. These areas then become attractive and colourful features in their own right. Such large-

Variegated ivy has been used here as a colourful and effective ground-cover subject in a shrub border.

scale planting of ground cover can, therefore, be used as a labour-saving alternative surface treatment in situations where large areas of hard surfaces or lawns are unsuitable.

BOUNDARIES

It is important to define the boundary of your garden not only to mark out the legal confines of your land but also to provide privacy, to act as a windbreak or just to provide an attractive back-ground for planting. Usually, some sort of boundary barrier will already exist around the plot. If you are lucky, this may be of a suitable type –

easily maintained informal hedges of slow-growing shrubs or attractively built stone walls are ideal surrounds for an easy-care garden. However, if the boundary barriers are found to be unsuitable, a decision will have to be taken about altering them.

If the established barrier is simply unattractive, as are some forms of fencing or walls built of new bricks or blocks, it can be easily disguised by screening with evergreen trees or shrubs or by climbers supported on a trellis. This will also have the effect of softening or obscuring the rigid boundary lines, which will be of benefit to many garden designs.

Changing a barrier that demands a great deal of maintenance to one that is less labour intensive needs more careful consideration, as the work involved in the alteration can itself often be time consuming and costly.

HEDGES

The first reaction is often to replace all the boundary hedges with walls or fences to eliminate the daunting prospect of endless trimming. If time or physical capability is very limited or if there is a need for complete privacy, this may well be the best solution. However, hedges do have advantages over walls and fences: they offer better protection against wind than do solid barriers, filtering the wind rather than blocking or redirecting it, which can produce strong, plant-damaging air turbulence in other parts of the garden. And where there are large areas of paving, a living boundary can act as a counter-balance and enhance the beauty of the garden.

Formal hedges

One of the greatest problems confronting the easy-care gardener is to inherit a garden already bounded by well-grown, formal hedges, of the type so beloved of keen gardeners. You may well be reluctant to lose them, but, left unclipped, such hedges will soon grow into unattractive shapes and become unsightly. They can, however, be re-modelled by selective hard pruning to make their maintenance less arduous. Prune back most of the stems to ground level, leaving only two or three of the main ones. The shrubs will recover and thicken into a pleasing shape. They will then need only occasional clipping to keep them tidy. Alternatively, if the hedge is of a type that would still demand too much attention after this treatment – a formal hedge of privet, for example – it is best replaced. Privet deserves a special mention. It is commonly used for hedging in built-up areas because it is tolerant of pollution and is evergreen. However, it does demand clipping several times a year, which is a tiring task even with an electric hedge trimmer, and it must also be cut back hard to the old wood from time to time to keep it within bounds. Such a job requires the use of secateurs or even a saw, which is not only time consuming but may be beyond the capability of gardeners with weak hands and arms.

Completely removing an unsuitable formal hedge and replacing it with a more manageable one or with a wall or fence is extremely hard work and very costly. However, there is an easier, if slow, method of transforming an unsuitable formal hedge into a more suitable one. Provided your soil is not a heavy clay, young seedlings of the common holly (*Ilex aquifolium*) or its varieties can be planted in gaps at the base of the existing hedge. If necessary, create suitable gaps by cutting back the plants to form arches 45cm (18in) wide and 60cm (2ft) high. As the holly seedlings grow, more and more of the existing hedge can be cut back, until eventually the old hedging plants can be removed. The common holly is particularly useful for this purpose as it readily sets fruit, providing a continual source of seedlings for planting in further gaps, and, when fully grown, it makes an attractive hedge that needs only one light clip a year.

Informal hedges

Informal hedges are an ideal choice for the easy-care gardener in situations where a living boundary as opposed to a wall or fence is required. Although a hedge will require more attention than a non-living boundary, informal hedges require much less attention than do formal ones. While formal hedges are regularly clipped so that the individuality of each shrub or tree is lost, trees and shrubs making up an informal hedge are allowed to grow and take on their natural shapes so that the outline of each plant is preserved. Informal hedges need no clipping as such, therefore, and if shrubs that need little or no pruning are selected, the hedge will be comparatively easy to manage.

Informal hedges should be of a height and spread appropriate for their purpose and for the size of the garden, and the hedging plants should be chosen accordingly. Avoid the temptation of planting rapidly growing shrubs to make an effective barrier more quickly; unless they are cut back regularly, these will soon get out of hand and become untidy or overhang or block pathways, making access difficult. In gardens where a living barrier is preferred but it is essential to provide privacy or screening quickly, rapidly growing shrubs should be interplanted with slower growing subjects. This will produce a quick barrier in the short term, until the slower growing shrubs grow taller and mature, when the more rapidly growing subjects should be removed.

WALLS

Boundary walls of brick or stone tend to give the garden a more formal and secure feel than do either fences or hedges. Although expensive to build, walls are virtually maintenance free and should last a lifetime. As with any material introduced into the garden, however, care must be taken in selecting a style and type of walling material that harmonizes well with its surroundings and is suitable for the purpose intended.

Natural stone walls

There is an almost infinite variety of types of natural

stone available for walling purposes. Most stone is available rough cut (in irregular shapes and sizes), squared (shaped into more regular blocks) or ashlar (smoothly finished, squared blocks). Rough-cut stones are laid in a random fashion, while the more regularly cut stones are laid in courses. Stone walls can be built either with or without mortar. Mortared random walls are more stable than dry stone walls (those without mortar), and they therefore not only have a longer life but are also easier to build.

Dry stone construction is not recommended for amateurs if the wall is to exceed 90cm (3ft) in height. Dry stone walling is a skill, which can be difficult for the novice to acquire, and it takes a great deal of time and effort. It is far easier to create the effect of a dry stone wall by carefully wiping out the mortar from the visible joints of a conventionally built, mortared wall.

Natural stone walls look best in rural settings, especially when local stone is used, and they are seldom used in urban gardens except where the setting is particularly traditional.

Brick

Brick is a versatile, easily maintained and readily obtainable walling material. Unlike natural stone, which imposes a particular style on a garden, brick is available in a wide range of shapes, sizes, textures and colours, and it is, therefore, flexible in character and can be used in a wide variety of settings, urban and rural, formal and informal. The appearance of brick walls can be further enhanced by colouring the mortar, combining other materials such as slate with the bricks or topping low walls with fencing.

Unless you have a readily available, cheap supply, bricks can be at least as expensive as natural stone. To ensure stability, a single brick wall over 90cm (3ft) in height must be reinforced with buttresses built into it at intervals of at least 3.6m (12ft). Taller walls, over 1.3m (4ft 6in), should be of double thickness, and if they are over 1.8m (6ft) the walls will require additional strengthening. To reduce cost and the necessity of buttressing a single wall, sections of it can be staggered or overlapped, so that there are no long straight runs, the bonded overlapping corners strengthening the wall.

An alternative is to reduce costs by using single-thickness, open brickwork, the gaps providing a honeycombed effect. Although less private than solid walls, they allow light and air to pass through, filtering the wind, rather than redirecting it, and they have a lighter, less dominating appearance than do solid walls.

Concrete blocks

Concrete blocks are a cheap and easy alternative to natural stone or brick, being both durable and maintenance free. However, concrete 'breeze' blocks, commonly used for the cavity walls of buildings, although strong and easy to lay, are rather too unattractive for garden use. Their appearance can be improved by rendering the surface or by erecting a trellis on which climbing plants can be grown, but it is far better to choose blocks with an ornamental finish or those made from reconstituted stone. Tinted blocks weather into mellow colours, whereas ordinary grey concrete can take on a rather 'dirty' appearance as it ages.

Concrete screen blocks, perforated with a variety of traditional or geometric patterns, make useful screens that provide privacy but allow air to circulate. In addition, when they are used in combinaton with solid blocks, pierced blocks can lighten the otherwise heavy effect of a completely solid wall.

As concrete blocks cannot be cut, it will be necessary to make the length of wall a multiple of the block size used. Half-blocks must be specially purchased and, if blocks are laid in alternate courses, the number of half-blocks required must be calculated at the time of purchase. If you are using coloured or textured blocks, it is particularly important to buy all you need at the same time, as the colour or finish of the blocks can vary slightly from batch to batch.

FENCES

Fences are a much cheaper alternative to walls but are less durable, require more maintenance and cannot be expected to last as long. There are many types available. Solid fences offer the most privacy, but open-work types, such as spaced board, louvred or picket fencing, can look more decorative, especially in a small garden. Open-work fences also allow greater air circulation around plants and some can provide a useful frame for climbing plants.

Any fence made of timber, especially softwood, must be painted or treated with preservative if it is to withstand many years of exposure to the elements. Generally it is the supporting posts that are most prone to decay. Although expensive, treated hardwood posts give much longer trouble-free service than softwood ones. But any type of post that is set directly into the earth will rot relatively quickly. This can be overcome by using metal post-holders driven well into the ground. These keep the wood out of contact with the earth, so reducing the likelihood of rot, and they also make the eventual replacement of any rotten posts much easier. Some metal post holders are even adjustable, which makes the correct positioning of the posts, which is critical, much easier to achieve.

Unless the soil is particularly soft or the fence is to be higher than 1.5m (5ft), metal post holders can be hammered directly into the soil. For taller fences or on soft soils, it is best to set the posts in concrete, and special sockets are available for this purpose.

Panel fencing has become the most popular type in recent years. It is attractive and the easiest kind of fence to erect. Panels come in different types, with overlapping horizontal, vertical or diagonal strips. Panels are usually supplied in 1.8m (6ft) lengths and rise in 30cm (12in) increments from 60cm (2ft) to 1.8m (6ft) in height. Generally, unless lack of privacy is a particular problem, fences should be kept as low as possible, especially in a small garden, to avoid creating a boxy effect. If a tall panel fence is required, the dominating effect can be lessened by selecting shorter than necessary panels and topping these with one or two 30cm (12in) high trellising panels.

When erecting panel fencing, never put all the posts in first hoping to fit the panels later. Some posts will, inevitably, be a fraction out of position and you will either have to move other posts or, which is even more difficult, alter the size of the

Carefully selected trees and shrubs require little attention yet form an attractive screen. Bear in mind the ultimate height of the plants you select so that the mature border is of pleasing proportions.

Perforated concrete blocks make useful screens, affording privacy but at the same time avoiding the heavy effect of completely solid walls.

panels. Drive the first spike into the corner of your boundary line. The post can then be simply slotted into the socket and tightened up with a spanner. Once the post is firmly in position, offer up the panel, adjusting the height by blocking it underneath with bricks or blocks of wood. The bottom of the panel should not be in contact with the soil. Use a spirit level to ensure that the level is correct, then secure the panel to the post. Special fixing brackets, which are screwed, first to the post and then to the panel, are effective and simple to use, and there is no risk of splitting the wood with nails. Leave the panel supported, drive the next spike in position, slot in the post and attach it to the panel. The rest of the job is simple repetition.

If you are using the special concreting sockets, it is best to fix the posts into the sockets first. Dig holes at the approximate distances necessary and insert the post and socket. Fix the panel to the post to make sure of the spacing before concreting it in. Finally fit the wooden or metal caps to the top of the posts. This will prevent water from seeping into the end grain, which may cause rotting.

2. THE IMPORTANCE OF PLANT CHOICE

The correct selection of plants for an easy-care garden is all important. Good design, labour-saving techniques and mechanical aids can all reduce work, of course, but the correct choice of easy-care plants can actually help the gardener to keep the garden neat and weed free. This is achieved not only by selecting easily grown plants that require the minimum of routine maintenance such as staking and pruning, but also by selecting those plants that can compete successfully with weeds, inhibiting their germination and development.

Often recommended as the easiest plants to grow are hardy annuals. Seeds can be sown directly into the soil, and the resulting plants need little aftercare. However, annuals are only temporary residents in a garden, germinating, flowering and dying in the same year. Keen gardeners often have ambitious bedding schemes for annuals, raising from seed and planting out in feature beds a large variety of annual species each year. As the flowering period of these plants is usually short, the early-flowering annuals need to be replaced with later-flowering types to maintain colour throughout a season. This is obviously a very labour-intensive method of gardening, requiring frequent disturbance of the soil, which can allow weeds to gain a foothold. Unless it is necessary to provide temporary colour quickly, planting schemes that involve the raising and planting out of numerous annuals are best left to the enthusiastic gardener.

Selected hardy annuals
The following hardy annuals are easily grown and can be used where quick, temporary colour is required: *Anchusa capensis*; *Calendula officinalis* (pot marigold); *Eschscholzia caespitosa*; *Limnanthes douglasii* (poached-egg plant, meadow foam); *Malcolmia maritima* (virginia stock); *Nigella damascena* (love-in-a-mist); *Tropaeolum majus* (garden nasturtium, Indian cress).

Perennials are plants that grow for more than two years, eliminating the need to buy afresh each year or to spend time raising and tending new plants. Perennials include trees, shrubs, sub-shrubs, ever-greens and herbaceous plants. Herbaceous perennials differ from the other types of perennial in that their top-growth dies down in winter leaving a living, but dormant, rootstock, from which new growth is produced in spring. In recent years much has been made of the labour-saving advantages of growing trees and shrubs in place of herbaceous plants. However, if herbaceous plants are carefully selected and are well suited to the soil and situation in which they are grown, they demand little more attention than most shrubs, offering the gardener a range of colour and form that shrubs and trees alone cannot provide.

As all perennials are more or less permanent residents in the garden, they should be selected with particular care. A great deal of unnecessary work in gardens is created because the plants selected are unsuitable for the situation or purpose for which they are grown.

First, consider the growing conditions in your garden. Although most plants can be made to grow in a wide range of soil types and climatic conditions, few will flourish if they do not receive the growing medium and conditions they prefer. While the easy-care gardener does not aim to produce prize-winning blooms, a plant's health is still of prime importance. Attempts to grow plants that are wholly unsuited to the conditions found in the garden – acid soil-loving heathers in a soil with a high lime content, for example, or warmth-loving plants in too cool a climate or in a position exposed to cold winds – will result in poorly growing, unhealthy plants. Such plants, as they struggle to exist, will be unable to compete with plants that are better suited to the prevailing conditions, and they will be defenceless against weed invasion. Even though it is possible to overcome difficulties of soil type by providing isolated pockets of suitable soil for favourite plants that you may wish to grow, overstocking with such plants should be avoided. In the long term, this practice is rarely successful, involving additional and unnecessary work combined with an increased risk of invasion by weeds or other garden plants. It is far better for the gardener

Find out what kind of soil you have by collecting a sample from about 5cm (2in) down.

to cooperate with nature than to spend time fighting it and to accept the limitations of plant choice that are imposed by the soil and climatic conditions prevailing in the garden he or she owns.

KNOWING YOUR SOIL

In many cases you will already know the soil type of your garden or will be able to deduce it from the appearance and 'feel' of the soil or the species of plants already growing successfully on it. However, if you are in any doubt, it is a simple matter to find the exact physical and chemical nature of the soil.

A mechanical analysis of the soil will give you a good insight into its physical character. Take samples at a depth of 5cm (2in) from various areas of the garden. Put these through a sieve and put a small handful of the sifted mixture into a large jar, add water until three-quarters full and mix gently, taking care not to break up any lumps there may be. Leave the jar undisturbed for 24 hours, during which time the constituents of the soil will separate into layers of stones, sand, clay and organic materials. The heavier, coarser particles will settle quickly to the bottom, the lighter, finer particles settling more slowly. Coarse organic material will float on the water, while the finer, organic particles will be left as a dark residue on top of the sand and clays.

If no organic material is present, the soil will benefit from the addition of extra organic matter such as peat or compost. If the water above the

Plants suited to clay soils
Ajuga; *Alchemilla*; *Aster*; *Astilbe*; *Aucuba japonica* (shrub); *Berberis* species (shrubs); *Bergenia*; *Brunnera*; *Campanula*; *Chaenomeles*; *Choisya ternata* (shrub); *Clematis*; *Cotoneaster* species (shrubs); *Cytisus* (shrub); *Epimedium*; *Erigeron*; *Euonymus*; *Euphorbia amygdaloides* var. *robbiae*; *Genista*; *Geranium*; *Hedera*; *Hemerocallis*; *Hosta*; *Hypericum*; *Lamium*; *Lonicera*; *Lysimachia*; *Mahonia* species; *Nepeta*; *Polygonum*; *Potentilla*; *Prunus*; *Pulmonaria*; Roses; *Rudbeckia*; *Salix*; *Salvia*; *Saxifraga* × *urbium*; *Senecio*; *Skimmia japonica* (shrub); *Solidago*; *Viburnum* (shrub); *Vinca* species; *Waldsteinia* species.

sediment is clear this shows that the soil is light and free-draining. Cloudy water shows that the soil is clayey; clay soil is often acid, badly aerated and poorly draining.

A chemical analysis will give precise information about the chemical properties of the soil. There are many soil testing kits on the market, and these are simple and quite easy to use. They contain either indicator papers or liquids that change colour depending on the pH level (acidity or alkalinity) of the soil. Some can also measure the amounts of plant nutrients present. Soil samples are taken, moistened and an indicator paper dipped in, or the soil sample is mixed directly with indicator liquids. The changed colour of the paper or liquid can be

Plants requiring an acid (lime-free) soil
Azalea; *Calluna*; *Erica*; *Gaultheria*; *Pernettya*; *Rhododendron*.

Plants for alkaline or chalky soils (will also grow well on any fertile soil)
Acanthus; *Acer*; *Achillea*; *Aethionema*; *Alchemilla*; *Anaphalis*; *Anenome*; *Aster*; *Astilbe*; *Aucuba*; *Berberis*; *Bergenia*; *Brunnera*; *Campanula*; *Cistus*; *Clematis*; *Cornus alba*; *Cotoneaster*; *Crataegus*; *Crocosmia*; *Dianthus*; *Dicentra*; *Echinops*; *Elaeagnus*; *Epimedium*; *Erigeron*; *Euonymus*; *Euphorbia*; *Galanthus*; *Genista*; *Geranium*; *Geum*; *Hebe*; *Hedera*; *Helleborus*; *Hemerocallis*; *Hypericum*; *Ilex*; *Juniperus*; *Lavandula*; *Lonicera*; *Lupinus*; *Mahonia*; *Nepeta*; *Olearia*; *Paeonia*; *Philadelphus*; *Phlox*; *Polygonum*; *Potentilla*; *Prunus*; *Pulmonaria*; *Pyracantha*; *Rudbeckia*; *Salvia*; *Sedum*; *Senecio*; *Solidago*; *Stachys*; *Syringa*; *Thymus*; *Tulipa*; *Vinca*; *Weigela*.

A raised bed can be filled with lime-free or with alkaline soil if you want to grow varieties that will not thrive in the rest of your garden.

compared with a printed colour scale and the pH value read off. The neutral point, at which the soil is neither acid nor alkaline, is 7. The lower the pH the more acid is the soil. A soil with a pH value of 6 is ten times more acid than neutral soil; a soil with a pH of 5 is a hundred times more acid and so on. Generally, the most acid, peaty soils have a pH of 3. A pH value higher than 7 indicates an alkaline soil (although it is rare to find alkaline soils in areas of moderate rainfall with a pH higher than 8). The use of a testing kit is highly recommended if the nature of the soil is unknown. Doing this simple test can save a great deal of time, disappointment, work and expense, especially if you are contemplating the purchase of any lime-hating plants to include in your planting scheme.

Plants for very moist soils

Ajuga; *Astilbe*; *Brunnera*; *Crataegus*; *Hosta*; *Lysimachia*; *Polygonum bistorta*; *Salix*; *Viburnum opulus*.

CHOOSING PLANTS FOR CLIMATE AND ASPECT

Once you have found the characteristics of the soil, you can begin to make a selection from those plants that are known to grow well on your type of soil. When making these choices, further consideration must be given to whether the plant is suitable for the prevailing climatic conditions of the district and for the situation in the garden in which it is to be grown.

Hardy plants can usually survive all but the most severe of winter conditions. Half- or semi-hardy plants are more tender and can be divided into two categories: those plants that are completely frost-tender and can be grown only during the summer – runner beans, for example – and those shrubs and herbaceous perennials that will survive only mild winter conditions. In cold climates the amount of frost and wind to which plants are exposed during the winter can vary greatly within even the smallest of gardens depending on the plants' immediate surroundings. Walls, over-hanging branches of trees and the close proximity of other plants, as well as providing shelter from cold winds, can prevent the heat in the soil, built up during the day, from escaping into the atmosphere at night. A plant grown against a south-facing wall, for example, can benefit from an increased winter temperature of up to 3°C (5°F). These sheltered pockets of warmer air and soil can offer protection from the worst of the early winter or late spring frosts, which are often the most damaging to semi-hardy plants. Although it is always better to err on the side of caution, these temperature differences can, if carefully exploited, allow the successful cultivation of some semi-hardy plants in what would otherwise be too cold a climate.

Although all green plants require light to live, their individual requirements vary. Many plants need an unshaded, sunny position for optimum growth. Growing these sun-loving plants in shady situations can result in poorly growing, unattractive and less compact, often straggly, plants. This weaker growth can cause an otherwise robust plant to require additional staking to keep it upright. Select suitable shade-loving or, at least, shade-tolerant plants for those areas of the garden that are in more or less permanent shadow or for growing under trees and shrubs.

CHOOSING PLANTS FOR EASY MAINTENANCE

Easy maintenance will depend on the characteristics of the trees, shrubs and perennials that are to be included in the planting scheme. Stocking the garden with a high proportion of plants that do not require any regular pruning, lifting and dividing, staking, frequent spraying against pests and diseases, or checking to deter them from invading their neighbours' space will greatly reduce the amount of work necessary in a garden. Selecting evergreen subjects is also an important consideration, particularly when choosing trees and shrubs or ground-cover plants. Not only do evergreens provide foliage interest all year round, but evergreen trees and shrubs generally require less attention than do deciduous types, and as they lose their older foliage gradually, there is not the chore of having to sweep up vast quantities of fallen leaves every autumn. Evergreen plants also make more effective weed suppressors as their canopy of foliage prevents light from reaching the ground beneath.

Plants for shade

(The use of (Dry) after the name indicates that the plant is suitable for dry, shady conditions; (P) indicates that the plant is suitable for partially shaded positions only.)

Acaena (P); *Acanthus* (P); *Azalea* (P); *Ajuga reptans* 'Variegata' (P); *Alchemilla* (P); *Anemone*; *Arenaria balearica* (P); *Astrantia* (P); *Astilbe*; *Aucuba*; *Berberis* (P); *Bergenia* (Dry); *Brunnera* (P); *Campanula* (P); *Celastrus* (P); *Chaenomeles*; *Colchicum*; *Cornus* (P); *Cotoneaster* (P); *Crocus*; *Dicentra* (P); *Dodecatheon* (P); *Elaeagnus pungens*; *Epimedium* (Dry); *Eranthis*; *Euonymus*; *Euphorbia* (Dry); *Galanthus* (P); *Gaultheria procumbens*; *Geranium* (Dry); *Hedera* (Dry); *Helleborus*; *Hemerocallis* (P); *Heuchera*; *Hosta*; *Hydrangea* (P); *Hypericum* (Dry); *Ilex*; *Lamium*; *Lonicera*; *Lysimachia* (P); *Mahonia* (Dry); *Olearia*; *Philadelphus* (P); *Polygonum* (P); *Prunus*; *Pulmonaria*; *Pyracantha* (P); *Robinia* (P); *Rhododendron* species (shrubs); *Saxifraga* × *urbium* (P); *Schizophragma* (P); *Skimmia japonica* (shrub); *Solidago* (P); *Syringa* (P); *Tellima* (P); *Tiarella*; *Veronica* (P); *Vinca* (Dry); *Waldsteinia* (Dry); *Weigela* (P).

Plants for windy sites
Anenome; *Artemisia*; *Bergenia*; *Echinops*; *Euphorbia*; *Geranium*; *Hemerocallis*; *Kniphofia*; *Nepeta*; *Potentilla*; *Sedum*; *Stachys*.

A simple but eye-catching easy-care focal point in an otherwise dark corner of the garden is provided by this conifer and a carpet of weed-suppressing ground cover.

TREES

Trees give the garden the added dimension of height, and can make impressive focal points when planted singly or in groups. They are also useful for providing shelter or for screening purposes.

Apart from ensuring that it will grow well in your climate and soil, the most important consideration when choosing a tree is the ultimate size it will reach. Planting a too large or quickly growing tree for the size of plot should be avoided at all costs. Not only will the tree soon become too dominant a feature and look out of place, but the deep shade it casts over the rest of the garden will make a far less suitable environment for the other plants, making their care and attention much more difficult. This does not mean, however, that trees must be excluded from the smaller garden as many suitable and attractive compact or slow-growing trees are now available.

Trees for the easy-care garden
(C) = conifer; (D) = deciduous; (E) =evergreen; (SE) = semi-evergreen
Compact trees – up to 4.8m (16ft)
Buddleia alternifolia (D); *Chamaecyparis lawsoniana* (compact varieties) (E, C); *Euonymus europaeus*; *Ilex aquifolium* (compact varieties) (E); *Juniperus communis* (compact varieties) (E, C); *J. virginiana* (compact varieties) (E, C).
Medium sized trees – 4.8-7.6m (16-25ft)
Chamaecyparis lawsoniana (E, C); *Cornus florida*; *Genista aetnensis*; *Ilex aquifolium* (E); *Prunus subhirtella*.
Tall trees – 7.6m (25ft) or more
Acer davidii (D); *A. griseum* (D); *Chamaecyparis lawsoniana* (tall varieties) (E, C); *Juniperus virginiana*; *Robinia pseudoacacia*; *Salix caprea*.

SHRUBS

Many of the same criteria used in the selection of trees can be applied when it comes to choosing shrubs, but while almost all trees need no pruning, some species of shrub require regular pruning to maintain their shape or vigour or simply to keep them in bounds. Although, in terms of increased flowering or general vigour, most shrubs will benefit from an occasional pruning, some species or varieties of shrub will grow quite happily, flower well and maintain an attractive and pleasing shape if left unpruned. These should always be chosen in preference to their more demanding counterparts, especially if a large number of shrubs is to be grown. However, as with all plant selection, ensure

that any shrub chosen is suitable in size and habit for its purpose. This is particularly important when choosing subjects for informal hedging. If the shrub's eventual mature size is too large for the purpose intended, it will require regular cutting back to keep it at the desired height and spread, even if it does not normally require any pruning.

Shrubs that do not require regular pruning
(D) = deciduous; (E) = evergreen; (SE) = semi-evergreen
Artemisia abrotanum; *Aucuba japonica* (E); *Berberis* species (E and D types); *Chaenomeles* species; *Choisya ternata* (E); *Cistus* species; *Cotoneaster* species (E and D types); *Cytisus* species; *Euonymus* species (E and D types); *Gaultheria shallon* (E); *Genista* species; *Hebe* species (E); *Hydrangea* species; *Juniperus horizontalis* (E); *J. × media* (E); *Lonicera pileata* (SE); *Mahonia* species (E); *Olearia* species; *Osmanthus delavayi* (E); *Paeonia lutea*; *P. suffructicosa*; *Pernettya mucronata* (E); *Pyracantha rogersiana* (E); *Rhododendron* species (E); *Senecio laxifolius* (E); *Syringa patula*; *Ulex europaeus* (E); *Viburnum* species (E and D types); *Weigela florida*.

Some shrubs do not have a bushy habit but are low-growing or prostrate, often producing soft stems from a woody base. These are termed sub-shrubs, and many are useful substitutes for low-growing herbaceous plants while others are good ground-cover subjects.

Sub-shrubs
(E) = evergreen
Calluna vulgaris (E); *Erica carnea* (E); *Euphorbia polychroma* (E); *Gaultheria procumbens* (E); *Hypericum × moserianum* (E); *H. olympicum* (E); *Iberis sempervirens* (E); *Phlox subulata* (E); *Salvia officinalis* (E); *Vinca* (E).

HERBACEOUS PERENNIALS

The easiest to grow herbaceous perennials are those that do not require any regular lifting and dividing or staking. Some types of herbaceous plants – many of the varieties of Michaelmas daisy, for example – must be lifted and divided in order to remain vigorous, and the tall, upright growers such as heleniums and delphiniums, commonly used to provide height at the back of borders, require staking to prevent them flopping over, particularly in windy districts or when the plants are in full bloom and the foliage is heavy with rain. Such attention can be avoided if the less demanding, bushier types of plant are chosen. Not only will these be self-supporting, but the canopy of foliage they produce will also suppress weed growth.

For the back of the border select taller, bushier plants such as *Acanthus mollis, Anenome × hybrida* or *Aruncus dioicus*. Kniphofias, hemerocallis, solidago, dicentras and astilbes make excellent mid-border plants, while the front of the border can be planted with the lower growing herbaceous plants such as dwarf asters, erigerons, achilleas or *Campanula carpatica*.

CLIMBING PLANTS

Because climbing plants and wall shrubs take up little ground space in relation to their coverage, they are extremely useful for providing large areas of colour and foliage interest while demanding the minimum of maintenance. To produce an area of colour and foliage at ground level, similar to that given by a few climbers planted in a narrow strip of ground at the base of a wall or fence, for example, would require a very large bed or border, planted with a far greater number of plants, with the attendant extra maintenance.

Some climbing plants are self-clinging – that is, they do not require additional support and will attach themselves directly to any surface – and these plants need practically no attention or special requirements at all. Others climbers are self-clinging but must be given some support, such as a trellis or wires, to which they can cling by means of their twining stems or tendrils. Wall shrubs, however, generally need to have their new growths tied on to the supports. Although this means extra work, this need be done only once or twice a season, and it is a relatively easy task if plastic-coated wire is used.

Climbers
Self-clinging
Hedera helix; *Hydrangea petiolaris*; *Parthenocissus henryana*; *P. quinquefolia*; *P. tricuspidata*; *Schizophragma hydrangoides*; *S. integrifolia*.

Self-clinging with extra support
Celastrus orbiculatus; *Clematis* species; *Euonymus fortunei* var. *radicans*; *Lonicera* species; *Polygonum baldshuanicum*; *Wisteria floribunda*; *W. sinensis*.

Wall shrubs
Pyracantha rogersiana; Roses, climbing.

GROUND-COVER PLANTS

Many plants form dense clumps or mats of foliage that blanket the ground or have such colonizing natures that they compete with weeds so successfully that they considerably reduce the chance of weed invasion. The use of plants for ground cover has long been known, but it is rarely exploited to its fullest extent by the home gardener. Ground-cover plants are often used only to clothe difficult or inaccessible areas, such as steep banks, while areas of bare soil around shrubs or trees are assiduously maintained. In nature any areas of newly exposed, bare soil are rapidly covered by vegetation. Similarly in the garden, these bare areas provide an ideal environment for germinating weeds and, in the struggle to keep nature at bay, must be constantly kept weed free by manual or chemical means. In addition, bare soil has little aesthetic appeal, and it can dry out quickly, offering little protection to plant roots from hot sun or drying winds. The planting of suitable ground-cover subjects, which provide a weed-supressing blanket between shrubs or under trees as well as the more difficult or wilder areas of the garden, can greatly reduce the work involved in keeping a garden free from weeds, can prevent the soil and roots of plants from drying out too quickly during dry spells and can provide an attractive background for specimen plants.

When ground cover is mentioned, many gardeners think of large, featureless areas planted with only a few species of low-growing shrubs such as potentillas, cotoneasters and prostrate junipers or carpeting plants such as vincas, ivies and hypericums. There is, however, a great variety of ground-cover plants, which not only effectively supress weed growth but can also provide the garden with an interesting range of colour and form in their own right. Indeed, many herbaceous plants, such as *Anenome × hybrida* or *Campanula glomerata*, or shrubs, such as the dwarf azaleas, which are commonly used as border plants and not as ground coverers, make effective weed suppressors because of their clump-forming, bushy or colonizing natures. Once established, any herbaceous or shrub border planted with such plants will require little weeding.

Unfortunately, the labour-saving benefits of ground cover cannot be obtained immediately. It takes time before the plants establish themselves, grow together and form a complete and effective cover.

Before planting, the ground must be prepared carefully, ridding it of any perennial weeds and enriching the soil where necessary with compost, peat or manure. Immediately before planting,

Left: *Wisteria sinensis* is justifiably one of the most popular of all climbing plants; above: mixed borders of shrubs and herbaceous perennials require little attention but provide interest throughout the year; right: ericas are effective ground-cover subjects that can provide year-round colour.

lightly dress the soil with a suitable fertilizer. Careful preparation is amply repaid by the plants' early vigour, which enables them to form continuous cover more quickly. During this time it will be necessary to control any weeds that grow in the gaps between plants, but provided that the ground has been adequately cleared, this should not be a particularly difficult or time-consuming task. This weeding is usually best done by hand. Using a hoe can damage shoots or roots, which can check the plants' spread and so slow down the process of establishing ground cover. Contact chemical herbicides can be difficult to apply accurately between closely growing plants, and any splashes can damage the plants, especially softer, non-woody species. The application of residual weedkillers to the soil may inhibit the plants' spread.

Slower growing ground-cover shrubs will take longer to form a complete covering than either the herbaceous or sub-shrubby types. While they are becoming established, therefore, apply a light organic mulch, such as peat or pulverized tree bark, between plants to suppress weed growth. As an alternative, low-growing ground-cover subjects can be planted under and between the shrubs. These will gradually be replaced as the shrubs increase in size and spread and prevent light from reaching the lower growing plants.

Do not be tempted to plant ground-cover subjects more closely than is recommended. Although a complete covering is achieved more quickly, too close planting will result in increased competition between the plants later on. This can cause a rapid depletion of the soil nutrients and loss of vigour of the plants.

When selecting plants for their weed-suppressing qualities, take care not to introduce into the garden plants that are so successful in competing with other types that they become problems themselves,

spreading throughout the garden at the expense of all the other desired types. Clump-forming ground coverers, once they reach a certain size, generally do not spread further but only increase in area. Colonizing plants and some carpeting ground coverers, however, spread by sending out suckers or runners. The spread of most of the recommended species of colonizers and carpeters is easily checked once they have filled their allotted space, but if you use some of the more vigorous spreaders, a surround of vertical slates or tiles below ground level will help to keep them within bounds.

Ground-cover subjects
(D) = deciduous; (E) = evergreen; (SE) = semi-evergreen

Ground-cover shrubs
Artemisia (SE); *Berberis* (E and D types); *Calluna* (E); *Chaenomeles japonica*; *Cotoneaster congestus*; *C. dammeri*; *C. horizontalis*; *Cytisus × beanii*; *C. × kewensis*; *Erica* (E); *Euonymus fortunei* (E); *Gaultheria* (E); *Genista hispanica*; *G. lydia*; *Hebe albicans* (E); *H.* 'Youngii' (E); *Juniperus horizontalis* (E); *Lavandula angustifolia* 'Hidcote' (E); *Lonicera pileata* (SE); *Mahonia* (E); *Pernettya* (E); *Potentilla*; Roses (prostrate varieties); *Viburnum davidii* (E).

Clump-forming ground coverers
Alchemilla mollis; *Anenome × hybrida*; *Brunnera macrophylla*; *Campanula carpatica*; *Dicentra*; *Epimedium* (E and SE types); *Geranium*; *Heuchera* (E); *Hosta*; *Nepeta × faassenii*; *Pulmonaria*; *Tellima grandiflora* (E).

Carpet-forming ground coverers
Acaena 'Blue Haze'; *Ajuga reptans* (SE); *Iberis* (E); *Lysimachia nummularia*; *Polygonum* (E and D types); *Saxifraga × urbium* (E); *Sedum* (E); *Stachys*; *Thymus serpyllum* (E); *Tiarella cordifolia* (E); *Waldsteinia* (E).

Colonizing ground coverers
Bergenia (E); *Campanula glomerata*; *Euphorbia* (E); *Geranium*; *Hedera helix* (E); *Hypericum × moserianum* (E); *Lamium maculatum* (E); *Lysimachia punctata*; *Parthenocissus quinquefolia*; *P. tricuspidata*; *Symphytum grandiflorum*; *Vinca* (E).

Plants to avoid
Some of the common species of garden plants that are readily available can rapidly become invasive 'weeds' because of their extremely vigorous spreading natures. Such plants are often recommended as ground coverers because of their abililty quickly to blanket an area, however, their rapid spread continues and has to be checked continually to stop them becoming an unwelcome nuisance in other areas of the garden. Controlling the spread of such plants can be a difficult and arduous task but one that, if neglected, can lead to the garden rapidly being overrun and to the loss of other, less vigorous cultivated plants. The following species should be avoided by the easy-care gardener as they all have strong, invasive natures and require regular and frequent attention to keep them in check: *Achillea ptarmica*; *Artemisia eriantha* (syn. *A. villarsii*); *A. ludoviciana*; *Euphorbia cyparissias*; *Hypericum calycinum* (Aaron's beard, rose of Sharon); *Mentha × piperata* (peppermint); *M. suaveolens* (syn. *M. rotundifolia*) (apple mint); *M. spicata* (garden mint); *Nepeta hederacea* (syn. *N. glechoma*, *Glechoma hederacea*, ground ivy); *Oxalis acetosella* (wood sorrel); *O. articulata* (syn. *O. floribunda*); *O. corniculata* (sleeping beauty); *Petasites fragrans* (winter heliotrope); *Saponaria officinalis* (soapwort); *Sasaella ramosa* (syn. *Arundinaria vagans*); *Sedum acre* (biting stonecrop, common stonecrop); *S. anglicum* (English stonecrop); *Soleirolia soleirolii* (syn. *Helxine soleirolii*) (baby's tears, mind-your-own-business).

Some garden plants produce such a profusion of seed that they can become almost as much of a menace as annual weeds. Such plants self-sow and can develop in areas of the garden where they are not wanted. Prolific seeders are not as much of a threat to the garden as the invasive spreaders – indeed, their spread may actually be welcomed in less formal gardens – but in gardens where they are likely to be a problem they should be controlled by the removal of the flowers before the seeds set or not introduced at all. The following plants are prolific seeders and self-sow easily: *Calendula*; *Corydalis lutea*; *Digitalis purpurea* (foxglove); *Foeniculum vulgare* (fennel); *Lunaria annua* (syn. *L. biennis*) (honesty); *Meconopsis cambrica* (Welsh poppy); *Myosotis* (forget-me-not); *Papaver somniferum* (opium poppy); *Physalis alkekengi* var. *franchetii* (Chinese lantern, bladder cherry); *Salix caprea* (pussy willow, goat willow – female forms only).

BUYING PLANTS

As plants can take a very long time to recover – if at all – from a poor start in life, it is important to purchase the best quality stock possible. This may cost more initially but will save much wasted time and effort trying to grow poor stock. Whenever possible buy from a reputable nursery that specializes in container-grown plants so that you can inspect each plant before you buy it. Go with a list of the plants you want to purchase, and, unless you know your plants well, stick to it. Do not buy on impulse. If a plant that is not on your list appeals to you, make a note of the name and check its suitability for your garden and planting scheme when you return home. If it proves to be suitable, you can buy it later.

CONTAINER-GROWN PLANTS

Container-grown subjects are the most expensive, but the most convenient, kind of plants to buy, the main advantage being that container-grown trees, shrubs or perennials can be planted out at any time of year provided the plant is hardy and the ground is neither frosty nor waterlogged. In addition, if there is a delay in planting, container-grown plants can be left unplanted for several weeks if the soil around the roots is kept moist.

Any plant described as container-grown should have been raised from a seedling, cutting or grafted variety in a container and potted on as it becomes larger. It should not have been lifted from open ground and merely replanted into a container for sale.

Examine any plant you are contemplating buying carefully. Do not necessarily buy the largest specimen you find, as older and larger plants, especially trees and shrubs, can be more difficult and take longer to establish than smaller, younger and more vigorously growing specimens. Make sure that the plant is well-established in its container by gently lifting the plant by the stem near soil level. If the soil ball moves out of the container easily, do not buy the plant. Look also for any thick roots growing downwards from the base of the pot or exposed on the soil surface. These indicate that the plant has been in the container too long and that it may also be starved of nutrients. Small white roots projecting through the container or the drainage holes, on the other hand, are a good sign, indicating that the plant is well established. The foliage should not be blanched, discoloured, wilted or undersized. Any browning or reddening of the leaves may indicate starvation. The plant should show no sign of uneven, lop-sided or leggy growth, shown by long, leafless stems. Reject any plant that has evidence of pests and diseases, such as shrivelled leaves or cankered stems, or plants with numerous pruning cuts, which indicate that it has been drastically cut back. Finally, check that the container is in good condition and is not split. The soil should not be dried out or be covered in dense weed growth, although a few weeds, moss or algae growing on the surface indicate a well-established plant.

BARE-ROOTED PLANTS

Bare-rooted plants are those that have been lifted at the nursery and are transported without soil, although damp peat, straw or sacking should be packed around the roots to stop them drying out. Bare-rooted trees and shrubs are cheaper than their container-grown counterparts and generally establish themselves just as easily. However, they must be lifted and planted during their dormant season (from October to the end of March), and the roots must never be allowed to dry out. The best time to buy is when you are ready for immediate planting, but if there is a delay, heel in the plants temporarily in a shallow, V-shaped trench until you are ready.

When choosing bare-rooted subjects, select trees and shrubs that have well-developed and undamaged root systems and shapely, evenly branched crowns. Avoid plants that show signs of advanced new growth, such as opening leaf buds or small young white roots growing into the peat, and those that have diseased or shrivelled stems.

BALLED PLANTS

Evergreen trees and shrubs, including conifers, are often sold as balled plants. These have been lifted but the soil ball kept intact and wrapped in sacking, netting or polythene sheets. Before you buy, make sure that the wrapping is intact, that the root ball is firm and large and that it has not been allowed to dry out. Evergreens should have sturdy stems with a good covering of healthy leaves. Avoid plants with lop-sided growth or with large patches of brown foliage. Conifers should not have forked leading shoots. Tall-growing conifers are best bought as young specimens; dwarf types can be bought as

Tulipa humilis, a dwarf species, flowers in early spring and is an ideal subject for well-drained soils and rock gardens.

older plants. Finally, check that there are no roots growing horizontally around the stem at the top of the soil ball; these can usually be felt through the wrapping. The time to buy and plant balled evergreens is September and October or April and early May, although they may be left unplanted for several weeks if the soil ball is kept moist and the covering is not removed.

PRE-PACKAGED PLANTS
Herbaceous perennials and shrubs are often sold pre-packaged in stores and supermarkets as well as in garden centres. They are bare-rooted subjects, with moistened peat, compost or moss packed around their roots, and the whole plant is contained in a polythene bag or box. They are cheaper than container-grown plants, but the packaging does not allow you to inspect what you are buying very closely. Pre-packaged plants should be bought and planted when dormant. However the warm conditions of shops can often encourage premature growth, so check that growth has not started and avoid any plants with opening leaf buds or with small white roots growing into the damp peat. Check also for any diseased or shrivelled stems.

BULBS
Do not buy bulbs that have started to grow and make sure that they are free of any surface mould or evidence of attack by boring insects. A certain amount of peeling of the dry outer skin is normal and does not indicate a defect. Large bulbs are usually the best choice, but check that they are firm at the base. Plant bulbs as soon as possible after purchase.

3. WEEDS AND THEIR CONTROL

Weeds are the enemies of all gardeners but especially of the easy-care gardener who aims to reduce to the minimum the time spent tending the garden. The broad definition of a weed is any plant that is growing where it is not wanted. Good garden design and careful plant choice make it possible to reduce the risk of garden plants spreading to areas they are not wanted or of wind-blown seeds germinating. However, the garden is continually bombarded with seeds from outside, and inevitably from time to time a few weeds will be successful in establishing themselves and will then have to be controlled.

TYPES OF WEED

Weeds can be divided into two distinct groups: annual and perennial. Annual weeds are shallow rooted and live for only one season, and they are the easiest kind to control. They propagate solely by seed produced when the plant is mature, so that, if control measures are taken before the plants set seed, any spread can be effectively prevented.

Perennial weeds are usually deep rooted and can live for many years, growing larger each year. They spread by their roots or by shoots that travel under or over the soil's surface as well as by seed. Perennial weeds are harder to control than annual weeds, as the root as well as the top growth has to be killed to prevent regrowth and spreading.

CLEANING THE GROUND

Before starting to plant, it is vital that any new ground is totally cleared of perennial weeds. Failure to do so will make it far more difficult to keep weeds under control in the future. The weeds will benefit from the improved growing conditions of newly cultivated land and will grow even more strongly than before. Moreover, access to them will be difficult when they are growing among cultivated plants and shrubs.

If you are clearing large areas of neglected ground where there would be no danger to cultivated plants, the whole area can be treated with a suitable translocated herbicide such as glyphosate. The ground should be left uncultivated for at least 12 weeks after application to give the chemical time to act. If there will be no risk of causing fire to neighbouring land or property, the dead weed-growth can be burnt off to make cultivation easier.

In those cases where chemical weed clearance is not practicable, the ground will have to be cleared manually. The plot should be dug to a depth of at least 30cm (12in), and particular care should be taken to sift the soil with a garden fork to ensure that every scrap of root broken off when the weeds are lifted is removed, as they are liable to grow again.

Although digging in this way, if done thoroughly, will rid the ground of almost all perennial weeds, fallowing the ground – that is, leaving it bare and undisturbed for several months after digging – will allow any surviving perennial weeds or any annual weeds that develop from seeds brought to the surface to be easily removed. Although not always practicable, fallowing the ground is especially useful if a motorized cultivator has been used. These tend

---

Common annual weeds

Annual meadow-grass (*Poa annua*); Black bindweed (*Bilderdykia convolvulus*); Chickweed (*Stellaria media*); Common speedwell (*Veronica officinalis*); Groundsel (*Senecio vulgaris*); Hairy bittercress (*Cardamine hirsuta*); Marsh cudweed (*Filaginella uliginosa*, syn. *Graphalium uliginosum*); Petty spurge (*Euphorbia peplus*); Prickly sow-thistle (*Sonchus asper*); Red dead-nettle (*Lamium purpureum*); Shepherd's purse (*Capsella bursa-pastoris*); Smooth sow-thistle (*Sonchus oleraceus*).

Common perennial weeds

Bindweed (*Convolvulus arvensis*); Broad-leaved dock (*Rumex obtusifolius*); Buck's-horn plantain (*Plantago coronopus*); Colt's-foot (*Tussilago farfara*); Common (stinging) nettle (*Urtica dioica*); Cotton thistle (*Onopordon acanthium*); Couch grass (*Elymus repens*); Creeping buttercup (*Ranunculus repens*); Creeping thistle (*Cirsium arvense*); Curled dock (*Rumex crispus*); Daisy (*Bellis perennis*); Dandelion (*Taraxacum officinale*); Dog's mercury (*Mercurialis perennis*); Germander speedwell (*Veronica chamaedrys*); Ground elder (*Aegopodium podagraria*); Hedge bindweed (*Calystegia sepium*); Hoary plantain (*Plantago media*); Horsetail (*Equisetum arvense*); Lesser celandine (*Ranunculus ficaria*); Meadow buttercup (*Ranunculus acris*); Red clover (*Trifolium pratense*); Ribwort (*Plantago lanceolata*); Rosebay willowherb (*Epilobium angustifolium*); Sorrel (*Rumex acetosa*); White clover (*Trifolium repens*); White dead-nettle (*Lamium album*); Yarrow (*Achillea millefolium*).

to chop up any root material left in the soil into easily missed small pieces, which may be capable of producing new growth. Any perennial weeds that develop after cultivation should be removed by hand or treated with applications of glyphosate. Annual weeds can be controlled by hoeing at six-weekly intervals or by the application of glyphosate or a suitable contact weedkiller. Alternatively, the plot can be covered with black polythene sheeting or old carpets. Any developing weeds will quickly die from lack of light.

NON-CHEMICAL WEED CONTROL

Until comparatively recently, before the advent of modern herbicides, hand and hoe were the usual means of weed control. It was known that cultivated plants could smother and prevent weeds, but the concept of ground cover and the specialized use of plants for this purpose was not generally practised. Mulches were used primarily for their moisture-conserving or soil-improving properties, not for their effective weed-suppressing qualities. Even now, however, with the availability of the wide variety of modern herbicides, there is still a place for the control of weeds by manual methods, even in easy-care gardens. This does not necessarily mean long, back-breaking sessions hoeing or hand weeding. Often, in an established, well-designed and well-planted garden the only measure of weed control necessary throughout the growing season will be the removal, by hand, of the occasional weed seedling noticed when walking through the garden.

HOEING

Although many gardeners commend the use of the hoe for producing a moisture-retentive tilth and for its role in improving the texture of the soil, the disturbance caused by the hoe can bring to the surface many dormant weed seeds and enable them to germinate. Nevertheless, in places where the application of herbicides may be difficult, hoeing can be a most convenient method of weed control between newly planted subjects, until the plants become established and grow together to form a weed-suppressing cover. The best time to hoe is when the weather is dry and warm, so that the uprooted weeds scorch and wither. In damp or cool conditions, care must be taken to rake or pick up the weeds, otherwise there is a danger that they will again take root and all that will have been achieved is that the weeds will have been transplanted to different positions.

MULCHING

A mulch is a layer of organic or inorganic material that is spread over the soil's surface, directly controlling weeds by smothering them and blocking off their light. It can also have the indirect effect of promoting the healthier growth of cultivated plants by reducing moisture loss from the soil and, in the case of an organic mulch, by providing an additional supply of nutrients to the soil, thus aiding cultivated plants to compete more successfully with the weeds and to make effective ground cover more quickly. If it is to be fully effective, a mulch needs to be of sufficient depth to prevent weed seeds germinating, and it must itself contain no such seeds. As mulches tend to insulate the soil from the extremes of hot and cold weather, they should be applied when the soil is warm, in late spring or when plants start new growth, otherwise the soil will be slow to warm up during the summer months.

Organic mulches

Peat An excellent mulch for shrubberies and borders, peat is widely available, looks natural and can improve the soil's structure. To be an effective weed suppressor, it needs to be at least 2.5cm (1in) deep, and, as it loses approximately 15 per cent of its volume each year (more in a hot climate), it may require topping up from time to time. If it is allowed to dry out completely, it will form an impermeable crust that can prevent light rain from reaching the soil and may blow about in windy conditions.

Coarse tree bark The application of woody material to soil used to be discouraged as it was believed that it could introduce and promote fungal diseases. However, this is no longer thought to be the case, and tree bark of varying grades has become widely available for use as a mulch. Tree bark has an attractive, natural appearance, and, when it is applied to a depth of 5–7.5cm (2–3in), provides an excellent weed suppressor and conserves soil moisture. Because it rots down slowly, tree bark needs topping up only once every two years or so. Tree bark is, however, expensive, and it should not be used around plants that are especially prone to attack from slugs.

Well-rotted manure A mulch of well-rotted farm-yard manure – horse manure is best – will enrich the soil more than any other organic mulch. It is also quite an effective weed suppressor, provided that the manure does not itself contain weed seeds. This is difficult to guarantee, but, notwithstanding, manure mulches generally prevent more weeds than they introduce. As farmyard manure tends to break down and dissipate fairly quickly, it will require more frequent renewal than other types of weed-suppressing organic mulches. Farmyard manure is freely available and relatively cheap in rural districts, but it is important that the manure is well rotted, otherwise it can be acid and smelly.

Hop manure Spent hops, a by-product of beer making, make an attractive mulch, which can quickly improve the soil's texture. However, to be an effective suppressor of weeds, the mulch must be renewed annually. In addition, on windy sites it can be blown about and should be mixed with peat to prevent this.

Sawdust A light-to-handle mulch, composted sawdust can be used on herbaceous borders and in shrubberies. It darkens as it weathers, taking on an attractive, natural appearance.

Compost Spent mushroom or tomato compost, well-composted seaweed or home-made compost provide humus, improving soil texture and providing a good source of nutrients. To be an effective weed suppressor, compost must be renewed annually, and some types must be mixed with peat to prevent them blowing about. Spent mushroom compost is suitable only for lime-tolerant plants.

Inorganic mulches
Black plastic Heavy-grade black polythene sheeting stretched over the soil and anchored at the edges by stones or gravel acts as a good weed suppressor and also warms the soil and conserves moisture. Plants can easily be introduced and grown through holes made in the plastic. It is, therefore, ideal for use in the vegetable garden, where cover may only be needed for part of the year; the sheeting should be removed in winter. Its appearance makes it less suitable for the ornamental garden, although it can be used in a shrubbery if it is completely covered with a thin layer of gravel, stones or coarse tree bark to disguise it. If polythene sheeting is used around permanent shrubs, make a small well around each plant so that water can reach the soil. Annual weeds will stop growing, and no maintenance will be required. You will, however, have to keep an eye out for slugs and woodlice, which can thrive in the dark, moist conditions under plastic; slugs can be controlled by scattering slug pellets on the ground before laying the sheeting.

Tree spats The germination and development of weeds around the bases of young trees and shrubs can be prevented by the use of tree spats. These are slotted squares of bituminous felt that fit around the stem or trunk of the plant and cover the immediate

Making your own compost
Making compost from garden and kitchen waste requires little effort and provides the gardener with a readily available source of mulching or soil-improving material that is also rich in plant nutrients. Many waste materials can go on the compost heap, including vegetable peelings, the contents of vacuum-cleaners, coffee grounds and tea leaves, straw, grass clippings and dead leaves. Diseased material, the roots of perennial weeds, pine needles, woody stems and plants that have been treated with a weed killer are best burnt.

The successful decomposition of waste plant materials into useful compost depends on the action of bacteria, which must receive an adequate supply of air, water and nitrogenous matter in order for the fermentation process to work well. A simple container, at least 1.2 × 1.5m (4 × 5ft), with open sides to allow the free passage of air into the compost, is the most practical and tidy method of making compost in the domestic garden. It is best to start with a layer of dry material, such as straw or stalks, which should be well firmed down. As waste matter becomes available, add it to the pile and firm down after every 30cm (12in) or so. Sprinkle a proprietary compost activator or ammonium sulphate between layers and, if it is available, bonfire ash, which will prevent the compost becoming too acid. If possible, balance the amount of soft green material with a similar amount of dry material to keep the compost 'open' and to aid aeration. Water the compost as necessary to keep it moist; if its dries out it will not rot down. Turn the compost every six weeks or so to ensure that the matter on the outside is moved to the inside, watering any dry patches that are revealed to speed up decomposition.

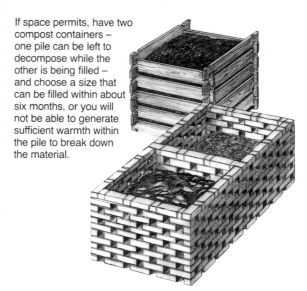

If space permits, have two compost containers – one pile can be left to decompose while the other is being filled – and choose a size that can be filled within about six months, or you will not be able to generate sufficient warmth within the pile to break down the material.

area of soil around it. Their appearance can be improved by a light covering of gravel or soil. Although ready-made tree spats can be bought, they are easily made at home from ordinary roofing felt. A cheap and effective alternative is old carpet, preferably made from woven, natural fibres, which can easily be cut into the required shapes.

Gravel A thick mulch of gravel – to a depth of 5cm (2in) – spread over the soil will be quite effective in suppressing weeds. It is, however, best used in areas where it will not be spread about by people or animals. For mulching use relatively small grade stones – small enough to pass through a 12mm (½in) sieve – as these will pack more closely together and be more effective in stopping light reaching the soil's surface. Wash the gravel before use to rid it of any particles of soil that may bind it together, harbour weed seeds or make it less permeable to water. Choose the type of gravel carefully: those kinds that contain crushed limestone should not be used around acid-loving plants.

CHEMICAL WEEDKILLERS
There is a huge variety of chemical weedkillers on the market. Although some gardeners have, in the past, been reluctant to use chemicals in their gardens, modern herbicides are far less toxic than their predecessors and can be of great assistance to the easy-care gardener. They are perfectly safe provided that they are used responsibly and the manufacturer's directions are carefully followed. It is, however, important to select the correct type of weedkiller for specific purposes. There are three main types of weedkiller, each distinct in its mode of action and use: contact, translocated and residual. Each type can be further divided into selective and total (that is, non-selective) kinds. Selective weedkillers kill only specific types of plant when they are applied to an area of the garden; total weedkillers will kill all types of plant in the treated area. Burn all plants killed by chemical means; do not add them to the compost heap.

APPLYING WEEDKILLERS
The commonest method of applying weedkillers that are diluted or dissolved in water is by watering can, fitted with either a fine rose for localized application or a dribble or sprinkler bar for larger areas such as lawns, drives and paved areas or for clearing uncultivated land. Accurate distribution is difficult, and watering cans are not, therefore, suitable for treating weeds growing between susceptible cultivated plants. They can, however, be used for the overall treatment of beds, borders and

In an established bed or border where the plants are growing closely together, a weedwiper may be the best method of controling weeds.

lawns by selective weedkillers (provided that no susceptible cultivated plants are present) or for applying residual weedkillers to the ground.

The simplest and most accurate method of applying non-selective weedkillers such as glyphosate to weeds that are growing among closely spaced, cultivated plants is to use a 'weedwiper' applicator. This greatly reduces the risk of any accidental splashing of the chemical on to a cherished plant. The applicator consists of a container set into a handle into which the chemical solution is poured. The solution is gravity-fed to a wick at the base, and the moistened wick is then simply brushed over the weed's leaves.

A variety of sprayers is also available. These are designed mainly for the application of insecticides or fungicides, and most have an adjustable nozzle, which can produce a coarse or fine spray, and can be fitted with a hood for more selective use. These can be used for weedkillers, but extreme care must be exercised, even when a hood is used, to prevent spray drifting on to cultivated plants. Sprays are best used only for clearing large areas of neglected ground well away from cultivated plants.

Contact weedkillers

Contact weedkillers, which are also sometimes known as chemical hoes, are most useful for the removal of short-rooted annual weeds. They act by killing any green top-growth with which they come directly in contact; they are not transported through the plant and have no effect on the root system. When they are applied to established perennial weeds, therefore, the top-growth will die and the plant will appear to be dead, but new growth will subsequently appear from the roots.

Contact weedkillers do not affect woody tissue, and they become harmless on contact with the soil. They are most useful for the treatment of annual weeds growing close to cultivated plants or around the bases of woody shrubs. They can also be used to clear a plot shortly before planting or sowing, which can be done 24 hours after treatment. They are generally available in concentrated liquid or powder form and diluted or dissolved in water for application as an overall treatment to an area or to individual plants.

Translocated weedkillers

Capable of destroying deeply rooted perennials as well as annual weeds, translocated, or systemic, weedkillers are absorbed by the foliage and transported to all parts of the plant's system. It is not, therefore, essential to treat the entire foliage, as with contact weedkillers, and weeds can be controlled by 'spot treatment' – that is, by applying the chemical to only a few leaves. As well as the usual liquid and powder forms, translocated weedkillers are available in the form of paint-on gels or aerosol sprays. They are an effective and safe method of controlling difficult weeds growing among cherished cultivated plants, and they are often the easiest and most practical means of chemical weed control in herbaceous borders for the handicapped gardener as they do not need diluting in large quantities of water.

Residual weedkillers

As they are applied directly to the soil, residual weedkillers are translocated in action, being absorbed by the plant through the root system. Although they will kill established shallow-rooted weeds, residual weedkillers are most useful in treating areas in advance of weed growth, destroying any weed seedlings as they germinate. They remain mostly in the top-soil, forming a chemical, weed-destroying barrier. Any disturbance of the soil after their application, however, may break this barrier and reduce their effectiveness by bringing to the surface untreated soil in which weed seedlings may root.

When used in high doses they act as total weedkillers and are useful for keeping uncropped areas such as paths and drives weed free for up to a year. In low doses their action is more selective, and they can be used to kill germinating weeds between established cultivated woody plants such as roses, shrubs and trees, although they are not recommended for this use on light, sandy soils, when they may penetrate to the roots of established plants, nor are they suitable for treatment around newly planted or small specimens.

Residual pre-emergent weedkillers prevent weed seeds germinating for up to eight weeks, and they can be used immediately after young plants have been bedded out or on the established herbaceous border in spring.

All containers used for applying weedkillers should be clearly marked and kept solely for that purpose. The slightest neglect in careful cleansing can result in damage to cultivated plants if containers are used for watering or for applying fungicides or pesticides. If weedkiller is mixed but not used in a single application, it should be further diluted and poured onto waste ground as far away from water courses as possible. Always follow the manufacturer's instruction to the letter in the mixing and storage of weedkillers.

4. PATIO GARDENING

Areas of hard surface such as terraces and patios, as well as providing space for sitting and dining outside, entertaining or simply relaxing, also make an ideal environment for growing containerized or feature plants. Not only are these easily maintained, but they can greatly contribute to the garden's overall appearance, especially if the patio area is large or if it has been necessary to replace a lawn or other areas of planting with an inert surfacing material such as paving or gravel for ease of maintenance.

Growing plants in containers has a number of advantages over ordinary garden planting. Weeds do not present a problem nor is any heavy cultivation of the soil required. In addition, species

Containers give the easy-care gardener opportunities to grow annuals to provide a temporary splash of colour without the problems associated with bedding out and potting on.

that might not normally do well in the garden, can sometimes be successfully grown in containers. Very tender plants such as palms and orange trees can be grown in quite cold climates provided they are brought indoors during the cold winter months, and, as the growing medium in the container can easily be tailored to the plant's specific needs, types of plant that are not suited to the soil found in the garden can be grown.

A containerized display is also flexible. As long as some containers are light enough to be moved easily, the arrangement can be altered during the year to give the best possible show, plants that reach their best being moved to a prominent position while those that are fading are put in a less conspicuous place. Some vegetables, fruit and herbs are also well suited to patio gardens, and quite large crops can be grown with much less effort than in a special vegetable or fruit bed.

As well as growing plants in containers, feature plants, such as small trees and shrubs underplanted with ground cover, can be grown in gaps left in paving. Such plants can give the extra dimension of height to a large patio and can be used as eye-catching focal points in a patio garden.

GROWING PLANTS IN CONTAINERS

Containers for plants can be found in all shapes and sizes, ranging from simple flower pots, window boxes or hanging baskets to large tubs, half barrels and very ornate vases. Whatever type of container you choose, however, it should be a suitable size for the plant (or plants) to be grown in it. Plants look far more attractive when they are in containers that are in proportion with their top-growth. The style of container and the material it is made from are also important. Containers should always be in keeping with their surroundings – stone urns, for example, are well suited to a period town patio but would look out of place in a rural setting, where clay pots or wooden tubs would be more appropriate. Containers made from non-porous materials such as glass-fibre and plastic help to keep the soil moist for longer and so reduce the need to water quite so often; indeed, some containers have built-in water reservoirs, which reduce the burden of frequent watering still further.

In general, the larger the container the better, for not only does this allow more impressive displays to be planted but it also enables the plants to be more easily maintained and means that they will be less prone to drying out, which will, in turn, mean that they are more likely to thrive. However, containers must not be too large or the plants may eventually suffer from root problems caused by too much compost being left unpenetrated by the roots, becoming waterlogged and turning sour. Moreover, once filled with compost, large containers are generally too heavy to move easily, and they should be given a more or less permanent position in the garden. If you are choosing a single plant for a large container, therefore, make sure that it will remain attractive for a long period during the season. An alternative to growing a single specimen plant in a large container is to group several smaller plants together. If you do this, you may find it convenient to keep them in their original small pots, which can be plunged into the large container filled with moisture-retentive peat or bark, so that they can be replaced without disturbing the other plants.

It is usually better to use special potting compost for pots and tubs as it compacts less than ordinary garden soil, is guaranteed sterile and weed free and can be more easily tailored to suit the specific needs

The delicately scented *Narcissus* 'Silver Chimes' flowers in late spring.

of particular plants. However, while the soil in a garden tends to become progressively more acid over the years as rain washes the calcium away, the soil or compost in containers tends to become more alkaline. It will, therefore, be necessary to restore the natural acid balance of the compost by a dose of sequestrene (chelated iron), especially if acid-loving plants are grown.

There are two distinct types of potting compost – soil based and peat based (or soil-less). Soil-based potting composts are generally available in three formulations (in the UK, John Innes Nos. 1, 2 and 3), each of which has a different amount of fertilizer added. The composts with low fertilizer mixes (John Innes No. 1) are best for raising seeds and growing small plants. The composts with higher fertilizer content (John Innes Nos. 2 and 3) should be used for larger, more permanent plants. Greedy feeders such as tomatoes, shrubs or small trees should always be planted in the composts with the highest fertilizer content. Peat-based composts are also available with different fertilizer contents to suit different categories of plant.

Choosing the type of compost to use can depend on your specific situation and the type of plants grown. Peat-based composts are the cleanest and easiest to handle and, being lighter, are more suitable if weight is a problem, such as for hanging baskets or in roof-top patios, or if pots have to moved around a good deal. However, this lightness can be a disadvantage if large, top-heavy plants are being potted up. Peat-based composts also become depleted of nutrients more quickly, having less than half the life of soil-based composts, and they therefore require regular feeding with artificial fertilizer. Peat-based compost must never be allowed to dry out, as remoistening can be difficult. On the whole, therefore, unless weight is the deciding factor, soil-based composts are more suitable for longer term planting.

Before filling the container, clean it thoroughly and add a layer of crocks. Correct crocking is essential for adequate drainage and aeration, and it also prevents fine soil being washed out through the draining holes. First, cover any large holes with zinc gauze or mesh and add a layer of stones or pieces of broken clay pots (concave side down). Cover this with a layer, 12–50mm (½–2in) deep, of chippings or small stones, making sure that they are not limestone if lime-hating plants are to be grown. If the plant is to stay in the container more or less permanently, add a further layer, 12mm (½in) deep, of fine pulverized bark, sphagnum peat or leaf mould. Add the compost until it reaches a level at which the plant, standing on the compost, reaches the correct height relative to the rim of the container. Add more compost around the plant and gently firm it in. Water well and place the container in a sheltered spot until the plant is established.

After a time it will become necessary to pot on plants in small containers whose roots have completely filled the container into larger ones. The time before repotting becomes necessary will depend on the speed with which the plant grows. Some quicker growing plants may need repotting annually, while some slower growing types – azaleas, for example – may need potting on only once every several years. It is possible to tell if a plant needs to be repotted by watering it thoroughly, removing it from its container and examining the rootball. Smaller pots can be inverted, the plant stem supported between the middle and forefinger of one hand and the pot removed. Removing larger plants is best done by laying the container on its side and carefully rolling it to and fro. This loosens the rootball in the container and eases removal. When the plant is out of its pot, examine the roots: if they are wound tightly round the outside or bottom of the rootball, repotting is necessary. If there are no, or only very few, roots showing on the outside of the rootball,

carefully replace the plant in its original container and top up with new compost if required.

If repotting is necessary, choose an appropriately sized new container. As a guide, when repotting from a pot of up to 10cm (4in), an increase in size of 12mm (½in) is about right; if the pot is 12.5cm (5in) or larger, choose a new pot that is 2.5–3.5cm (1–1½in) larger. Finally, when repotting from a container that is 30cm (12in) or more, increase the size by 7.5–10cm (3–4in).

To repot, place crocks in the container and add a layer of fresh potting compost. Gently remove any crocking material buried in the old compost around the rootball, set the plant firmly on the layer of fresh compost and pour more mixture around the rootball. Pack down the new compost with your fingers, taking care not to overdo the pressure or the mixture will become too compacted and impenetrable to the roots, and gradually add more mixture. As you fill the container, tap it on a hard surface from time to time to eliminate any air pockets and to help the mixture to settle. Finally, water thoroughly around the edges of the pot.

Eventually, the largest convenient container size will be reached and further potting will be impracticable. The easiest and most effective alternative to repotting is to give an annual top-dressing. Use a trowel to remove as much as possible of the top layer of potting mix without exposing major roots, and refill the container with standard potting mix with some slow-release fertilizer added to it.

> **Easy shrubs for containers**
> *Aucuba japonica*; *Berberis* species; *Chamaecyparis lawsoniana* 'Ellwoodii'; *Hydrangea macrophylla* var. *serrata*; *Juniperus* × *media* 'Old Gold'; *Rhododendron* species; Roses, miniature varieties.

STRAWBERRY AND PARSLEY POTS

These pots have small lipped openings set in the sides, and they are an attractive and easy way of growing strawberries, herbs or some annual flowers and small bulbs. Proprietary strawberry pots made of terracotta or of glass-fibre are most suitable, but they can be expensive. A cheaper, but less durable alternative is to convert old wooden barrels or water butts by boring a series of holes, 2.5cm (1in) in diameter, in their sides and several drainage holes in their bases. Wooden containers should always be cleaned carefully and treated with a horticultural wood preservative (never creosote, which is harmful to plants) to prevent rotting. Wooden barrels should

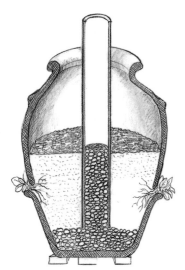

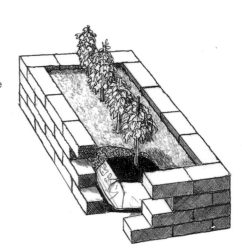

Left: Make sure that water penetrates evenly through a container by placing a length of drainpipe in the centre before you begin to fill it with compost and plants. Fill the pipe with gravel or pebbles as the compost is added around it until the column of pebbles is about 15cm (6in) below the final level of the soil. Withdraw the pipe and fill the container with the growing medium.

Right: A growing bag can be disguised by building a three- or four-tier course of un-mortared bricks around it and by covering its surface with pebbles or bark. The whole thing can be quickly dismantled when necessary.

not be allowed to dry out as prolonged or excessive dryness will make the staves shrink and fall out.

To ensure a good crop, use a rich growing mixture and keep it moist. Tall pots should be kept level or water will permeate unevenly through the growing medium, allowing some plants to dry out while others become waterlogged. Even watering and good drainage can be assured by placing a plastic drainpipe, 7.5–10cm (3–4in) in diameter, vertically in the pot. As you carefully fill the container with compost, fill the drainpipe with small pebbles and insert the plants through the holes from the outside of the pot, gently firming the mixture around the roots as each level of holes is reached. Continue to add more mixture, and when the container is full, gradually pull out the drainpipe to leave a core of pebbles running down the centre of the pot. The pebbles should stop about 15cm (6in) below the surface of the compost. When water is poured into the pot, it will spread evenly through-out the soil. Alternatively, terracotta pots, being porous, can be kept in a saucer filled with water, which will be slowly drawn up into the container and thence the soil by capillary action.

HANGING BASKETS

Hanging baskets can be used to provide splashes of colour in unorthodox places, such as brightening a dull façade or for use over a doorway. They can be either ordinary pots or tubs, which can be planted in the normal way and hung up or wall-mounted, or the wire-frame type, which have special foam-rubber liners. The wire-frame baskets are not suitable for permanent planting as they afford little protection to plant roots from winter frosts, and if they are used, they must be replanted each spring.

TROUGH OR SINK GARDENS

These make attractive permanent containers for the patio or for placing in or around the garden. They are ideal for dwarf conifers or alpine or rock plants that may otherwise demand too much work if grown in a conventional alpine garden where weeds can be a real menace. Trough or sink gardens should be raised off the ground to make tending them easier and to keep out pests such as slugs and snails. Set the trough on brick piers or a low wall before filling it with soil or it will be too heavy to move. If supporting bricks are used, the trough should overlap these by 15cm (6in) all round, partly to hide the bricks and partly to allow the feet to go underneath, which will make tending the trough easier, especially for the handicapped gardener.

Troughs can be bought or made. Old glazed sinks are especially suitable if they are covered with hypertufta, a mixture of equal parts of builder's sand, peat and cement, which gives an attractive brown, stone-like finish. Before covering a con-tainer in hypertufta, make sure it is absolutely clean. If you are using a sink, there will already be a plug-hole for drainage, but if there is no hole, you will have to drill one or more holes in the base. Apply one or two coats of a waterproof, bonding, builder's glue with a paint brush. Mix the sand, peat and cement with just enough water to make a stiff consistency and apply it, using a trowel or gloved hand and while the glue is still tacky, to all the parts of the sink that will remain exposed when it is finally filled with soil. Do not forget to treat the inside of the top edge to a depth of about 7.5cm (3in) from the top. A final rough finish can be given by stippling with a brush. The hypertufta should not be allowed to dry too quickly or it will turn grey

Container-grown fuchsias and geraniums.

rather than the desired more natural-looking, weathered brown. To give an even more natural appearance, encourage algae and moss to grow on the outside of the trough by painting it with milk.

Before filling the trough or sink, cover the drainage hole or holes with wire gauze (an old wire saucepan cleaner could be used). If the sink is particularly deep, insert a piece of metal piping, 12mm (½in) in diameter, to half the depth of the soil at the opposite end to the drainage hole, leaving 12mm (½in) of pipe projecting above the soil's surface. This will make it easier to water the lower levels of soil.

GROWING BAGS

These large plastic bags, filled with a soil-less growing medium, can be used for growing spring and summer flowers, although they are probably most useful as a clean and easy way of growing tomatoes, courgettes, marrows, cucumbers and other vegetables on a patio or in gardens where it is impracticable to cultivate vegetables by any other means. Growing bags should be laid on a hard, level surface so that water will reach all parts of the bag equally. Young plants can be inserted through three or four equally spaced holes or slits made in the top of the bag. Alternatively, one large rectangular hole

may be made, but as this increases the area of growing mixture exposed to the atmosphere, it makes the bag more prone to drying out and more frequent watering necessary.

When individual holes for each plant have been made, watering will be easier through two 12.5cm (5in) flowers pots sunk into the mixture. Make two additional holes in the top of the bag between plants and gently push the compost aside, inserting a flower pot in each hole so that the base of the pot is just above the bottom of the growing bag. The whole of the growing bag can be watered simply by pouring water into the pots. Growing bags can be watered automatically by a proprietary drip-feed system with five or six nozzles.

After harvesting, the soil-less compost makes an ideal mulch for using around the garden.

Growing bags on the patio can be disguised by building an unmortared, low brick wall of about three courses around them. If the top of the bag is covered with peat, pebbles or coarse tree bark, it will be an attractive temporary bed for flowers and vegetables and can be easily dismantled if the layout of the patio needs to be changed.

PLANT CARE

Correct watering and feeding of plants in containers – and in raised beds – is vital to ensure good health and vigour. The frequency of watering and the

An old sink covered with hypertufta has a new lease of life.

amount of water required will, of course, depend on the weather, time of year, type of container (plants grown in plastic or glass-fibre containers are less prone to drying out than plants in clay or terracotta pots), the plant's specific needs and its position on the patio. A moisture-loving plant grown in a position exposed to drying winds or the mid-day sun will, for example, demand more water than a plant grown in a more sheltered spot. Before positioning plants, therefore, give some thought to their individual needs.

WATERING

If containers with a built-in watering system are used, only occasional attention is needed to keep them fully topped up. Porous containers – those made of clay or terracotta – can be stood in shallow bowls of water. The container will take up the water, which will travel through the growing medium. If non-porous containers are used, it is possible to ensure a steady supply of water by inserting one end of a wick of capillary matting into the mixture through a drainage hole while the other end is in a bowl of water. This system will work only if the compost or soil is thoroughly moist before the wick is introduced. Larger containers such as sink gardens or raised beds can be watered

by hand with a watering can fitted with a fine rose or by a low-pressure hose with a spray attachment. When you are using a hose, make sure that the pressure is not too high or the soil will be washed out of the container. Hanging baskets or high containers can be watered with a hose if a bamboo cane is tied to the end section to keep it rigid.

If an automatic watering system has been installed in the garden (see Chapter 7), small-bore branch pipes can be led off from the system to keep pots, tubs, troughs, sink gardens and raised beds well watered.

FEEDING

During the first year container plants grown in a proprietary potting mixture will not require feeding. After that time, however, it will be necessary to supplement the nutrients of the compost with a suitable fertilizer. Organic fertilizers can smell and are generally unsuitable for container plants, especially when they are grown near to the house. The most usual method is to use a proprietary soluble or liquid feed, which can be watered in according to the manufacturer's directions. If the handling of large quantities of liquid is difficult, slow-release fertilizers can be used. These are available in pelleted form or as spikes, which are especially designed for pot-grown plants and are simply inserted into the potting medium.

5. DESIGN AND TECHNIQUES FOR HANDICAPPED AND ELDERLY GARDENERS

Gardening can be a most pleasurable out-of-doors activity for the handicapped. Like the home and car, the garden can be adapted to overcome a wide variety of physical disabilities, ranging from those associated with increasing age that can affect us all to more serious disabilities that may result in confinement to a wheelchair. Adaptations to the garden and the use of specialized tools often allow even the most

severely handicapped person to tend and create a most satisfying and successful garden safely and largely independently of help.

Before any major alterations are undertaken, decisions will have to be made on the garden's layout and on the type, number and relative sizes of the features to be included in it. The decisions will depend on the amount of time available for gardening and on your present and, if they are likely to change, future physical abilities. For the easiest-care garden, only those features that can be comfortably managed and are well within your physical capabilities should be included. However, some gardeners may welcome a challenge, and there

When planning the layout of a garden for an elderly or handicapped gardener. the prime consideration must be the provision of safe and easy access to all parts of the garden. Make sure that paths are wide and level and that, where steps or ramps are necessary, sturdy hand rails are provided.

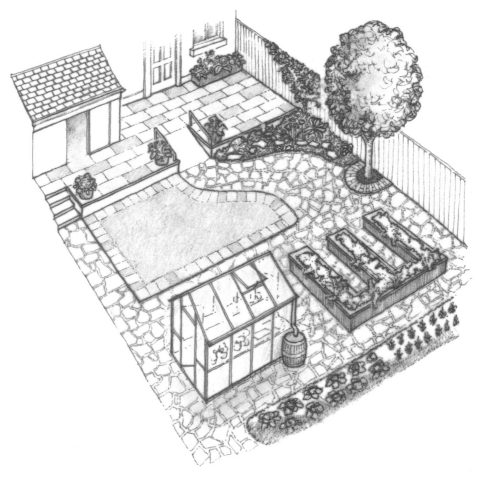

is plenty of scope for variety and personal expression in the design of a suitable garden. An adapted garden can be as individual as the person who adapts it. It is possible for a wheelchair gardener with a strong upper body to mow a lawn with a suitable mower, or even, if he or she wishes, to dig the ground, although it would be difficult to attend to tall plants or shrubs that require an annual pruning. Similarly, a person who has difficulty bending may not be able to tend low-growing plants at ground level, while taller plants, or plants in raised beds, will be quite easily maintained from an upright position.

THE ADAPTED GARDEN

Ideally, the entire garden should be planned and laid out to suit an individual's needs in one go. This is rarely possible, however, as it can involve a great deal of work, most of which is likely to be beyond the capabilities of a handicapped gardener, and the help of friends, relatives or a paid garden contractor will often be required. Most probably, alterations will have to be made a little at a time, in which case it is advisable initially to concentrate on the area of the garden closest to the house, and to provide or improve suitable access to and around the garden.

PATHS AND TERRACES

Safe and easy access to and around the garden is vital. Many hard surfacing materials commonly used for garden paths and terraces are not suitable for the handicapped gardener. Cobbles, stone setts and natural stone paving are too uneven for either safe walking or for the comfortable and easy passage of wheelchairs. Brick paths are liable to become uneven after a time, as frost and hard wear chip and crack their surfaces. Gravel and pebbles can make walking difficult and clog the wheels of wheelchairs.

When choosing a suitable hard surfacing material, some aesthetic considerations may have to be sacrificed for the sake of practicality. However, paving slabs provide a suitable attractive surface for the handicapped gardener, and they are available in a variety of shapes, colours and sizes. If a range of types is selected with care and used for different areas of the garden, paving alone can provide an interesting variety of visual effects. The choice of paving is a matter of personal taste, but it is essential to choose slabs that have non-slip surfaces. Surface treatments vary, and some may be more suitable than others. It is therefore advisable to try walking on some before buying if at all possible.

It is particularly important for the handicapped that paving is correctly laid, as even the slightest raised edge or unevenness can cause a fall. For this reason too, plants should not be introduced into the paving or between stones, for although they may make large paved areas more attractive, they can be a hazard to walking.

Concrete is probably the cheapest suitable material for paths. Colour the concrete during mixing with a special weatherproof colourant to make it more attractive and lightly brush the surface before it sets to give a textured, non-slip finish.

Tarmacadam, which is available in a variety of colours, may also be considered. However, tarmacadam paths can be broken up by the roots of nearby plants and shrubs growing through them, making the surface uneven and unsafe. It can also be difficult to handle and is best laid by a specialist contractor.

Situate terraces so that they are readily accessible from the house and, where possible, sheltered from cold winds. Some raised beds adjoining the terrace can be both attractive and functional. They can be quickly reached and easily tended from the hard surface of the terrace, and they therefore provide an opportunity to garden without the need to travel far from the house, which is a useful consideration for days when the weather is bad or unpredictable.

Paths should be wide and have no sharp bends or steep gradients. The width of the path will depend on the mobility of the gardener. Any path should allow an ambulant gardener easy access for the transportation of implements such as mowers and loaded wheelbarrows without their becoming entangled in the bordering plants. Gardeners using two sticks or a walking frame and those who may need the assistance of another person walking alongside from time to time will require a minimum width of 90cm (3ft). The width required by wheelchair gardeners will, of course, depend on the size of the wheelchair, but a minimum width of 90cm (3ft), with wider areas for easy turning, is often necessary.

Slopes in the garden will necessitate the construction of steps or ramps. Most ambulant gardeners will find that steps are easier to negotiate than ramps. Steps should be as wide and shallow as possible, as they will not only be easier to climb but will allow planks to be laid over them to ease the transportation of wheeled garden equipment. Alternatively, sloping ramps can be built at the side of the steps for this purpose. For wheelchair gardeners, ramps are essential. Where possible, make slopes no steeper than 1:15, a gradient that should be manageable by both ambulant and wheelchair gardeners alike (although it may be possible to have slightly steeper slopes if a powered wheelchair is used). If a ramp has to be longer than about 10m (33ft), a level area should be provided every 4.6m (15ft) along it to enable a wheelchair gardener to rest.

It may be necessary to erect a handrail on one or both sides of the path, especially near to steps or ramps. Many materials can be used for handrails, but galvanized piping, although perhaps a little unattractive, is the most practical. It is, however, vital that any handrail is strong, is securely fixed and is free from any play or movement so that it can safely bear the gardener's weight.

Ground-level Beds

It is likely that the ground-level beds already present in the garden will need some modification if they are to be tended easily. Because uneven soil is difficult to walk on and will not support a stick or walking frame, it will be necessary to have access to all parts of the bed from a hard surface.

The existing beds will often be found to be too wide to be worked easily, and this can best be overcome by laying paths along one or both sides of the bed. The maximum practical width of a bed allowing easy access from a path is 60cm (2ft); if there is a path on both sides, 1.2m (4ft) is the optimum width. These paths can also act as useful weed barriers if the bed adjoins a lawn or other similar feature. It is perfectly possible for a wheelchair gardener with a strong upper body to work ground-level beds of this width from the path by using long-handled tools.

Closely placed stepping stones leading to a hard surface such as a large paving slab, which will give the gardener a firm surface on which to stand and work, can be laid throughout the bed to give access for tasks that might be difficult to carry out from the path, such as the pruning of shrubs and roses.

However, if the gardener has to use any form of walking aid, stepping stones are not really suitable because of the ever-present danger that the stick will be placed on, and sink into, the soil, which could cause a fall. If access is required, it is better to construct a small path, wide enough for the walking aid, leading into the bed.

Raised Beds

There are various methods of raising beds to enable the gardener to tend plants from a seated or standing position. It is not always necessary to have raised beds especially built, as it can be possible to adapt existing garden features, such as banks, low walls and terraces, to suit the gardener's special requirements.

Banks can provide a conveniently accessible habitat for a variety of small plants, and if there is a

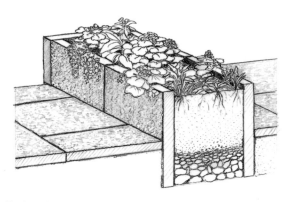

Paving slabs can be used to make a simple raised bed if they can be held upright against a paved area such as the edge of a patio. Line the slabs with heavy-duty polythene, making holes in the bottom for drainage, and make sure that you pack hardcore in the bottom one-third before adding soil.

retaining wall, plants can be grown either between the stones or in holes made at intervals in it by the removal of the occasional stone or brick. If the bank or wall is of a convenient working height – usually no more than 60cm (2ft) – it is also possible for a border to be made to run along the top of it. Similarly, terraced gardens provide natural raised beds, which can be worked from the lower level.

Plants can often be grown in a cavity between two brick walls that has been filled with drainage material and soil. This is particularly useful for plants such as herbs and alpines that like freely draining conditions, but if the cavity is wide enough it is perfectly possible to grow some of the larger herbaceous plants, small shrubs or even a low hedge in this way.

Where the garden is flat or where there are no existing features that can be easily utilized, raised beds will have to be specially constructed. They should be of a height and width that will enable the gardener to reach all parts comfortably, but the dimensions will vary depending on the capabilities of the individual, and it may be wise to experiment with a small bed at first to find the optimum size that can be easily managed. Generally, a bed 60cm (2ft) high would be suitable for a wheelchair user, while 85cm (2ft 10in) might be more appropriate for the ambulant disabled; the width should be 60cm (2ft), or 1.2m (4ft) if there is access from both sides. The construction of raised beds of differing heights can make a garden more visually interesting, and this might be considered by an ambulant gardener who finds bending easier on some days than on others. There should always be a firm and level non-slip surface of at least 1.2m (4ft) in front of all raised beds to allow adequate space for unhindered movement when working.

Plants particularly suited to raised-bed cultivation

Achillea × lewisii 'King Edward'; *Azalea*; *Calluna*; *Campanula carpactica*; *C. glomerata*; *Crocus chrysanthus*; *Dianthus*; *Erica carnea*; *Eryngium planum*; *Euphorbia polychroma*; *Hebe* 'Youngii'; *Helleborus*; Herbs; *Hypericum olympicum*; *Iberis sempervirens* 'Weisser Zwerg'/'Little Gem'; *Juniperus communis* 'Compressa'; *Mahonia aquifolium*; *Narcissus*; *Pernettya mucronata*; *Phlox subulata*; *Rhododendron impeditum*; Roses; *Salix × boydii*; *Saxifraga burseriana*; *S. × urbium primuloides*; *Sedum spathulifolium*; *Solidago* (shorter varieties); *Thymus serpyllum*.

Raised beds can be made in a number of ways and from a variety of materials. Sink gardens or troughs set on brick piers make attractive, small raised beds, which are easy to manage. Larger beds of brick or natural stone can be built in a variety of interesting shapes and are probably the most visually attractive. However, they require some effort to build. The walls will require a hardcore and concrete foundation and, if the bed is to be longer than 1.2m (4ft), it is essential to key in buttresses at 1.2m (4ft) intervals to give the walls the necessary strength to support the weight of soil.

If they are not going to be exposed to direct sunlight, raised beds can be built of peat blocks. These beds have a natural appearance and are easily built as the blocks are light to handle, but if the blocks are exposed to continual sunlight they will become dry and brittle, and the walls of the bed will gradually disintegrate. Regular watering of the blocks can prevent this, but that is an additional task, which should be avoided if possible. Before building with peat blocks it is necessary to moisten them thoroughly. A small trench, the outline of the bed, is dug and the first course of peat blocks laid in it so that the top of each block protrudes about 2.5cm (1in) above soil level. Further courses of peat blocks are built up on this so that the walls gently slope inwards. After each successive layer of blocks is set in position, soil must be put into the bed and firmly compressed behind the blocks until the required height is reached.

A quickly erected raised bed can be made from up-ended paving slabs and heavy duty polythene sheeting. Although these beds can have a rather utilitarian appearance, they are a good choice for the vegetable garden. Paving slabs, 60 × 90cm (2 × 3ft), are placed on end, and one-third of the longer end is dug in and fixed into the soil. Drainage material is spread over the bottom to a depth of

about 20cm (8in), and the sides are lined with polythene to prevent the soil from escaping through the joints between the paving stones. The remaining space is filled with soil.

When a raised bed is being prepared for planting, about one-third of the depth should be filled with drainage material such as broken bricks or rubble; if the soil is heavy, further drainage should be installed below soil level, and if the bed is standing on a solid base, this should be broken up. Ideally, the drainage material should be covered with inverted grass turves to prevent the compost from being washed through and eventually clogging the drainage. If turves are unavailable, peat blocks or coarse peat are effective substitutes. The soil or compost is put on top of this and gently firmed so that it comes to about 5–7.5cm (2–3in) below the top. Allow some time for the soil level to settle before planting and add more soil if necessary. Generally, the type of soil used in a raised bed will depend on the type of plants that are to be grown in it. Ordinary garden soil is suitable for most types of plants. Peat or sharp sand can be added to improve its texture if it is very heavy or clayey. If acid-loving plants such as ericas, callunas or azaleas are to be grown, however, a lime-free mixture should be used. These acid-lovers are particularly well suited to raised-bed cultivation, and a raised bed of peat blocks containing such plants is especially attractive and, being easy to construct and care for, should be well within the capabilities of most gardeners, whatever their degree of handicap or infirmity.

GROWING VEGETABLES IN RAISED BEDS

For wheelchair gardeners or those who have difficulty in bending, vegetables are most easily grown in a raised bed. Not only can they be more easily tended when they are at a higher level, but the gathering and harvesting of the crop is also much easier. However, the limitations of space make rotation of crops, which is essential for brassicas, difficult, and, because of the relative shallowness of the soil in a raised bed, the selection of vegetables that can be grown successfully will be more limited than for ground-level beds.

Many of the deep-rooting vegetables such as parsnips are unsuitable, as are some taller growing vegetable such as Brussels sprouts, runner beans and broad beans, which are difficult to tend and harvest and can also be prone to wind damage and being blown over. A raised bed used for vegetables should be in an open, sunny position and close to a convenient water supply. Vegetables need far more light and moisture than do most flowers, and they tend to dry out more quickly when grown in a raised bed. As space is more limited in a raised bed, it must be put to optimum use. It is, therefore, always wise to grow some of the more unusual varieties and to stagger the planting of a crop over a period so that the plants do not all mature at the same time, especially with perishable crops such as cabbages and lettuces, otherwise much produce can be wasted.

Vegetables suited to raised-bed cultivation
Beetroot: 'Detroit Little Ball', 'Sutton's Globe'; cabbage: 'Primo', 'Hispi'; carrot: 'Parisian Rondo', 'Chantenay', 'Scarla'; celeriac; lettuce: 'Tom Thumb', 'Little Gem'; onions; peas (early low-growing varieties): 'Little Marvel', 'Kelvedon Wonder'; annual spinach: 'Greenmarket', 'Sigma-leaf'; tomatoes: 'The Amateur'; turnip: 'Snowball'.

Special Tools and Techniques

As well as thoughtful design and the eradication of those features that are too difficult to manage, the careful selection of suitable garden tools and the employment of special gardening techniques can greatly ease specific tasks, making them more easily managed and, therefore, more enjoyable. As with design, the type of tools chosen and techniques employed will depend on the particular capabilities of the gardener. There is a variety of specialized equipment available to suit a wide range of disabilities, but think for a few minutes before buying, as it may be possible to adapt some existing equipment. The handles of forks and trowels can be padded to make their use easier for people with weak or arthritic hands, for instance, or small fork- or trowel-heads can be fitted to longer handles. However, where there is a mixture of raised and ground-level beds in the garden it is often more suitable to purchase a single, multi-purpose tool with an adjustable, telescopic handle and a number of interchangeable heads. This can be used for a variety of purposes and is invaluable for the handicapped or elderly gardener, for not only can the angle of work be varied, but the tool can be adjusted for work from a seated or standing position.

Cultivating the Soil

Soil cultivation is probably the most physically demanding task in the garden, often requiring a great deal of bending and strength, and it therefore presents the greatest challenge to the handicapped gardener. Frequent deep digging in a well-planned and planted adapted garden will, on the whole, be unnecessary, but if digging is contemplated at some point – during the initial preparation of the site or when annual vegetables are to be grown in ground-level beds, for example – specialized equipment should be considered.

MECHANICAL ROTAVATORS

Neglected areas of ground that would otherwise be difficult for a handicapped or elderly person to cultivate easily by other means can be quickly covered with a mechanical rotavator. The smaller, lightweight, petrol-engined models can be managed by most ambulant gardeners, and they may be either hired or purchased. Most suitable are those fitted with a clutch, which allows more control over the speed of travel, so enabling the gardener to proceed at his or her own pace and to stop for rests whenever necessary without having to restart the engine.

'TERREX' SPADE (AUTOMATIC SPADE)

The use of a 'Terrex' spade, with its unique lever action, allows a gardener to dig without the need either to bend his or her back or to lift spadefuls of soil. As well as being particularly useful for elderly or disabled gardeners, these spades are also time-savers for the able-bodied, allowing them to dig a larger area of ground at one time than if they were using a conventional spade. The spade is pushed into the ground with the foot plate, and the handle is then levered backwards. The spring action propels the soil fowards away from the trench. On light soils it is possible to dig with this spade using the hands alone. There is also an optional fork attachment available.

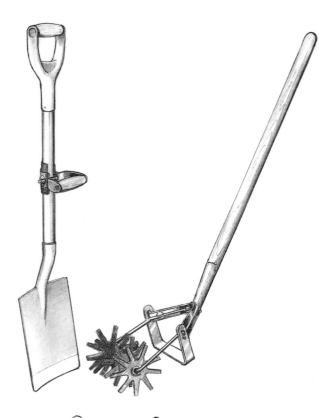

CONVENTIONAL DIGGING TOOLS

It is possible to adapt conventional spades and forks by fitting a D-shaped handle half-way down the shaft. This helps with lifting the weight of soil before turning it over and eliminates the need to bend quite as much. A D-shaped handle fitted to smaller, 'junior' forks and spades can allow wheelchair or seated gardeners to dig the soil.

SOIL TILLER

A good tilth can be produced by using a soil tiller, which can be used by gardeners who are unable to dig at all. These consist of two, three or four star-shaped wheels with a hoe-like blade behind, and when they are pushed and pulled through the soil, the hoe blade digs into the surface and the starred wheels chop the soil. The depth of cultivation can be controlled by raising or lowering the shaft. Using a soil tiller is not heavy work and involves no bending at all.

Opposite: one of the most useful tools for a gardener is a 'Terrex' or terrain spade; left: a D-shaped handle attached to an ordinary spade or fork and a scuffle hoe; below (from left to right): a long-handled weeder, a 'cut and hold' flower cutter, a long-handled trowel, a double hoe, a wheel-type seed sower, a dibber, a long-handled garden line, a scissor-action grabber for clearing refuse and an 'Easi-Kneeler' stool.

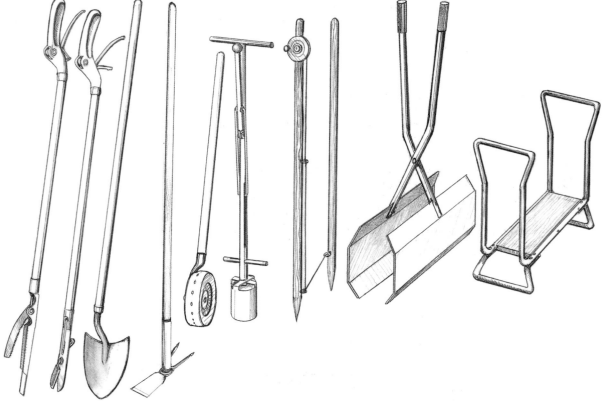

Providing safe, easy access around the garden is vital, but make sure that paths are free of all uneven edges .

SOWING SEED

Sowing and planting ground-level beds can be a major problem for those gardeners who have difficulty in bending. To make it easier to put down a line before sowing or planting, consider making a special garden line fixed to two broom handles, each about 90cm (3ft) long and sharpened at one end, to replace the usual shorter ones, which do require the gardener to bend. The line can be kept tidy by using a fishing reel attached to the top of one handle, and feeding the line down the handle through screw eyes. The line can be attached to another screw eye at the bottom of the other handle.

Drills or holes can be easily made using the back of a rake, a light draw-hoe or simply a sharpened broom handle. Small seeds can be sown using a wheel-type seed-sower with a long handle. Larger or pelleted seeds can be accurately directed into position by dropping them through rigid plastic piping, 2.5cm (1in) in diameter and cut to a comfortable length.

PLANTING

Most gardeners prefer to plant from a kneeling position, using a short-handled trowel. If it is difficult to get into or up from this position, an

'Easi-Kneeler' stool can be a used. This has a platform on which the gardener can kneel, and arm supports to help the gardener return to a standing position. It can also be used as an easily transportable seat, and can be recommended for gardeners who have difficulty standing in one place for any length of time.

When it is necessary to plant from an upright position, a trowel head attached to a handle 1.2m (4ft) long can be used. A hole can be easily made, and the plant either dropped into it or placed on the trowel and guided into it, and the soil firmed around it. Alternatively, a dibber, which makes a neat circular hole without the need to bend or kneel, can be used for planting bulbs or pot-grown plants. Small pot-grown plants can be dropped through a length of lightweight plastic drainpipe placed over the hole.

WEEDING

Handicapped gardeners can usually employ most, if not all, of the control measures described in Chapter 3 to keep weeds in check. However, some may find handling large quantities of diluted contact weed-killer difficult. In such cases the weedkiller can be applied from a small plastic container (such as a used liquid detergent bottle). When the bottle is squeezed, a jet of weedkiller can be easily directed through a hole made in the cap on to weeds either from a standing position or from a wheelchair.

A long-handled weed puller is a useful aid for removing isolated weeds complete with roots. The tool consists of a blade, which is pushed into the soil next to the weed. A 'jaw', operated by squeezing a trigger on the handle, closes around the weed, enabling the gardener to remove it with its root system intact. A weed puller, with its long reach and grip, can double as a general 'helping hand' in the garden, for picking up pots, dropped tools and so on, and it can also be of great help when planting, making the accurate placing of plants in their holes much easier.

PRUNING

Many disabled garders find conventional cutting tools such as secateurs difficult to manage. It is especially important, therefore, for gardeners with weak hands to select trees and shrubs that do not require any regular pruning. However, for light pruning, cutting flowers and dead-heading a floral

A feast for the eye perhaps, but a garden such as this could well prove a nightmare for an elderly or disabled gardener. Maintaining the low borders with a succession of colourful annuals and edging the lawn will make gardening into a chore rather than the enjoyable recreation it should be.

cutter can be a great aid. This is a lightweight cut-and-hold secateur, which can be used one-handed. The blade, which both cuts and holds the stem, is operated by a trigger in the grip, and as the handle is usually at least 75cm (30in) long, the cutter can be used over a wide area from a chair or when standing without the need to change position. For heavier pruning, ratchet secateurs enable the gardener to cut through quite large stems and branches without having to exert much pressure.

LAWN CARE

Any lawn that is to be tended by the handicapped or elderly must be well laid out to make its maintenance as easy as possible. Be sure to surround the lawn with mowing stones to eliminate the need to trim the edges, which is a wearisome task for any gardener, and to keep the shape simple to avoid difficult corners, which can make mowing more time consuming and arduous. The choice of mower for the handicapped gardener is particularly important. Generally, the smaller, electrically powered machines, in which only the blades are driven, are the most suitable. They are lighter than other types and, as the mower is not mechanically driven along, allow the lawn to be mowed at the gardener's own pace. However, when mains-powered machines are used, always take great care to ensure that the cable is safely handled. A rotary hover mower, which floats on a cushion of air, is the lightest to handle when mowing and the easiest to push; it can also be the most suitable type of mower for most wheelchair gardeners, as it can be moved sideways in an arc, allowing a much larger area of lawn to be cut before the chair has to be moved to a new position.

ROUTINE MAINTENANCE

As with any easy-care garden much of the routine work can be eliminated by good design and careful plant choice. Because tying in and supporting plants can be particularly difficult for the handicapped or elderly, it is especially important to avoid plants that require this attention (although a number of ways of making this easier are given in Chapter 7).

The collection of garden debris and rubbish can be facilitated by the use of long-handled grabs, which allow the disabled gardener to pick up quite large amounts of garden waste in much the same way as an able-bodied person using two boards, except that the 1m (3ft 6in) long, scissor-action handles preclude the need to bend. Small amounts of garden debris can be collected and transported in buckets, although it is often more convenient for

wheelchair gardeners to use polythene carrier bags instead. These can be hooked on to the arm of the wheelchair, and they take up far less space than rigid buckets, which is an important factor when the wheelchair is parked close to a raised bed.

Transporting heavier loads can present more of a problem. Gardeners who can use a wheelbarrow should choose one constructed of light materials to keep weight to a minimum and one that is a good shape for tipping out, or picking up, heavy loads. Barrows that take the weight over two wheels and are equipped with a pram handle are much more suitable than the more conventional single-wheel, two-handled types, as they can be pushed either single-handed or double-handed. Many handicapped gardeners, such as those with bad backs, cannot use a conventional wheelbarrow because they cannot lift any heavy loads into or out of the barrow. A wheelbarrow that can be lowered to ground level by a lever action of the handles is now available, and this makes any lifting unnecessary when filling or emptying the barrow. The wheelbarrow is simply lowered, filled, by rolling, sliding or brushing the load into it, then raised again.

In situations where wheelbarrows cannot be used, it may be possible for the ambulant gardener to move items that are too heavy to lift – large stones or slabs for example – by rolling or sliding them over the ground. This is easier if some strong sacking or old carpet is inserted under the load. This can be dragged along by the corners without too much bending.

Watering can present a problem to the handicapped gardener, especially as raised beds can dry out more quickly than ground-level beds and so require more frequent watering. Handling and refilling watering cans is heavy and difficult work as well as being inefficient. Using a hose can also present the handicapped gardener with problems. Long lengths of hose can become entangled around plants or make the manoeuvring of wheelchairs almost impossible. When a hose is used, keep it wound on a hose reel of the type that allows water to flow while the hose is still coiled. The hose reel should ideally be connected to a standpipe situated in the centre of the garden. This will allow all parts of the garden to be reached with the minimum amount of hose un-coiled. After watering, the hose can easily be re-wound by turning the reel handle.

The easiest and most practical method of watering is by an automatic watering system (see Chapter 7). This can be installed quite easily and cheaply and will keep all parts of the garden, including raised beds, adequately supplied with water without any effort from the gardener.

6. The Lawn

It is perfectly feasible for a lawn to occupy a large area of the easy-care garden, for a well-designed lawn can be a most labour-efficient feature. Once established, a lawn requires little maintenance apart from mowing when the grass is growing actively and watering during periods of drought.

It is true that a lawn can be hard work. A pristine, closely-mown, luxury lawn composed entirely of the compact, fine-leaved grasses, the bents and fescues, which has a characteristic 'bowling green' appearance, involves far too much work to interest the easy-care gardener. This type of lawn requires careful site preparation, is hard to establish, will not stand up to hard wear or any neglect and demands a continual programme of heavy maintenance. Far better for the easy-care gardener is a utility-grade lawn consisting of a mixture of broad-leaved turf grasses plus some bents and fescues. Such a lawn will appear attractive, will be low in maintenance and will stand up well to hard wear and some neglect, without losing its vitality or becoming unsightly. It establishes itself easily on a wide variety of soils and quickly forms a dense, healthy sward, which will prevent any wind-blown weed seeds from germinating.

Creating the Lawn

If some grass is already growing well on the site it may be unnecessary to create a new lawn from scratch, as it can be possible to improve the existing grass by good cultivation alone, thus avoiding the work and time involved in preparing the ground. If the site is reasonably level, little or no soil disturbance will be necessary. However, if it is uneven it will be necessary to level the bumpy areas of the lawn by first removing the turf, either by using a spade or, better still, a turfing iron. Dig and level the soil and replace the turf. Once it is level, the character of the site grass can be improved by following the lawn renovation programme described later in this chapter.

Where there is no suitable grass the site must be prepared, and then seeded or turfed. If a lawn is planned on a new, empty site it is often best to use

When you plan a lawn, keep the layout simple. Lay bricks or narrow paving stones around the whole area to eliminate the time-consuming task of having to trim the edges and where a lawn runs right up to a vertical surface mowing stones are essential or a strip of grass, inaccessible to the mower, will need to be trimmed by hand.

seed to put the whole site down to grass. The grass will act as an attractive and effective temporary ground cover, giving you time to create other features such as beds and borders at leisure.

To prepare the ground for seeding or turfing, clear it of all weeds and dig it over, removing any debris or stones. Incorporate as much organic, humus-making material as possible and, if possible, improve heavy soils by adding lime-free sand and light soils by adding peat. Level the ground and break down any large clods of soil. Leave to settle for a week or so, and on a day when the ground is reasonably dry, consolidate the soil by walking on it with short, overlapping steps with your weight on your heels. Any soft spots will be revealed by deep foot prints. Lightly rake to level the surface and repeat the treading and raking until the soil is firm (garden rollers are not recommended for consolidating the soil as they can leave air pockets, which eventually settle and give an uneven surface).

The site can now be grassed, either by sowing seed or laying turf, the main difference being that a lawn grown from seed takes time to become established while laying turf produces an 'instant' lawn. However, this is the only major advantage of turfing. Quality turf is difficult to obtain, much of the turf on sale being of meadow grass, which comes complete with weeds and 'weed grasses'. The advantage of seed is that the type of grass being used is known and can, therefore, be chosen to suit your particular needs.

Seed Mixtures

A large range of utility lawn seed mixtures is now available, and these can succeed under most conditions and on a wide range of soils. However, it is still important to select a good quality mixture

suitable for the conditions of your particular site, especially if your soil is a heavy clay or a very light sand. If the site is shaded a special mixture can be used, but it is better for the easy-care gardener to use an ordinary utility mixture and keep the grass rather longer than normal by mowing less frequently and with the mower blades set at a slightly higher than usual cutting height.

A utility lawn seed mixture will typically contain some compact, fine-leaved grasses such as brown top bent (*Agrostis tenuis*), Chewing's fescue (*Festuca rubra-commutata*) or creeping red fescue (*Festuca rubra rubra*) and one or more of the broad-leaved grasses.

Broad-leaved grasses

Smooth-stalked meadow grass (*Poa pratensis*) A good turf-producing grass, which is hard wearing and resistant to drought; particularly useful for light sandy soils and shady situations, it suits most conditions, with the exception of wet, chalky sites.

Rough-stalked meadow grass (*Poa trivalis*) Quick to establish but not as hardy, hard wearing or drought resistant as other varieties. Useful for wet, shady sites.

Wood meadow grass (*Poa nemoralis*) The most shade tolerant of all lawn grasses, it is useful for damp situations under trees; it will not tolerate close or frequent mowing, which eventually causes it to die out.

Timothy or **cat's tail** (*Phleum pratense*) A quick to germinate, hardy and hard-wearing broad-leaved grass, which thrives on heavy, wet soils, but cannot tolerate dry, sandy soils or close mowing.

Lesser timothy or **small cat's tail** (*Phleum bertolonii*) A very hardy, hard-wearing fine-leaved grass, which thrives on heavy wet soils.

Crested dog's-tail (*Cynosurus cristatus*) Very hard wearing and resistant to drought and suitable for all types of soil.

Perennial rye grass (*Lolium perenne*) Quick to establish, hard wearing and suitable for all soil types. Although found in many seed mixtures, rye grasses used to be considered unsuitable for lawns because of their rapid vertical growth and intolerance of close mowing. However, with the development of the modern slow-growing, dwarf, finer leaved strains such as Arno and Manhattan, or the very recently introduced and excellent Barclay and Elka strains, this is no longer true. To avoid frequent mowing, therefore, the easy-care gardener should not use a seed mixture containing perennial rye grass unless he or she is certain that only modern, slow-growing dwarf varieties have been included.

SOWING

The best time of year for sowing is between late August and early October, when the soil is still warm. Choose a fine, calm day when the top of the soil is dry but the ground is moist just below the surface. Carefully rake the surface of the soil to form small, straight furrows. Calculate the amount of seed required for an application rate of 40–55gm per sq m (1½–2oz per sq yard); higher rates encourage damping off, lower rates produce a thin, sparse growth. To ensure an even distribution of seed, sow a quarter over the whole plot as evenly as possible, and then repeat with the other quarters, each time sowing in a different direction. Once the seed has been sown the whole area should either be gently raked or a very light layer of fine peat scattered over the seed. This is to prevent excessive moisture loss, but it is important not to bury the seed, as this will result in patchy germination.

The seedlings should appear 7–21 days after sowing. The bed will have to be watered during any prolonged dry spells, and this should be done

Make sure that paving stones are sunk into the ground so that they do not interfere with grass cutting.

Although more expensive than turves cut from grassland or meadow, seeded turf is of a known type of grass, and it also has the advantage of being lighter and, therefore, easier to lay than other kinds of turf.

carefully with a fine spray so that the seedlings are not washed out of the ground.

Do not walk on or attempt to cut the grass until it is 5–7.5cm (2–3in) high. Three or four days before making the first cut, the grass will benefit from a light rolling, using, for example, the back roller of a cylinder mower with the blades held up. Although not essential, this 'breaks' the grass and firms the soil around the roots, encouraging the production of new shoots and helping the grass to establish itself quickly and withstand the first cut. The grass should be 'topped' on the first cut and only the top 12mm (½in) removed. If the bed is small and time and trouble will allow, this is best done with a pair of sharp shears, but if you use a mower, make sure that the blades are sharp, otherwise the seedlings may be pulled out of the soil or the roots sufficiently damaged to hinder development. No further mowing of an autumn-sown lawn will be required until the following spring, but a spring-sown lawn will require regular mowing throughout the summer, gradually lowering the cutting height.

TURFING

All turfing can be heavy work, but generally small turves are easier to lay than large ones. Turves are most usually supplied in separate pieces, 30 × 90cm

(1 × 3ft) in size, although smaller pieces may be available. The size should be considered if lifting is a problem. Measure and mark out the area to be grassed, bearing in mind that it will be necessary to order approximately 5 per cent extra to allow for any wastage. The ideal time to lay turf is on a fine, dry day in October or November, but provided that the soil is not waterlogged or frozen, turf can be laid at any time throughout the winter. If it is laid in the spring, great care must be taken to water regularly in warm or dry weather to prevent drying out and shrinkage of the turves.

Start with a straight row close to the stack of turves. Stand on a board so that you do not compact the soil as you lay the turf. Place the piece of turf in position and gently but firmly press it down with the back of a spade or a clean plasterer's hawk to ensure good contact between the roots and the soil. Start the second row with a half-sized turf so as to stagger the joints – rows of turves are laid like bricks in a wall. When the laying is complete, spread over and brush into the joints a light top-dressing (a mixture of one part peat, two parts loam and four parts sand is best) to fill any cracks. Do not subject the lawn to any heavy traffic until it becomes well established. When mowing becomes necessary, just 'top' the grass with the first cut, gradually reducing the cutting height for subsequent cuts.

LAWN MAINTENANCE

A number of tasks have to be carried out on established lawns, which, if done correctly, not only enhance their appearance but help the grass to form and maintain a dense, disease-resistant, healthy sward, which will be an effective barrier against weed invasion.

MOWING

All lawns have to be mowed, but, provided that the lawn has been well designed and has no awkward corners or inaccessible areas to make mowing difficult, this need not be a time-consuming or particularly arduous job.

Start mowing in spring (March or April depending on climate) when the grass begins active growth. The optimum height and frequency of the cut depends on the type of lawn, weather and time of year. Generally, the grass in a utility-grade lawn should be maintained at a height of approximately 2.5cm (1in) throughout summer and slightly longer, 3cm (1¼in), in spring and autumn and during periods of drought. Luxury-grade lawn should be 12mm (½in) in summer and 20mm (¾in) in spring and autumn. Keeping the grass longer than the recommended height over a prolonged period will encourage the growth of coarser grasses, which will eventually replace the more desirable fine lawn grasses. Mowing shorter than the recommended height will greatly reduce the vigour of the grass, increasing the risk of weed invasion and disease.

WEEDING

Good lawn management can greatly reduce the risk of weeds establishing themselves in the turf, but any broad-leaved lawn weeds that do gain a foothold are easily and quickly controlled thanks to the many selective chemical herbicides that are now available specifically for lawns. When used at their recommended dosage rate, these are harmless to established grasses but will destroy a wide range of lawn weeds. Because no single chemical can control all types of weed, it is best to choose a manufactured preparation that contains at least two or preferably three of the common lawn herbicides such as 2,4-D, MCPA, mecoprop or dicamba. However, these chemicals should not be used on newly sown lawns, as they can do a great deal of harm to grass seedlings. If weeds are a problem on new lawns, use a specially formulated herbicide.

Before using any weedkiller always read and follow the maker's instuctions. Choose a still day when there is little possibility of rain for several hours. Ideally, the lawn should not have been mown for at least two days before application, and the grass should be dry but the soil moist. Do not use any lawn weedkiller in times of drought. Liquid weedkillers can be applied using a watering can fitted with a fine rose or a sprinkler bar. A sprayer may be more suitable for larger lawns, but guard against the ever-present danger of the fine spray drifting over neighbouring shrubs or flowers.

Renovating a neglected lawn

When you move house you may inherit a neglected lawn or perhaps, because of long illness or absence from home, your own lawn may become overgrown and full of weeds. If some desirable lawn grasses are still present, the lawn can be reclaimed by carrying out a renovation programme.

The best time to start is spring. Cut down the tall weeds and grasses to a height of about 7.5cm (3in), using a billhook, scythe, strimmer or a rotary mower set at the highest possible cutting height. Rake out the dead vegetation. Over the next few weeks continue to mow, gradually lowering the height of each cut until the recommended height for the type of lawn is reached. Apply a combined lawn feed and weedkiller in the early summer and treat any patches of moss with a proprietary moss killer. Repeat applications can be given six weeks later if necessary. Any further weeds that may appear can be destroyed by spot treatment using an aerosol or paint-on weedkiller. In early September apply a suitable autumn lawn feed and scarify the lawn to remove any thatch. Clumps of weed grasses should be dug out and any bare patches reseeded. Top-dress the whole lawn with a mixture of peat, loam and sand with a little grass seed added, working the dressing well into the surface with the back of a rake. Apply evenly and take care not to smother the grass. The following season usual lawn maintenance only will be required.

FEEDING

At first sight it may seem odd to recommend the application of lawn fertilizers, which encourage grass to grow quickly and thereby increase the amount of mowing required. However, it is much more important and labour-saving in the long run to replace the soil nutrients that have been depleted by a season's mowing, otherwise the grass becomes pale green and the turf thin and sparse and more prone to invasion by moss and weeds and susceptible to drought and diseases.

Apply a fertilizer with a high nitrogen content in spring or summer. This will rapidly produce a rich green colour and increase the vigour of the grass.

7. Beds and Borders

Beds and borders usually represent the main decorative planting in a garden. In an easy-care garden, however, the total area given over to beds and borders may well have to be less than in a conventional garden to reduce maintenance. It is particularly important, therefore, that any beds and borders created are well planned and planted so that the best possible decorative effect can be achieved throughout the year. Concentrate the main planting in one or two main beds or borders. These will allow greater scope for planting, will look more imposing and will be easier to maintain than a large number of smaller beds or borders.

Siting

Beds and borders should ideally be situated where plants will receive sufficient amounts of light, air and moisture to allow optimum growth. Small beds can be created in almost any suitable space that is not overhung by large trees, but larger borders can be more difficult to site because of the limitations of size and shape of the garden. South- or west-facing aspects are best, as they allow the widest selection of plants to be grown. A north-facing border is the most difficult to plant, as the choice of suitable plants is more limited.

Although a bank of shrubs, a wall or a hedge will make an excellent backdrop for showing off a border to best advantage, these barriers can adversely affect the growing conditions for plants at the back of the border. The soil can remain exceptionally dry near the footings of a wall, and a wall or the overhanging branches of hedging plants can considerably reduce the amount of light the border receives. This causes the plants at the back of the border, in their quest for light, to produce weak and spindly growth, which may require staking even though the plants may normally be self-supporting. Where space permits, extend the border outwards by 90–120cm (3–4ft) and lay paving of this width between the back of the border and the wall or hedge. This will help prevent the rearmost border plants becoming starved of light and moisture and will also greatly aid access to the back of the border.

Borders look far more imposing when viewed down their length rather than straight on, as even the best planted border will have a few seasonal gaps. Site the border so that it runs directly or obliquely away from the windows of the house or any other viewing points, so that it appears to best advantage as one looks or walks down its length.

Planning

When planning a bed or border it is always best to work out the scheme on graph paper, as a haphazard approach is rarely successful. The most important consideration in positioning plants is their size. Beds are generally designed to be viewed from all sides, and are planted accordingly, with the tallest plants being given a more or less central position and increasingly shorter subjects planted towards the sides. Borders are usually long and narrow and traditionally back on to a hedge, wall or fence, and they are designed to be viewed from the front and sides only. The tallest subjects should, therefore, be positioned at the back and the shorter ones towards the front. However, these rules should not be applied too strictly. Perfect grading by size, although presenting an unbroken view, can look very artificial. An occasional group of tall or clump-forming subjects cutting into the foreground can add interest and create a more natural effect.

Although less important for flowering shrubs and trees, flower colour is of prime importance when positioning herbaceous plants in a bed or border. It is sometimes held that no colours clash in nature, but it has to be said that some colour combinations do look better than others. In particular, avoid planting strong, hot colours, such as the brighter shades of red, cerise and orange, close to each other. These colours do not harmonize well and are best separated by later-flowering plants, which provide a barrier of foliage between clashing colours. Experiments can be made to find the best colour combinations by arranging cut-out shapes of coloured paper on the plan of the bed.

As well as flower colour, the most impressive plantings are those designed with contrast in foliage and flower form in mind. For example, lacy foliage appears much more delicate and refined when grown close to plants with large, undissected or leathery leaves. And large groups of plants with round, daisy-like flowers, such as erigerons or asters, can be contrasted with groups of irregularly shaped flower types, such as salvias or polygonums and the tall flowery spikes of such plants as *Acanthus mollis*, kniphofias and lupins.

Planting

Before planting, mark out the planting position with canes for each plant to check the spacing. Dig a hole for each plant, making sure that it is neither too deep nor too narrow. Improve drainage by breaking up the soil at the bottom of the hole and mix in some peat, bonemeal and slow-release fertilizer.

Bare-rooted or pre-packaged plants

If the roots of pre-packaged plants are dry, stand them in water for about two hours before planting; this is especially necessary when planting dry-rooted herbaceous perennials. If you are planting a bare-rooted tree that will require support until it becomes well established, it is important to take this into account before planting, as is discussed later in this chapter.

Place the plant in the hole. The old soil mark on the stem should be at or just below the soil's surface, and this can be accurately checked by placing a piece of wood across the hole. Add a little soil or planting mixture and work it in around the roots. Shake the plant up and down, work in more soil and gently firm it in with your fists. Half-fill the hole with more soil and firm it by treading lightly around the outside of the hole, gradually working inwards. Add more soil until the hole is filled and again firm by light treading.

Balled or container-grown plants

Water the plants well 24 hours before planting. The hole should be large and deep enough to allow the soil ball to be surrounded by a 5–10cm (2–4in) layer of planting mixture. When planting container-grown subjects, do not use ordinary garden soil; instead use a mixture of equal parts peat and soil with perhaps a little bonemeal or slow-release fertilizer added. If ordinary soil is used, the roots may not grow from the potting compost into the soil, particularly if the potting compost used in the container is peat based. Cover the bottom of the hole with a 7.5–10cm (3–4in) layer of planting mixture. If the plant is container-grown, remove it by inverting the container and gently tapping the sides while supporting the rootball with the fingers. If you are planting a balled plant, untie and carefully cut away the covering when the plant is positioned in the hole.

Tease out a few roots, taking care not to break up the soil ball, fill the remaining space with planting mixture and gently firm down with the hands. Leave a saucer-shaped depression to collect water if it is a moisture-loving subject.

General aftercare

Water in immediately after planting. The next day, hoe the ground around the plant to break up any compacted soil caused by footprints or watering. Keep moist until well established. A mulch applied to the soil both inhibits weed growth and helps to retain moisture. Weeds or grass should not be allowed to grow around the base of a newly planted shrub.

TYPES OF BED OR BORDER

In the past it was customary to divide the garden into sections and to have several formal beds or borders, each dedicated to specific groups of plants. These ranged from the very labour-intensive half-hardy annual beds to the much more easily managed informal tree and shrub beds. Nowadays, gardens are far less regimented as the value of mixed planting has become appreciated. It is now common to include other types of plants, such as bulbs or sub-shrubs, in predominantly herbaceous or shrub beds and borders to give a more prolonged variety of display. Growing herbaceous plants, bulbs, sub-shrubs, shrubs and trees in a single mixed bed is a space-saving and labour-efficient method of growing a wide range of plants that will provide interest throughout the year.

Left and below: before planting an herbaceous border, experimenting with different colour combinations of cut-out paper will enable you to avoid colour clashes and make sure that taller plants and shrubs are positioned appropriately.

HERBACEOUS

The herbaceous border has developed something of a reputation for being a labour-intensive garden feature in recent times, but this need not be so provided that it is well planned and planted.

Because the choice of herbicides for use on herbaceous borders is much more limited than it is for shrubberies, it is important to select plants that will form a dense, continuous canopy of foliage when mature to suppress weed growth by denying the weeds light and air. Choose the bushier types with a spreading habit, and plant these slightly closer together than their maximum spread. Use bold groupings for maximum visual effect, which helps to avoid a 'spotty' appearance when the bed is in flower. Unless a plant is very substantial or the bed or border is exceptionally small, a grouping of five plants of the same species or variety should be the minimum.

Most herbaceous plants need an annual tidying to remove the dead stems that are left above the ground as the plants die back in autumn. This is not

a particularly arduous job, taking only one or two hours each year. Cut the stems to ground level in autumn or spring. Cutting back the stems in autumn, after the last flowers have faded, will make the garden look tidier in winter, but in cold gardens or if tender varieties are grown, leave the stems uncut throughout the winter and remove them in spring. The dead vegetation will help to protect the crowns from the worst of the winter weather.

Flowering times

The careful selection of bulbous and herbaceous plants and flowering shrubs makes it quite easy to prolong the flowering season of beds and borders and to create a garden in which some plants will be in bloom almost every month of the year.

Easy-care herbaceous plants and bulbs

(B) = bulb

January
Galanthus nivalis (B); *Helleborus niger*.

February
Anenome blanda (B); *Crocus chrysanthus* (B).

March
Anenome coronaria (B); *A. nemorosa* (B); *Bergenia cordifolia*; *Crocus vernus* (B); *Helleborus orientalis*; *Narcissus* (B).

April
Brunnera macrophylla; *Epimedium perralderianum*; *Paeonia mlokosewitschii*; *Phlox subulata*; *Pulmonaria officinalis*; Tulips (B); *Waldsteinia ternata*.

May
Ajuga reptans; *Dianthus deltoides*; *Dicentra eximia*; *D. formosa*; *D. spectabilis*; *Dodecatheon meadia*; *Geranium macrorrhizum*; *G. renardii*; *Muscari armeniacum* (B); *Nepeta* × *faassenii*; *Sedum spathulifolium*; *Tiarella cordifolia*.

June
Astilbe × *arendsii*; *Eremurus* (Shelford hybrids); *Geum chiloense*; *Heuchera sanguinea*; *Kniphofia* (June-flowering varieties); *Lupinus* (Russell hybrids); *Lysimachia nummularia*; *L. punctata*; *Paeonia lactiflora*; *Saxifraga* × *urbium*.

July
Achillea filipendulina; *Alchemilla mollis*; *Aster alpinus*; *Campanula carpatica*; *C. glomerata*; *Crocosmia* × *crocosmiiflora*; *Echinops ritro*; *Erigeron speciosus*; *Eryngium planum*; *Geranium* 'Russell Prichard'; *Hemerocallis* hybrids; *Kniphofia* (July-flowering varieties); *Stachys byzantina*.

August
Anenome × *hybrida*; *Aster amellus*; *A.* × *frikartii*; *A.* × *thomsonii* 'Nanus'.

September
Colchium speciosum (B); *Kniphofia* (September-flowering varieties).

Easy-care flowering shrubs and sub-shrubs

(E) = evergreen; (SE) = semi-evergreen

January
Erica carnea (E); *Viburnum* × *bodnantense*.

February
Chaenomeles speciosa.

March
Chaenomeles japonica; *C.* × *superba*; *Mahonia aquifolium* (E); *Rosmarinus officinalis* (E); *Salix* × *boydii*.

April
Berberis darwinii (E); *B.* × *stenophylla* (E); *B. thunbergii*; *Lonicera nitida* (E); *Osmanthus delavayi* (E); *Prunus* × *blireana*; *P. cerasifera*; *P. subhirtella*; *Skimmia japonica* (E); *Ulex europaeus* (E).

May
Berberis verruculosa (E); *Choisya ternata* (E); *Cornus florida*; *Gaultheria shallon* (E); *Genista lydia*; *Olearia* × *scilloniensis* (E); *Paeonia lactiflora*; *P. lutea*; *P. mlokosewitschii*; *P. suffruticosa*; *Pernettya mucronata* (E); *Philadelphus coronarius*; *P. microphyllus*; *Rhododendron augustinii*; *R. impeditum*; *Syringa meyeri*; *Viburnum opulus*; *Weigela florida*.

June
Buddleia alternifolia; *Cistus* × *aguilari* (E); *C.* × *corbariensis* (E); *C.* × *cyprius* (E); *C.* × *lusitanicus* (E); *C.* × *purpureus* (E); *Cotoneaster congestus* (E); *C. dammeri* (E); *C. horizontalis*; *C. lacteus* (E); *Cytisus* × *beanii*; *C.* × *kewensis*; *C.* × *praecox*; *Genista hispanica*; *Hebe albicans* (E); *H. cupressoides* (E); *H. pinguifolia* (E); *Pyracantha rogersiana* (E); *Viburnum davidii* (E).

July
Artemisia abrotanum (SE); *Calluna vulgaris* (E); *Erica vagans* (E); *Genista aetnensis*; *Hypericum* × *moserianum*; *H. olympicum*; *Lavandula angustifolia* (E); *Olearia* × *haastii* (E); *Potentilla fruticosa*; *Senecio laxifolius* (E).

August
Gaultheria procumbens (E); *Hydrangea macrophylla*; *H. petiolaris*; *Vinca major* (E); *V. minor* (E).

September
Hypericum patulum (SE).

November
Mahonia × *media* 'Charity' (E); *Viburnum farreri* (E); *V. tinus* (E).

December
Erica erigena (E).

BULBS TO PLANT AND FORGET

Hardy bulbous, cormous or tuberous plants are ideally suited to the easy-care garden. They are easy to handle and to plant, and, as long as good quality stock is purchased, success is almost guaranteed. Once established, they need little attention apart from occasional dead-heading and feeding, but they provide the garden with a rich and almost limitless diversity of colour and form year after year and often when little else in the garden is in flower. Most spread themselves easily, either by seed, offsets (in the case of bulbs) or by simply extending their underground growth (as is the case with corms and tubers).

Because most bulbous subjects do not provide much defence against weed invasion, it is best to grow them, not in beds of their own, but in association with other plants, which will more effectively clothe the ground and reinforce the bulbous plants against invasion by weeds. These plants should either make most of their growth after the bulbs have flowered or be of such a type that the bulbous subjects can grow up through them. In this way the flowers of bulbous subjects will be shown off to their best effect, weeds will be inhibited, and, as the ground will always be covered by planting, there will be no need to cultivate the soil, thus eliminating the risk of accidentally damaging unseen, dormant bulbs. Dwarf bulbs are ideally suited for growing in a blanket of low-growing plants, and taller types grow well among carpeting ground coverers. A special problem with some bulbous subjects, especially taller types such as the larger varieties of narcissus and tulip, is the unkempt appearance of the foliage as it dies back after flowering. This cannot be removed until it has completely died back, or vigour will be lost. Plant these types, therefore, where their dying foliage will not be an eyesore, such as in the middle or back of the border, where they will be covered by the developing foliage of other plants.

Suitable blanketing plants for dwarf bulbs
Acaena 'Blue Haze'; Ajuga reptans; Sedum spathuli-folium; Thymus serpyllum.

Suitable carpeting plants for bulbs
Gaultheria procumbens; Lamium maculatum; Polygonum affine; Saxifraga × urbium; Tiarella cordifolia; Waldsteinia ternata.

NATURALIZING BULBS

As well as using bulbs in beds and borders some can be naturalized in wild or woodland areas of the garden, or in turf, rough grass or areas of ground cover. Best suited for naturalizing are varieties of narcissus, snowdrop (Galanthus), or crocus (although the smaller types are, of course, un-suitable for naturalizing in tall, rampant grasses). A pleasantly natural effect can be achieved by scattering the bulbs casually within the prescribed area, and planting them directly where they fall.

PLANTING BULBS

When planting bulbs singly, make holes with a dibber, trowel or special bulb planter. The hole should be slightly deeper than the recommended planting depth. Add a little sand to the hole and set the bulb firmly into this to ensure that there is no air pocket left between the base of the bulb and the soil, which is a common cause of failure. Refill the hole and gently firm in. Water well after planting.

When planting large areas of bulbs, it is easier to dig out the soil to the required depth from the entire area to be planted. Cover the base with sand, place the bulbs at the desired spacing and press into the sand. Return the soil and tread down lightly to remove any air pockets that may have been created.

TREES AND SHRUBS

Trees and shrubs are most useful in the garden as they can extend the period of interest throughout the winter months when almost all perennial plants have either died back or have long since finished flowering. A flowering shrub can be found for practically every month of the year, and evergreen shrubs will, of course, give all year round foliage interest.

A border composed of carefully selected, easily maintained and long-lived trees and shrubs is an extremely labour-efficient garden feature and can be particularly useful for providing visual barriers within the garden, separating one part from another, dividing off the end of a long, narrow plot or bridging the transition between the formal and the informal, wilder areas of planting.

Planning a tree and shrub border requires a slightly different approach from that adopted for other types of border. While perennial subjects are best planted in large groups, many trees and shrubs are substantial enough to be planted singly, although smaller shrubs may still be grouped to give a more dramatic effect. However, it is still important that neighbouring plants complement each other. Loosely group plants that provide interest during the same season to stop the border having a 'bitty' appearance at different times of the year. Intersperse these groups with some evergreen subjects to give year-round foliage interest. The inclusion of a high proportion of evergreens is particularly important if the border is in permanent view from the house. On the whole, shape, form and texture are more important than flower colour, although it is always advisable to include some late-

flowering or berrying subjects or shrubs with foliage that colours well in autumn to provide a variety of colourful effects in the garden late in the year.

Shrubs must be allowed sufficient space if they are to show their form to best advantage when they are mature, although they should always be planted at a distance that will allow them just to merge with their neighbours when at maximum spread to form a canopy of foliage under which weeds will be unable to gain a foothold. However, this complete coverage can take several years to achieve, during which time the areas of bare soil between plants will not only be unattractive but will become rapidly colonized by weeds, an inevitable consequence of leaving any area of soil uncovered. Because of their size, dislike of disturbance and the permanency of shrubs, it is unwise to try to shorten this time by closer planting, as recommended for herbaceous borders, because shrubs are not easily replanted. Instead, a weed-suppressing mulch can be applied to the soil or, for a more attractive effect, dwarf ground-cover subjects can be planted between the shrubs. The ground cover can be kept clear of the new trees or shrubs, if necessary by using tree spats (see Chapter 3), until the shrubs become well established. Eventually the ground cover can be removed or will die out as the shrubs grow together. Alternatively, additional shrubs or herbaceous plants can be planted in the spaces and any remaining bare soil covered with a suitable mulch. This gives an almost immediate impression of maturity to the border, although as the permanent shrubs mature and demand more space, the filling plants must be removed and either discarded or planted in other areas of the garden.

MIXED BEDS OR BORDERS
Nothing can compare with the length of display provided by a mixed bed or border. While there is no shortage of colourful herbaceous plants that flower between late spring and early autumn, the choice for the rest of the year is more limited. Mixed planting can overcome this. Including other types of plant – bulbs, shrubs and trees – in a border can provide colour and interest while herbaceous plants are dormant. A mixed border is the best choice for a gardener who wishes to grow a wide variety of plants but does not have the luxury of separate borders devoted to different groups of plants because of lack of space or time.

When choosing plants for mixed planting the aim is to achieve an all-year-round effect. This need not

A mixed bed or border can provide colour and interest throughout the year.

be by flowers alone. Coloured foliage, bark and berries can all add interest to the display. To provide foliage effect throughout the winter, a high proportion of evergreens should be included. These will form the framework of the border, with other plants growing in bays or pockets among them.

MAINTAINING BEDS AND BORDERS

WEED CONTROL
Because the choice of herbicide for use on beds and borders is limited by the ever-present danger of damaging cultivated plants, full use should be made of the close-planting techniques already discussed to reduce to a minimum the risks of weed invasion. Applying a suitable and attractive mulch, such as peat, pulverized bark, compost or sawdust, to the entire bed will also add to the garden's defences against weeds.

If the plants have not yet grown too closely together to prevent easy access, any weeds growing between plants can be controlled by applying a translocated herbicide, such as glyphosate, with a weedwiper. Although translocated weedkillers take some time to enter a plant's system, always take care not to allow the herbicide to come into contact with the foliage of any cultivated plants. Accidental splashes on cultivated plants should be immediately and thoroughly washed off.

Provided there are no cultivated grasses nearby, grass growing among shrubs or herbaceous perennials can be controlled by an overall spray of an alloxydim-sodium based selective weedkiller. However, there is no such overall treatment for the control of broad-leaved weeds growing among herbaceous plants, although propachlor granules applied to established borders during early spring will prevent any germinating weeds for six to eight weeks. Any isolated persistent weeds growing among established herbaceous plants are best controlled manually or by careful spot treatment with a paint-on gel herbicide.

Some herbicides may, however, be used as overall treatments on well-established shrubberies if no other non-woody plants are present. Existing annual weeds can be destroyed by applying a contact weedkiller such as diquat or paraquat to their foliage, and simazine, applied to the soil at a low-dosage rate in early spring, will prevent any annual weeds developing during the season if the ground is not disturbed. Persistent perennial weeds in some shrubberies can be controlled by an application of dichlobenil early in the year. As an overall treatment, however, dichlobenil must be used with great selectivity and care. Some species of shrubs and ornamental trees are susceptible to it, and it is important to heed any warnings on the packaging about its suitablility and use. Dichlobenil has also proved to be unsuitable when used around shrubs growing on very light, sandy soils. If in doubt, do not use it except as a spot treatment for the occasional perennial weed.

SUPPORTING PLANTS

Providing extra support for plants can be a tiresome chore, but one that can be avoided if plants are well selected and not grown in too shady positions for their needs. In windy or exposed gardens it is particularly important to choose your plants carefully. If you have inherited a garden full of tall or weak-stemmed herbaceous plants, it will be necessary to support them until they can be replaced, at your leisure, with more robust subjects. For a small number of plants, producing only a few stems, bamboo canes can be used to support each stem or the whole plant can be supported by a few canes securely arranged around the plant and joined with string or wire.

If a large number of plants needs supporting it is much better to employ a more permanent method to eliminate the need to re-stake each plant season after season. Patent metal supports, consisting of a height-adjustable, horizontal metal grill on legs, are ideal and can be used for individual specimens or for groups of plants, depending on their size. These can be left in place throughout the winter, the new growth growing through, and being supported by, the grill. A similar method of providing support for a large number of plants growing together in a bed or border is to stretch a wide-meshed nylon net, attached to stakes, horizontally over the whole area.

Newly planted trees and shrubs may need staking until their roots become properly established to prevent them being rocked or toppled by strong winds. Staking a tree is best done at the time of planting. If the tree is bare-rooted, a stout stake should be hammered into the bottom of the planting hole to a depth of about 30cm (1ft) before the tree is placed in the hole. The stake should be about 10cm (4in) away from the main stem of the tree, to the side of the tree nearest to the direction from which the prevailing wind blows. Container-grown trees should be staked immediately after planting. A stake should be driven at a fairly acute angle into the soil on the side of the tree away from the direction of the prevailing wind so that it misses the root ball and crosses the main stem about a third of the way up. In both cases the stem should be secured to the stakes using proprietary rubber ties, which should be adjusted as the stem thickens.

FEEDING YOUR PLANTS

After some time, the plant nutrients in the soil – nitrogen, phosphorus, potassium and some trace elements – can become seriously depleted and must be replaced to secure continued healthy and vigorous growth. This is vital for the easy-care garden, where the most rapid growing together of plants is sought and the densest possible canopy of foliage is necessary to ensure the effective suppression of weeds.

Nitrogen, which is available to the plant as nitrates, is necessary for a rapid rate of growth, and the production of lush green foliage and of fruit and seeds. Phosphorus, which is available to the plant as phosphates, is particularly important for healthy root growth, germination and seed formation. Potassium, which is available as potash, improves resistance to disease and frost and promotes the production of good quality flowers and fruit. All fertilizers should contain these nutrients together with the essential trace elements. Special formulations containing a higher proportion of one element can be applied for specific purposes – a high nitrogen feed for lawns in spring and summer, for example, or a high potash feed for increasing fruit yield.

Fertilizers can be divided into two main classes: organic and inorganic. Organic fertilizers come mainly from animal and plant wastes and include all types of manure, bonemeal, seaweed and spent hops. Organic manures are slow to act but are long-lasting. Although some make useful organic mulches (see Chapter 3) and can be used to improve the texture of the soil, used as a sole source of nutrients, they can be less convenient than some of the inorganic fertilizers. Organic fertilizers are often bulky and can be difficult to handle, and, as their nutrient content is generally rather low, large quantities have to be applied.

Inorganic fertilizers either come from natural mineral sources or are manufactured. Ordinary inorganic fertilizers are generally quick acting and are highly concentrated; they must, therefore, be applied with care or plants may be overdosed and harmed. They readily dissolve in water, which may make application easy, but this has the disadvantage that they are leached out of the soil quite quickly, so that repeated applications become necessary.

For most situations, by far the most appropriate and convenient method of feeding plants is to use one of the concentrated slow-release types of inorganic fertilizer. When moistened, these release their fertilizer, which is encased in a semi-permeable capsule of resin, into the soil over a long period, thus reducing the risk of harming the plants

An architectural plant such as a phormium can be used to provide a focal point in an area of low-growing subjects.

by overdosing and eliminating the need for re-application at frequent intervals. Different formulations of slow-release fertilizers are available for different plant requirements, and there are also formulations that release the fertilizer at different rates. Three- to four-month formulations are most suitable for using around herbaceous plants, while longer lasting formulations, which release their contents over nine months or more, are ideal for trees and shrubs. Application is almost effortless. The fertilizer can be scattered by hand over a whole bed of closely growing herbaceous plants, or applied, at the rate recommended on the packet, to the soil around individual herbaceous plants, shrubs or trees and raked in.

WATERING

Newly planted subjects must be kept well watered until they are established, and mature garden plants will need watering to maintain healthy and vigorous growth throughout prolonged spells of dry weather, although the frequency of necessary watering can be reduced by covering the soil with a mulch.

Any watering must be gentle, so as not to wash away surface soil, and yet thorough. It is no good giving parched plants small splashes of water. This will do more harm than good. Always water copiously, ensuring that the water permeates well down to the roots. Surface wetting merely draws the fine rootlets upwards, increases transpiration and makes the problem worse.

When a hose is used, thorough watering can be achieved only if a rain- or mist-forming attachment is fitted. Give a steady and prolonged soaking to each area to ensure that it is well watered before moving on. Unfortunately, when done thoroughly, watering with a hose is a slow process and involves a great deal of standing about. For saving time and labour, automatic watering systems are far superior. These can be either by sprinklers or by a specially installed drip-irrigation system. Sprinklers can be of the rotating or oscillating head type, which is attached to a hose and sprays water over a given area, or they can consist of a specially perforated length of piping, which sends up jets of spray. They are an efficient means of watering but take time to lay out and must be moved from time to time in all but the smallest of gardens so that all the garden is watered evenly.

By far the most labour efficient method of watering the whole garden is to install a drip-irrigation system. Once installed, all that will be required of the gardener is to turn on the tap! These systems consist of a network of flexible plastic hoses into which drip-emitters are fitted at intervals. Each emitter allows water to pass into the soil at a steady rate to a radius of about 45cm (18in). They are cheap and easy to install, although their layout will need some planning. The large diameter, 12mm (½in), supply pipe should run around the garden. Numerous smaller diameter branch pipes, fitted with emitters, can be attached to the supply pipe by means of special T-joints and then led off among the plants in the beds and borders or carried up to supply raised beds, pots or tubs. As the piping is lightweight and the joints are simply push-fitted, the layout can be easily altered to suit changing requirements. If desired, the pipes can be hidden from view by burying them in the soil or covering them with a mulch.

Renovating neglected beds and borders

Some gardeners will have the luxury of planting easy-care borders from scratch on a new plot; others may inherit established borders, which can be gradually altered to suit their needs. However, some gardeners, on moving house perhaps, will find a neglected garden, complete with overgrown beds and borders. If the borders are very large and are likely to remain unmanageable, they should be made smaller or even replaced with more suitable and less labour-intensive features. If the borders are to be kept, they must be renovated and cleared of all weeds.

In many neglected herbaceous borders weeds will not be the only problem to be tackled. The more vigorous and spreading border plants – Michaelmas daisies, for instance – may be smothering less vigorous subjects, and the crowns of the plants may be so closely packed that there is little or no room for further development. The border may be so overgrown that a new border is the only solution, but where this is not possible, because of the limitations of space or time, a renovation programme should be followed. This is best started in late winter or spring to reduce the risk of plant loss.

Start by cutting down all growth to ground level and dig out any obvious weeds. A more detailed examination can then be made. If time and energy permit, dig out the dormant crowns and temporarily heel them in in another part of the garden. When replanting, divide the crowns into small pieces, and remove any weeds or couch grass that may be mixed with them. Replant only the divisions from the outside of the clump, these should be healthier and more vigorous than the older, central portions. Not all subjects lend themselves to division, but in a renovation programme of this kind, all have to be treated equally.

Where time and energy do not allow wholesale lifting, dig around the established crowns in spring, when growth is just starting. Some reduction of the size of crowns can be made and many weeds dug out. If perennial weeds continue to be a problem, treat them with a translocated herbicide applied directly to the weeds with a brush or a weedwiper.

Neglected shrubberies should be thinned out. This is best done in winter. Dig out the less desirable shrubs, leaving only the choicest, most suitable types. If these are too tall, cut them back by about half in late winter or early spring. Do not worry about the specific pruning requirements of particular shrubs. The initial object is to create space for renovation. During the spring and summer, cut down all the weed growth to soil level and treat with a suitable herbicide.

8. ROSES

Roses are the most popular of all garden plants, and they can be successfully included in the easy-care garden. They require little or no maintenance apart from annual pruning and provide so much colour over such a long period that they can be considered an almost essential element of the easy-care garden.

TYPES OF ROSE

Although all roses belong to the same genus, *Rosa*, a wide range of varieties has been developed, and consequently a rose can be found to suit almost any situation or purpose in the garden. Roses can be used in beds of their own or in mixed borders; they can be used for hedging or screening; and they can be grown as climbers or even for ground cover. The gardener is, therefore, confronted with a bewilderingly large assortment of types and varieties.

Roses are divided into three groups – species, old garden and modern – which are further divided according to the characteristics of each plant, although the boundaries between the divisions are becoming increasingly indistinct as new varieties are introduced, and some overlap does occur.

SPECIES ROSES

This group includes the species, wild roses, and the species hybrids, which exhibit many of the characteristics of the species – flowers are borne in one flush in summer and hips appear in autumn. The flowers are usually single, although some semi-double and double forms are available. Species roses are generally hardy and deciduous, and they have good resistance to pests and diseases.

OLD GARDEN ROSES

This large group is further divided into several types of rose, including Bourbon, Centifolia (or Provence), China, Damask, Hybrid Perpetual, Moss, Noisette, Portland, Sempervirens and Tea roses. The types that are specifically recommended for the easy-care garden are the Albas, Gallicas, Hybrid Musks and Rugosas.

MODERN ROSES

Roses in this group are divided into climbing, cluster-flowered bush (Floribunda), ground cover, large-flowered bush (Hybrid Tea), miniature bush, patio (dwarf cluster-flowered bush or miniature Floribunda), Polyantha, rambling and shrub roses.

USING ROSES

Entire beds or borders can be devoted to growing roses. These can be in addition to other shrub, herbaceous or mixed borders in the larger garden or they can be used as the main or only decorative display in the smaller garden.

Where roses are to be grown together in a single bed, take care over the positioning and the different colour combinations. The best display will be obtained if bushes are planted in groups of three to five of the same variety and if the colour of each neighbouring group harmonizes well together. Pleasing colour combinations are largely a matter of personal taste, but groups of different red varieties, which can clash, are best kept apart by planting a group of a white, cream or pale yellow variety between them.

Although there are no hard and fast rules, island rose beds are usually formally planted, and the roses positioned in a strict geometric pattern. The shape of such beds should, therefore, be regular and kept simple. A rectangular bed, no wider than 1.5m (5ft), is ideal as this allows the plants in the centre of the bed to be tended without the need to stretch or tread on the bed between plants. The varieties should be selected so that their eventual height will be appropriate for the size of bed, although some standards or tall-growing varieties should be planted in the centre of larger beds to avoid the feeling of 'flatness'. For formal planting only large-flowered or cluster-flowered bush roses (Hybrid Teas or Floribundas) should be used. If the bed is near to the house so that the beauty of each individual bloom can be seen, large-flowered bush roses make the best display; if the bed is further away or large splashes of bold colour are required, use cluster-flowered bush roses. If ease of maintenance is a prime consideration or the growing conditions are not ideal, cluster-flowered bush roses should be chosen, regardless of position, as these are hardier than large-flowered bush varieties.

Rose borders are generally less formal than island beds, and a wider range of types of rose can be grown. Climbers and ramblers can be included in a large border as well as shrub roses and large-flowered and cluster-flowered bush roses. Many of the same principles for planting island beds apply to rose borders, except that the taller subjects will be planted towards the rear of the border instead of the

Rosa 'Alpine Sunset' is a compact large-flowered bush rose with a rounded habit and fully double blooms.

centre. As producing a mass of colour will be the aim in the border, cluster-flowered bush roses should predominate, with shrub, climbing and, perhaps, a few large-flowered bush roses included to provide interest and variety. Of the shrub roses, the early-flowering *R. xanthina spontanea* 'Canary Bird' will produce flowers in spring and some Rugosa hybrids, with their red hips, will give the border extra interest in winter.

Traditionally, rose beds were kept free of any other planting so as not to detract from the beauty of their flowers, but it is now often recommended that dwarf bulbs and carpeting ground coverers are grown beneath roses, either to suppress weeds or to produce a more varied and colourful effect, which can maintain a display when the roses are either leafless or flowerless. However, such underplanting can make access to the roses for pruning, spraying or dead-heading much more difficult, and it can make applying or renewing a mulch almost impossible. This is a situation where ground coverers can cause more work than they save. If ground cover is definitely required, space the rose bushes a little further apart than normal and choose shallow-rooted ground-cover plants that die-down in winter, as they will interfere least with the spring-time routine of pruning and feeding and will also allow any diseased rose leaves that have been shed during the season to be easily removed during winter, reducing the risk of reinfection. Otherwise, keep the rose bed free of other types of plant and control weeds by mulching and by applying a suitable herbicide if and when necessary.

MAINTAINING ROSES
PRUNING

Established shrub, miniature and climbing roses need not be pruned except to remove any dead or diseased wood. Large-flowered and cluster-flowered bush roses and ramblers require an annual prune to produce well-shaped bushes and to encourage strong, healthy growth. Provided there is easy

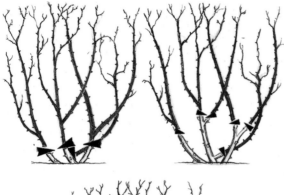

Above left: cut back a newly planted large-flowered bush rose to two or three buds; above right: prune a newly planted cluster-flowered bush rose to four buds; below: on light soils or in exposed areas, light pruning only is necessary.

access and gloves are worn, the pruning of large-flowered and cluster-flowered bushes is neither time-consuming nor arduous. The regular and often extensive pruning required by ramblers, however, can be much more difficult.

Large-flowered and cluster-flowered bushes should be pruned in spring when growth is just beginning but before any leaves have appeared. Unless the soil is very light, the first pruning of newly planted bush roses should be harder than

usual to encourage sturdy shoots to develop from the base and to build a strong root system. Prune the shoots of young large-flowered bush roses to between 10 and 15cm (4-6in) of the ground, and cluster-flowered bushes to 15cm (6in). On sandy

---

Less disease-resistant varieties

Several recommended varieties are included under *Rosa* in Part 2. However, a wider selection may be required, in which case you will have to choose from a catalogue or when you are at the garden centre. As the following varieties now seem to be becoming increasingly prone to such diseases as black spot, mildew and rust, careful consideration must given before planting them, especially if you live in an area where diseases are common, as they may well require more frequent spraying and attention than other, more disease-resistant roses.

Large-flowered bush roses (Hybrid Teas)
'Apricot Silk'; 'Beauté'; 'Belle Blonde'; 'Bettina'; 'Blue Moon'; 'Bobby Charlton'; 'Champion'; 'Diorama'; 'Doris Tysterman'; 'Double Delight'; 'Duke of Windsor'; 'Gay Gordons'; 'Harry Wheatcroft'; 'Josephine Bruce'; 'Message'; 'Mischief'; 'Mullard Jubilee'; 'Papa Meilland'; 'Paul Shirville'; 'Peer Gynt'; 'Piccadilly'; 'Prima Ballerina'; 'Royal Highness'; 'Silver Lining'; 'Super Star'; 'Tenerife'; 'Virgo'; 'Whisky Mac'.
Cluster-flowered bush roses (Floribundas)
'Dearest'; 'Dorothy Wheatcroft'; 'Elizabeth of Glamis'; 'Europeana'; 'Frensham'; 'Greensleeves'; 'Iceberg'; 'Lilli Marlene'; 'Megiddo'; 'Orange Sensation'; 'Orangeade'; 'Paddy McGredy'; 'Picasso'; 'Redgold'; 'Rob Roy'; 'Rosemary Rose'; 'Woburn Abbey'.
Miniature roses
Note: no miniature rose is very resistant to disease, especially when grown on its own roots 'Rise 'n' Shine'; 'Scarlet Gem'; 'Yellow Doll'.
Climbing and rambling roses
Note: no rambler rose is very resistant to disease; (R) = rambler
'Albertine' (R); 'American Pillar' (R); 'Climbing Crimson Glory'; 'Climbing Iceberg'; 'Climbing Mrs Sam McCredy'; 'Climbing Super Star'; 'Dorothy Perkins' (R); 'Gloire de Dijon'; 'Guinée'; 'Handel'; 'Parkdirektor Riggers'; 'Pink Perpétué'; 'Swan Lake'; 'Zéphirine Drouhin'.
Shrub roses
'Austrian Copper' (syn. *R. foetida* 'Bicolor'); 'Boule de Neige'; 'Buff Beauty'; 'Chapeau de Napoléon' (syn. *R.* × *centifolia* 'Cristata'); Common moss rose (*R. centifolia* 'Mucosa'); 'Frau Karl Druschki'; *R. gallica officinalis*; *R. hugonis*; 'Marguerite Hilling'; *R. mundi* (*R. gallica* 'Versicolor'); 'Nevada'.

soils prune only moderately in the first year but hard the next.

When pruning established roses, first cut out any dead, or obviously diseased or damaged wood. The cut surface of living tissue appears white. If it is brown, cut back further. Remove any very thin or unripe stems; test the ripeness of stems by snapping off a few thorns – if they do not break off easily but merely bend or tear, the wood is not ripe and should be removed. Also cut out any branches that cross and rub against each other, which can cause wounds through which diseases can enter. There should now remain only ripe healthy growth, which can be pruned back according to the type of rose.

LARGE-FLOWERED BUSH ROSES

Most varieties of established large-flowered bush roses (Hybrid Teas) should be moderately pruned, the stems being cut back to about half their length to an outside-facing bud, although weaker stems may be cut back further to encourage stronger growth. Vigorous varieties such as 'Peace' should be given a light pruning only and the stems merely tipped, leaving them about two-thirds of their original length. Neglected or weak-growing large-flowered bush roses can be rejuvenated by hard pruning. Cut back the stems to three or four buds from the crown, leaving the stems about 12.5cm (5in) long.

CLUSTER-FLOWERED BUSH ROSES

Most stems of cluster-flowered bush roses (Floribundas) should be moderately pruned and cut back to about half their length. However, to produce stems of different lengths to ensure a long and more continuous flowering period, cut back some old stems to within a few inches of the ground, and only lightly prune any stems that arose from near the base in the previous year. Never prune back hard all the stems of established cluster-flowered bush roses.

RAMBLERS

Rambling roses are not recommended for the easy-care garden. Although their pruning requirements do vary depending on the variety, most need the old flowering stems cut back to ground level, and the younger stems, which are to flower next year, need to be tied to supports. The removal of so much wood is very difficult and rarely practicable. If rambling roses are already present in your garden, it is easier merely to prune back the lateral shoots to within 7.5cm (3in) of the main stem when flowering has finished in late summer or autumn.

DEALING WITH SUCKERS

Suckers are shoots arising from the rootstock on grafted roses below the joint between the rootstock and the named variety. A sucker can easily be recognized as its leaf form and colour are often quite distinct from that of the named variety. If in doubt, trace it back to check that it does originate from below the bud union.

Suckers must always be removed, otherwise they will gradually take over the bush, the named variety disappearing and the whole plant reverting to the rootstock type.

The production of suckers is encouraged by loose planting, frosts and root damage caused by careless hoeing or the incomplete removal of previous suckers. It is no use merely cutting suckers off at soil level as this will cause them to grow more strongly and to produce even more shoots.

The correct removal of suckers is a simple job and one that is best tackled as soon as the sucker is noticed. Trace the sucker back, removing some soil if necessary. Pull or cut the sucker off at its point of origin with the rootstock, being careful to inflict only the minimum of damage to the roots, and replace and firm down any soil removed.

WEED CONTROL

Clear the ground before planting using a suitable herbicide such as glyphosate and make full use of mulches after planting. If the roses have not been underplanted with herbaceous subjects, simazine applied at a low-dosage rate in spring will control annual weeds throughout the season providing the soil is not disturbed, and dichlobenil, applied to all but the very lightest of soils in early February, before bud-growth starts, has proved safe for controlling perennial weeds around roses that have been planted for least two years. Until that time or on very light soils, control perennial weeds by painting glyphosate on their foliage.

DEAD-HEADING

Removing the dead blooms of large-flowered and cluster-flowered bush roses will encourage a regular succession of new flowering shoots. When the flowers have faded, remove the whole truss by cutting the stem to the first healthy bud below where the flowers were. Do not dead-head the hip-producing shrub roses. These generally flower only once in a season, and if they are dead-headed, the autumn display of hips will be lost.

9. Something to Eat

There is a great deal of satisfaction to be gained from eating home-grown produce, whether it be vegetables, fruit or just a few herbs. A large kitchen garden can, however, demand a great deal of effort and regular attention, often when time can be least conveniently spared. It is therefore advisable for the easy-care gardener who wishes to grow home produce to do so on a much smaller scale than a conventional gardener, limiting the choice of crops to those that are most easily managed and that demand the least attention.

Herbs

Although some herbs – sage, thyme and hyssop, for example – can be grown in the mixed border, herbs grown together in a special bed are, in general, easier to pick and to care for. Most do best on light soils in a sunny position, and the easiest and most convenient method of growing a selection of a herbs is in a raised bed or sink garden where perfect drainage can be obtained.

Most herbs can be harvested and dried for year-round use. Harvest on a sunny day, tie in bunches and hang in a cool dry room.

Chervil (*Anthriscus cerefolium*) An attractive biennial that grows to a height of 30–45cm (12–18in). It is an easy plant to grow and, once established, will seed itself. The aromatic, fern-like leaves can be used for flavouring salads, soups and sauces.

Chives (*Allium schoenoprasum*) A perennial plant, 20-30cm (8-12in) tall, with onion-like leaves. It will tolerate some shade. Although decorative, the flower heads should be removed to increase leaf production. The leaves have a mild onion flavour and are usually used fresh in salads, or for flavouring soups, or egg and cheese dishes.

Fennel (*Foeniculum vulgare*) Achieving a height of 1.8m (6ft), fennel is too tall for raised-bed cultivation. It can also become a menace in the garden as it seeds prolifically. Although it is an attractive plant, especially the bronze-leaved form, only grow it if you are prepared to keep its seeding nature under control by removing the flower-heads as soon as they appear. The leaves are used for flavouring sauces, fish and pickles.

Hyssop (*Hyssopus offcinalis*) A shrubby perennial, 50cm (20in) tall, with blue flowers. Both the flowers and the leaves have a mint-like flavour and can be used for flavouring salads, stuffings and soups.

Pot marjoram (*Oregano onites*) A perennial sub-shrub, which forms sprawling mounds of aromatic foliage some 30cm (12in) high. Seeds can be sown directly into the soil where it is to grow. Use the leaves fresh or dried for stuffings, flavouring veal, omelettes or sausage meat.

Mint (*Mentha spicata*) Mint, which is about 60cm (2ft) tall, is far too vigorous a grower for raised-bed cultivation. It also spreads rapidly by underground stems and can invade nearby plants when planted in a bed. Mint is best grown in a bottomless bucket sunk into the ground so that the rim stands just proud of the soil's surface. This will prevent it becoming a nuisance in the garden by confining its roots and restricting its spread.

Sage (*Salvia officinalis*) This decorative, evergreen sub-shrub, 60cm (2ft) tall, can be included in a mixed bed or border. It requires a sunny position and well-drained soil. The aromatic grey-green leaves can be used either fresh or dried to flavour meat or stuffings.

Thyme (*Thymus vulgaris*) An evergreen dwarf shrub, about 35cm (14in) tall, with aromatic, dark green leaves. Mauve flowers are produced in clusters in summer. The leaves can be used fresh or dried for stuffings, fish or casseroles. The plant makes an attractive ground-cover subject and may be grown as an edging plant or in crevices as well as in a raised bed.

Vegetables

Growing vegetables can be an extremely labour-intensive undertaking, and before you spend time and effort creating a special area for vegetables, you should carefully consider if this is really necessary or if you will be able to find the time and energy needed for its upkeep in the future. If only a very small amount of home produce is required or if space in the garden is strictly limited, some crops can be grown quite successfully in containers or in a variety of positions in the garden. Tomatoes and cucumbers can be grown against a sunny wall, for example, or crops that can be easily picked, cut off at ground level or simply pulled up without causing undue root disturbance to their neighbours can be grown among ornamental plants in existing beds. Lettuces, for example, can be grown between flowers or as edging plants.

Vegetables grown in small beds of uniform size separated by hard paths are much easier to tend and harvest than crops grown in the conventional long rows.

If the demands of maintenance allow and a large amount of produce is wanted, an area should be set aside for vegetables alone. A vegetable plot is best situated in a sunny position at the end of the garden furthest from the house, where it can be hidden from view, if desired, by screening plants such as rambling or climbing roses supported on pillars. However, even in a large garden where a great deal of space may be available, it is best to limit the size of the vegetable plot to ensure easy management; in general, the size of plot should not exceed 10 × 4.6m (30 × 15ft). Rather than growing crops in conventional rows, it is better to divide the plot into blocks measuring 1.5 × 1.2m (5 × 4ft), separated by hard paths 60cm (2ft) wide. This reduces the work involved in tending the plants, and the improved access makes it unnecessary to step on the bed between plants, which can compact the soil and hinder root growth.

The initial preparation of the plot must be thorough. The ground must cleared of all weeds (see Chapter 3), deeply dug over and improved by the addition of well-rotted, humus-making organic matter, such as good garden compost, well-decayed farmyard manure or spent mushroom or hop compost. Once the initial cultivation has been carried out, all that is required is the annual application and raking in of additional organic matter to keep the soil rich and in good condition.

As long as the soil is not frequently walked on so that it becomes compacted, no further heavy digging will be required for another five years or so.

Planting vegetables more closely together than is usually recommended can increase crop yield per unit area and help to suppress weeds. Water loss caused by evaporation from the soil is also reduced, and the plants will be more resistant to the effects of bad weather as they will afford each other some protection. Although close planting will usually result in smaller vegetables, they will taste just as good as larger ones, if not better. As an alternative, or in addition, to close planting, much labour can be saved by growing young plants through holes in heavy-duty, black plastic sheeting laid over the soil (see Chapter 3). This effectively warms the soil, prevents excessive water loss and suppresses weed growth; however, it can be used only on level sites or necessary moisture will be prevented from reaching the plants, rainwater merely being carried away and running off the plastic.

PROTECTING YOUR CROPS

Poorly growing or damaged crops are most often caused by pests and diseases or by exposure to too cold weather or strong winds. Therefore crops will need to be adequately protected if the best quality produce and highest possible yield is wanted.

The vegetables recommended in this chapter have been selected because they are particularly resistant to common garden pests and diseases. Good cultural conditions will also help to produce stronger plants that are better able to shrug off attacks that might kill or seriously distort weaker ones. But no vegetables can be said to be totally immune to pests and diseases. Bird damage can easily be prevented by erecting permanent or temporary netting cages over the whole crop, and these will also give the plants a considerable amount of extra protection against strong winds. However, unless you prefer to accept some loss or damage to crops rather than use chemicals on them, it may occasionally be necessary to control heavy infestations of insect pests or to prevent or control fungal diseases with sprays. Any chemical to be used on edible produce must be chosen and applied with care. Insecticides derived from plants, such as derris and pyrethrum, are regarded as being safer than man-made chemicals, but they are not persistent and repeat applications will be necessary. Permethrin is probably the safest general purpose insecticide for use in the vegetable garden, and suitable fungicides are best used as a preventative treatment rather than a cure.

To protect crops from the worst effects of winds or cold weather early or late in the season some form of screening can be provided around the plot and cloches used to cover particularly tender plants. Where a screen of plants or fencing would cut off too much light, use mesh or netting stretched over a frame. Netting is extremely effective in filtering and reducing prevailing wind.

Cloches can be used to cover plants or as a convenient way of warming the soil before planting or before applying a mulch. Most suitable is a cloche large enough to cover one complete vegetable block. This can be made from timber and a wire frame to which reinforced transparent plastic sheeting is fastened to form a protective covering.

Easy-to-grow vegetables

Perennial vegetables demand the minimum of attention as they can be planted in permanent beds and cropped year after year, thus eliminating the need to sow new crops every season. Whether or not you wish to confine your vegetable growing to these perennial types will depend on personal taste, requirements and availability of time, but some should certainly be included in any easy-care vegetable plot.

Asparagus (*Asparagus officinalis*) A perennial vegetable, asparagus should be given a convenient, permanent position in the garden. It is best to raise plants from purchased one-year-old, preferably male, crowns. Plants raised from seed cannot be harvested for three or four years, and older crowns, although they can be harvested quickly, are more difficult to establish and losses can result. Asparagus prefers a light, sandy soil. Plant crowns 38cm (15in) apart in 15–20cm (6–8in) deep holes in rows about 50cm (20in) apart. Cropping can usually begin the second year after planting. For the first crop, take only two or three shoots from each plant in mid-May. The harvesting period can be extended from early May to mid-June when the plants become more established. To harvest, cut 10–15cm (4–6in) tall shoots, at a point 10cm (4in) below ground level, taking care not to damage the other stems. Mulch with compost and cut back all remaining stems and foliage to within 2.5cm (1in) of ground level in autumn.

Beetroot (*Beta vulgaris*) Beetroot grows best in light soils. Sow a succession of seed between late March or early April and mid-July in 2cm (¾in) deep drills 15cm (6in) apart. Thin plants to 7.5cm (3in) apart and harvest when the beetroot is still quite small.

Calabrese (*Brassica oleriaceae italica*) Calabrese is a type of sprouting broccoli (see below), but it is less hardy and cannot be overwintered. It requires a rich soil and will benefit from a top-dressing of nitrogen when seedlings have six to eight leaves. Sow seed 12mm (½in) deep in rows 23cm (9in) apart from March to May. Calabrese resents root disturbance so either sow seed directly in final growing posiiton or in pots, from which seedlings should be carefully transplanted. Harvest when flower buds form between August and October.

Courgette (*Cucurbita pepo*) Sow seed in a warm place indoors in April or early May. When seedlings have developed two rough leaves, plant out 75cm (30in) apart and cover with a cloche until well hardened off. Water plants freely during any dry spells. Pinch out growing tips of trailing types to encourage bushier growth. Harvest when fruits are about 10cm (4in) long (if left on the plant they will develop into marrows).

Dwarf French beans (*Phaseolus vulgaris*) Sow seed 5cm (2in) deep in drills 30cm (12in) apart during late April or May. Thin plants to 30cm (12in) apart and keep well watered.

Egyptian onion (*Allium cepa aggregatum*) A perennial onion, which bears clusters of shallot-like bulbs on 90cm (3ft) stems in place of flowers. Plant bulbils, 23cm (9in) apart, in any well-drained soil in August or September. Crops may be taken from the following June onwards. Use in stews or salads. Established clumps can be divided and replanted in March.

Lettuce (*Lactuca sativa*) Thinly sow a succession of seed at three-weekly intervals between early April and August in shallow drills set 15cm (6in) apart. Thin plants to a spacing of 15cm (6in); plants that are not left to grow on may be eaten. Lettuces bolt readily if growth is checked for any reason, and they should not be overcrowded or disturbed once established and must be kept well-watered.

Onion (*Allium cepa*) Onions do best on a light, well-drained soil enriched with well-rotted manure. For maincrop onions, plant sets 10cm (4in) apart in rows in spring. They will be ready for harvesting in autumn after the leaves have turned yellow. Salad onions must be grown from seed. Thinly sow the seed in 12mm (½in) deep drills spaced 10cm (4in) apart from early spring onwards.

Potato (*Solanum tuberosum*) It is not really worth growing maincrop potatoes by the normal method, which involves a great deal of work. Early varieties can be easily grown under black plastic sheeting, however. Plant the seed potatoes through the plastic in March, about 12.5cm (5in) deep and 30cm (12in) apart. These will be ready for harvesting after about 12 weeks. To harvest simply lift the black plastic, remove the largest potatoes and allow the smaller ones to grow on. Recommended early varieties include 'Arran Pilot', 'Foremost' or, for heavy soils, 'Sharpe's Express'.

Radish (*Raphanus sativus*) Radishes do best in a fertile, well-drained soil enriched with well-rotted manure or peat. Sow seeds in succession from early spring to the end of the summer, in 12mm (½in) deep drills set 5cm (2in) apart. Thin plants to a spacing of 4cm (1½in). Harvest when large enough. Young roots are the most tender and have the most delicate flavour. Recommended varieties include 'French Breakfast' and 'Cherry Belle'.

Seakale (*Crambe maritima*) A hardy herbaceous perennial that produces a crop of edible leaf shoots every year. It will tolerate almost any soil but prefers a rich, sandy, well-drained loam. Seakale can be grown from seeds, but, as these take two to three years to mature, it is best to plant well-developed root crowns. Plant these in March, 5cm (2in) below soil level and 60cm (2ft) apart. Remove any flower stalks as they appear. To harvest, cut young shoots in spring, when they are about 20cm (8in) long and the leaves are just starting to develop. The harvesting period can be extended from December to late spring by forcing plants by covering them with pots after the leaves have died back in autumn. Seakale can be propagated by taking 15cm (6in) long root cuttings (thongs).

Spinach beet (*Beta vulgaris*) Also known as seakale beet or perpetual spinach, spinach beet does well on any well-drained garden soil. Sow seed thinly in 12mm (½in) deep drills 23cm (9in) apart in April for summer and autumn cropping or in July and August for winter and spring cropping.

Thin plants to 23cm (9in) apart. Harvest by pulling the largest leaves from each plant with the stalks attached. Thereafter, a fresh crop of new leaves will be produced.

Sprouting broccoli There are two types of sprouting broccoli – white and purple – which are similar, although purple sprouting broccoli is said to be the hardier. The soil should be rich, with well-rotted humus added the winter before planting and a top-dressing of nitrogen given to seedlings. Sow seed 12mm (½in) deep and 12.5-15cm (5-6in) apart in rows 10cm (4in) apart in April or May depending on the weather. Broccoli seedlings can be transplanted after about two months, when they should be planted 60cm (2ft) apart. Harvest before the buds begin to open, snapping off flower stalks about two-thirds down their length. 'Nine Star Perennial' produces cauliflower-like heads from late March until May, and the plants may last for several years if they are not allowed to go to seed.

Tomato (*Lycopersicon esculentum*) Outdoor bush varieties, such as 'Red Alert' and 'Sleaford Abundance', need no pinching out or other attention and are therefore an ideal choice for the easy-care gardener. Plant out young plants 40cm (16in) apart, through black plastic sheeting during early summer in, preferably, a warm, sheltered and sunny position. Tomatoes must be kept well watered. A frequently filled flower pot sunk into the soil next to each plant will ensure an adequate water supply. Crops will usually be ready for harvesting from late August onwards.

Turnip (*Brassica rapa*) Turnips do well on any rich fertile soil. Sow seeds in drills 12mm (½in) deep and 15cm (6in) apart in succession from mid-spring for summer cropping to late August for autumn and winter cropping. Thin plants to 7.5cm (3in) apart. Harvest when flower buds form.

Welsh onion (*Allium fistulosum*) Welsh onions are like perennial multi-stemmed spring onions. The stems grow to a height of about 30cm (12in) and form dense clumps or tufts. Use the shoots as a substitute for salad onions and the leaves as chives.

FRUIT

Growing fruit on a large scale takes up a considerable amount of space and, if an abundant supply of good quality produce is to be produced, fruit trees and bushes require protection from birds and regular pruning and spraying against pests and diseases. However, if you are willing to accept a lower than normal yield and fruit that, although as good in terms of taste and texture, may not be as perfect in appearance, an adequate supply of fruit can be grown without too much extra work.

FRUIT TREES

If apples, pears or plums are to be grown, always choose the smaller bush or dwarf bush trees. These have been grafted on to dwarfing rootstocks and will consequently never grow very large while still providing a good crop. When you plant grafted trees make sure that you do not bury the union, otherwise roots that will nullify the dwarfing effect of the rootstock may form from the grafted top-growth. Because they are more compact, the routine maintenance, such as pruning and harvesting, of these trees is much easier than for the taller and more wide-spreading half-standard and standard types, which often have to be tended from a ladder. However, even dwarf bush types grown as free-standing trees can take up a great deal of space, and it is much better to make a careful and considered choice as to the type and variety of fruit to be grown rather than growing a wide, and varied range of crops. Where only one apple, pear or plum tree is to be grown it is important to choose the variety with care. Although all varieties benefit from cross-pollination, most will give an adequate crop when planted in isolation. However, self-sterile varieties will not crop unless cross-pollinated, and such varieties should be considered only if two or more different varieties that bloom at the same time can be planted together or are present in nearby gardens. Where several varieties are required but space does not allow more than one tree, a 'family' tree is ideal. These have two or three cross-compatible varieties grafted on to the same trunk.

If a gardener is especially anxious to grow a fruit tree but space is extremely limited or he or she is confined to a wheelchair or has to tend the trees without stretching, fruit trees can be grown on a cordon system or as espaliers or fans. Although this training involves more work than growing a free-standing tree, the limited height and growth make access and care much easier and allow many more specimens to be grown. Varieties for training in this way, which must have been grafted on to a very dwarfing rootstock, are available from nurseries either ready trained or as a one-year-old 'maiden' or 'whip' plants with a single shoot. To maintain or form the desired shape, cordons, espaliers or fans need to be trained on taut, horizontal supporting wires. The easiest method is to plant the trees near to the base of a wall or fence. The wires can be stretched between straining eyes attached to the wall or fence at 30cm (1ft) intervals. If no wall or fence is suitable, wires can be stretched between specially erected posts.

CORDONS

Plant the maiden tree at an angle of 45°, pointing away from the sun. If more than one is to be grown, they should be about 75cm (30in) apart. Support each tree by tying it with a soft twine to a 1.8m (6ft) long cane, placed in the ground at the same angle as the tree. The cane should be secured to the horizontal wires. No pruning is needed until the end of the following summer, when the new lateral growths are ripe. These should be cut back to three or four buds. In the following years, prune back new laterals in the same way and cut extension growth from older laterals to two buds. Leave the main stem unpruned until the desired height is reached. When the stem reaches the top wire stop the terminal growth by cutting back the leader to within 12mm (½in) of the topmost wire.

ESPALIERS AND FANS

Plant espaliers and fans 3–4.6m (10–15ft) apart. If not already trained, plant the maiden tree so that a pair of buds is roughly in line with the first horizontal wire and cut back the stem to a bud above the chosen pair. Allow the centre shoot to grow vertically and train the two developing side-shoots horizontally by tying them to the lowest wire, one on either side of the main stem. The following year cut back the main stem to within 30cm (1ft) of the horizontal branches and train the two new side shoots horizontally along the wire to form an espalier or along a cane set diagonally if a fan shape is required. This treatment is repeated every year until the desired height and number of tiers is reached, when the central upright shoot should be cut right out. Any unwanted shoots that develop at any time from the vertical stem should be cut out

---

Apples
Apples should be planted in a sunny position, and if possible not exposed to strong winds or salt-laden air. They tolerate a wide range of soil types but prefer a deep, well-drained, loamy soil that does not dry out.

Recommended varieties
★ = unsuitable for training as cordon, espalier or fan
Dessert
'Cox's Orange Pippin'; 'Laxton's Fortune'; 'Lord Lambourne'; 'Sunset'; 'Worcester Pearmain'★.
Dual purpose
'Peasgood's Nonsuch'; 'Rival'.
Cooking
'Arthur Turner'; 'Grenadier'; 'Lanes's Prince Albert'.

Grown as cordons, apple trees can be fitted into the smallest
of gardens and are then easier to tend by gardeners who are
confined to a wheelchair or who find it difficult to stretch.

completely, or the cane should be untied and
lowered by 10° and retied securely.

'BALLERINA' APPLE TREES
A recent development in fruit horticulture,
'Ballerina' or columnar apple trees produce flowers
and fruit on short spurs on a single main stem.
These trees, which require far less space than
normal apple trees, are easy to manage and have
been specially bred to be resistant to mildew. At

Pears
Pears require a warmer, more sheltered position
than apples, and they are intolerant of salt-laden air
and chalky (alkaline) soils.

Recommended varieties
★ = unsuitable for training as cordon, espalier or
fan
Dessert
'Beurré Hardy'★; 'Conference'; 'Jargonelle'★;
'Louise Bonne of Jersey'.
Cooking
'Bellisme d'Hiver'★; 'Vicar of Winkfield'★.

present only four types are available; three bear dessert apples, while the fourth, 'Maypole', is an ornamental crab apple. They are grown like cordons but require much less pruning.

SOFT FRUIT
CURRANTS AND GOOSEBERRIES
Currants and gooseberries tolerate a wide range of soils but they grow best on a rich, free-draining but moisture-retentive loam. If grown on thin sandy soils, plants, especially blackcurrants, may be short lived and produce poor crops unless plenty of well-rotted manure is dug in and a heavy mulch applied to prevent excessive water loss from the soil. Currants dislike acid soils, while gooseberries prefer more acid conditions.

Grow bushes in an open, sunny position sheltered from strong winds. Earlier flowering varieties of blackcurrant and all red- and whitecurrants and gooseberries should be grown in positions that are sheltered from spring frosts and the early morning sun to prevent the flower buds being damaged.

Although usually grown as free-standing bushes, red- and whitecurrants and gooseberries can be trained against a wall or fence as double or single cordons. Blackcurrants, however, cannot be grown in this way because of their differing and less compact habit. Where garden space is limited and as an alternative to training, incorporate a few black-, red- or whitecurrant bushes into a informal hedge with other shrubs. The bushes will serve a dual purpose, and any crop will be an added bonus.

Avoid digging around bushes as they are shallow rooting. Control weeds by applying a mulch or covering the ground with plastic sheeting. Alternatively use paraquat or simazine.

Plant bushes in autumn or early spring. Blackcurrants should be planted 2.5–5cm (1–2in) deeper than the previous soil level mark on the stem. This will encourage new shoots to be produced from below the soil. Prune back hard to within 5cm (2in) of the soil level immediately after planting.

Red- and whitecurrants and gooseberries are usually grown on a short 'leg' or trunk, and they should be planted in the garden at the same depth they were planted at the nursery. After planting, prune shoots back by about half their length to a healthy bud. To achieve the best possible crops, regular feeding will be necessary. Apply a dressing of sulphate of ammonia in spring and sulphate of potash in the autumn.

Harvesting blackcurrants is easier if the fruiting wood is cut off and taken indoors, where the fruit can be picked. Thus harvesting and pruning are done in one simple operation. Red- and white-

currants can be treated in the same way when strong growth has been established two or three years after planting. Until such time, shorten the fruiting wood by only about one-third.

The harvesting and pruning of gooseberries are more difficult because of their thick, prickly growth. Cut back one-third of all fruited wood to nearly ground level each year.

CANE FRUITS
Blackberries, loganberries and raspberries are vigorous, scrambling plants that must be supported. They are, however, prolific fruit bearers and can be used as screening plants on a trellis or for clothing a pergola, or they can look quite decorative when grown up posts. They are useful fruits for low-lying, frost-prone areas as they flower long after the danger from spring frosts has passed, thus avoiding the problem of frost-damaged flower buds that is common on other, earlier flowering types of fruit.

Plums

Plums are loosely divided into two main groups, the gages, which produce better flavoured fruits but require more favourable growing conditions, and the damsons, which are ideal for cooking and jam-making.

Plums grow best on moisture-retentive but free-draining, medium to heavy, slightly alkaline loams, but they will tolerate slightly acid soils. Because they are early flowering, gages should not be planted in exposed positions but given a position that is warm and dry in summer. The best fruits are obtained when planted against a wall, either when fantrained or free-standing. Damsons are hardier, flower later and will succeed in colder, less sunny and wetter conditions.

Recommended varieties
Gages
'Denniston's Superb'; 'Early Transparent'; 'Golden Transparent'; 'Laxton's Gage'.
Damsons
'Merryweather'; 'Shropshire'.

Plant blackberries and raspberries in November or in March; loganberries should be planted any time between October and March when the soil is workable. Make sure that the ground is totally free of weeds before planting. Perennial weeds, especially bindweed, can be difficult to eradicate from among the canes of established plants. After planting, keep the ground clear by using paraquat or simazine at the recommended doses, rather than hoeing, which can damage shallow roots.

In early spring (or immediately after planting) cut back all the canes to within 25cm (10in) of ground level. Tie canes to supports when they have made enough growth. Cut out all the canes of established plants that have borne fruit after harvesting, leaving only the new young growth that was made that season. However, leave at full length all the strong canes produced by raspberries during their first season's growth.

Blackberries and loganberries

Well-drained but moisture-retentive, slightly acid or lime-free soil suits blackberries and loganberries best; an alkaline soil induces iron and manganese deficiency in loganberries. Both types are shade tolerant but do best in a sunny position sheltered from cold winds.

The Himalayan blackberry is the easiest fruit of all to grow against a tall wall or fence and does not need much attention. Tie the main shoots firmly to wire supports stretched through vine eyes attached to the wall during the first season. All that will be needed is the occasional thinning out of some of the branches from the thickest areas of growth to prevent them becoming a tangled mass. Loganberries can be grown against walls in a similar way provided the wall is not north-facing. Tie in the new young shoots once or twice during the summer.

Raspberries

Although raspberries prefer a moist heavy soil, they can be grown on light soils if a heavy mulch is applied and time and energy is available for regular watering. Raspberries will not, however, tolerate chalky (alkaline) or poorly draining soils. Give raspberries a sunny or shaded position sheltered from strong winds, which can break off the fruiting lateral shoots.

Raspberries can be made self-suporting if the canes are tied together into clumps, but they are best grown supported by wires stretched between posts or attached to a wall or fence.

Strawberries

Strawberries grown at ground level can be difficult to pick, especially for handicapped or elderly gardeners, and in such cases they should be grown in strawberry pots or barrels.

When grown in ground-level beds, they are best planted through plastic sheeting. Water the bed well and scatter a few slug pellets over it. Lay the plastic sheeting down and anchor the edges. Insert the plants through crossed slits made in the sheeting. Make sure that the crowns of the plants are exactly at soil level. If planted too deeply, they can rot, and too shallow planting can cause the roots to dry out. You should ensure that any plants you buy are certified virus-free. Healthy strawberry plants will give good crops for three or four years. Replace weakening plants with new stock obtained by rooting runners, either in pots or by staking them down into the soil. Runners are freely produced by most varieties from June onwards.

Although it will involve extra work, it is essential to provide some protection against birds. The easiest method is to fix heavy-gauge wire permanantly above the bed and lay netting temporarily over these supports whenever fruit is present.

RHUBARB

This useful hardy perennial will provide good crops over many years without requiring much attention. As rhubarb resents being moved, it should be given a convenient but permanent position from the start. If space is limited, rhubarb can be grown among other plants in a mixed bed or border, but it must be kept well fed as rhubarb is a greedy feeder.

Rhubarb does well on any rich garden soil, but prefers a sunny, sheltered site. It is best to grow rhubarb from purchased crowns – make sure each root has at least one bud. Growing rhubarb from seed usually results in inferior plants, which cannot be harvested for some years. Plant crowns in March, 75cm (30in) apart for small varieties, 90–120cm (3–4ft) apart for larger varieties, with the top bud 5cm (2in) below the soil's surface. Do not harvest the first year but thereafter pull three or four fully grown stems at a time from each plant, always leaving at least three strong stems remaining on the plant. Never eat the poisonous leaves. Lift, divide and replant the crowns after six to eight years.

PART 2
PLANT ENCYCLOPEDIA

The plants described in this section are organized alphabetically by genus. Species, varietal and common names are included in the Index on pages 157-9. Pests, diseases and methods of propagation named in CAPITAL letters are described in Part 3. If no pests or diseases are mentioned, the plant may be considered largely trouble free.

ACAENA   Rosaceae
New Zealand burr
A. 'Blue Haze'
Height: 5-10cm (2-4in)
Spread: 60cm (2ft) or more
A useful hardy herbaceous perennial for ground cover or as a carpet for dwarf bulbs. It can also be planted between paving stones as it is robust and tolerant of rough treatment and misplaced feet. 'Blue Haze' forms a dense mat of blue-green leaves, which are borne on red stems. Insignificant flowers appear in summer and are followed by red-brown burrs.
CULTIVATION
Planting time: September to March.
Soil: Well-drained.
Aspect: Partial shade to full sun.
Minimum temp: −15°C (5°F).
Propagation: By DIVISION between September and March; or sow SEED under glass between September and March and plant out in May.

ACANTHUS   Acanthaceae
Bear's breeches
A genus of herbaceous perennials. The species described are hardy and, although tall, require no staking; they make excellent clump-forming feature plants for easy-care herbaceous borders.
A. mollis
Height: 90cm (3ft)
Planting distance: 60cm (2ft)
A striking, semi-evergreen border plant with glossy, heart-shaped, mid-green leaves. Strong spires of white and purple flowers are produced in summer.
A. spinosus
Similar to *A. mollis* but with spiny leaves.
CULTIVATION
Planting time: October to March.
Soil: Well-drained.
Aspect: Full sun to partial shade.

Minimum temp: −10°C (14°F).
Pruning: After flowering, cut stems back almost to ground level.
Propagation: By DIVISION of large clumps in early autumn. Also, 7.5cm (3in) CUTTINGS of the thicker roots may be taken from December to February. Grow under glass until well rooted, pot on and plant out from October onwards.

ACER   Aceraceae
Maple
A genus of mostly deciduous trees and shrubs grown mainly for their ornamental bark and foliage. In autumn, the leaves often become brilliantly coloured.
A. davidii (snake-bark maple, Père David's maple)
Height: 15m (50ft)
Spread: 1.5 (5ft)
This deciduous tree has grey-green bark with white striations, which are more pronounced if the tree is grown in semi-shade. Leaves are tinted red when young, becoming darker green as they age and eventually turning bright red, yellow and purple in autumn.
Varieties: 'George Forrest'.
A. griseum (paper-bark maple)
Height: 10m (30ft)
Spread: 2.4m (8ft)
A slow-growing deciduous tree with an attractive, tan-coloured bark, which peels back to reveal patches of light orange bark beneath. The mid-green leaves assume bright red and scarlet hues before being shed in autumn.
CULTIVATION
Planting time: October to March.
Soil: Well-drained, but moist and cool.
Aspect: Full sun to partial shade.
Minimum temp: −18°C (0°F).
Pruning: None necessary, except initially to produce a main stem of the desired height.
Propagation: By SEED sown in either cold frames or the open ground in October.
Pests: Can be attacked by APHIDS, which cause the foliage to become sooty and sticky.
Diseases: CORAL SPOT, evidenced by pink-red pustules at the base of dead wood, can cause die-back of shoots. HONEY FUNGUS can cause death of the whole plant. TAR SPOT can cause

large black spots, often with bright yellow edges. VERTICILLIUM WILT produces a wilting of leaves and die-back of shoots; infected shoots may have brown streaks.

ACHILLEA   Compositae
A genus of hardy herbaceous perennials.
A. 'Coronation Gold'
Height: 90cm (3ft)
Spread: 60cm (2ft)
The fern-like leaves are silvery, and large, flat heads of small golden flowers are borne in summer.
A. filipendulina (syn. *A. eupatorium*)
Height: 90-120cm (3-4ft)
Spread: 60-90cm (2-3ft)
A useful border plant with fine, fern-like, mid-green foliage. Dense, flattened heads, 10-15cm (4-6in) wide, of bright yellow flowers are produced in summer.
Varieties: 'Cloth of Gold'; 'Gold Plate' (ht: 1.2-1.5m (4-5ft), sp: 60cm (2ft)).
A. x lewisii 'King Edward'
Height: 10-15cm (4-6in)
Spread: 20cm (8in) or more
A hummock-forming plant with semi-evergreen, grey-green foliage, particularly suitable for raised beds or rock gardens. Yellow flower heads are produced in summer.
A. millefolium (yarrow)
Height: 60-75cm (2ft-2ft 6in)
Spread: 38cm (15in)
This plant can be a lawn weed, but cultivated varieties make good border plants. The foliage is dark green with white to cerise flowers, which are borne in 10cm (4in) wide, flattened heads in summer.
Varieties: 'Cerise Queen' (cherry-red flowers); 'Fire King' (red flowers).
CULTIVATION
Planting time: October to March.
Soil: Well-drained.
Aspect: Sunny.
Minimum temp: −12°C (10°F).
Pruning: Remove stems after flowering.
Propagation: By DIVISION of clumps in autumn. By SEED sown in a cold frame in March; pot on and plant out between October and March. Also by 5cm (2in) CUTTINGS of non-flowering shoots taken in June/July and kept in a cold frame for planting out the following April.

AJUGA
Labiatae
A. reptans (bugle)
Height: 10-30cm (4-12in)
Planting distance: 30-45cm (12-18in)
An ideal hardy herbaceous perennial for low-growing ground cover. Although not wholly evergreen, ajugas do not die down completely in winter and enough of the leaves are retained to make effective spring cover for bulbs. Generally, however, the darker leaved forms lose more of their leaves than the lighter leaved varieties. Ajugas are grown mainly for their attractively coloured foliage, but whorls of blue flowers are produced in early summer.
Varieties: 'Atropurpurea' (purple foliage); 'Multicolor' (syn. 'Rainbow', 'Tricolor', bronze, pink and yellow foliage); 'Variegata' (syn. 'Argentea', grey-green foliage variegated with cream).
CULTIVATION
Planting time: Whenever the ground is not frozen or waterlogged.
Soil: Does well on heavy soil, but can grow in any moist soil.
Aspect: Shady.
Minimum temp: −22°C (−8°F).
Propagation: By DIVISION at any time.

ALCHEMILLA
Rosaceae
Lady's mantle
A. mollis
Height: 45cm (18in)
Planting distance: 38cm (15in)
A hardy herbaceous perennial that is a useful ground-cover plant, especially for shady positions. It forms spreading, flat-topped clumps of attractive, light green, velvety foliage, and heads of star-shaped, yellow-green flowers are produced in summer. If grown in very exposed positions, alchemillas may need supporting with twigs.
CULTIVATION
Planting time: October to March.
Soil: Moist and well-drained.
Aspect: Full sun to partial shade.
Minimum temp: −22°C (−8°F).
Pruning: Cut back to just above ground level after flowering.
Propagation: By SEED; *A. mollis* self-seeds readily, but seeds may also be sown in a cold frame in March, for planting in final positions from October onwards. By DIVISION of large clumps between October and March.

ANAPHALIS
Compositae
Pearl everlasting
A. triplinervis
Height: 30cm (12in)
Planting distance: 30-38cm (12-15in)

This hardy herbaceous perennial with silver-grey foliage looks particularly attractive when grown in a border among brightly coloured plants. Everlasting white flowers, borne in branched heads, are produced in late summer.
Varieties: 'Sommerschnee'/'Summer Snow'.
CULTIVATION
Planting time: September to April.
Soil: Well-drained.
Aspect: Prefers full sun but will tolerate shade if grown in freely draining soil.
Minimum temp: −20°C (−4°F).
Pruning: Can be cut back hard if plants become untidy in autumn.
Propagation: By DIVISION any time between September and April when soil is workable, or by 5-7.5cm (2-3in) BASAL CUTTINGS taken in April/May. Root under glass and plant out when established.

ANEMONE
Ranunculaceae
Windflower
A genus of hardy herbaceous perennials, which is divided into fibrous-rooted and tuberous-rooted types. These long-lived plants are easy to grow and free flowering.
Fibrous-rooted
A. × hybrida (syn. *A. japonica*)
Height: 60-90cm (2-3ft)
Planting distance: 30-45cm (12-18in)
An excellent clump-forming border plant with elegantly lobed foliage. Pink or white flowers with prominent yellow eyes are produced in late summer on 75cm (2ft 6in) stems. Plants need no staking and, once established, resent disturbance.
Varieties: 'Honorine Jobert' (ht: 1.2m (4ft), white flowers); 'Königen Charlotte'/'Queen Charlotte' (semi-double, pink flowers); 'Lorelei' (rose-pink flowers); 'Max Vogel' (semi-double, pink flowers); 'White Queen' (pure white flowers).
Tuberous-rooted
A. blanda
Height: 15cm (6in)
Planting distance: 10cm (4in)
Pale blue, blue, mauve, pink or white, daisy-like flowers, 2.5-5cm (1-2in) across, are borne in early spring. Plant in a sunny position as flowers close in shade.
Varieties: 'Atrocaerulea' (deep blue flowers); 'White Splendour' (white flowers).
A. coronaria
Height: 15-30cm (6-12in)
Planting distance: 7.5-10cm (3-4in)
Flowers, 5cm (2in) wide, in white or various shades of blue and red, are

produced in spring. Descended from this species are two popular strains of garden anemones, De Caen and St Brigid hybrids. **De Caen** hybrids can produce over 20 flowers to a plant over a long flowering season. Various named, as well as mixed, varieties of De Caen hybrids are available, including 'His Excellency' (syn. 'Hollandia', scarlet flowers); 'Mr Fokker' (blue flowers); 'Sylphide' (magenta flowers). **St Brigid** hybrids produce double or semi-double flowers. Varieties include 'Lord Lieutenant' (blue flowers); 'The Governor' (scarlet flowers).
A. nemorosa (wood anemone)
Height: 15-20cm (6-8in)
Planting distance: 15cm (6in)
An attractive woodland plant that provides some ground cover. It produces white flowers, sometimes tinged with pink, 2.5cm (1in) across, in spring.
Varieties: 'Robinsoniana' (lavender-blue flowers); 'Vestal' (pure white flowers).
CULTIVATION
Planting time: Fibrous-rooted, October to March; tuberous-rooted, September/October.
Soil: Well-drained but moisture-retentive; *A. blanda* does well in chalky soils.
Aspect: Full sun to partial shade; *A. × hybrida* does best in partial shade; *A. blanda* requires full sun.
Minimum temp: −14°C (7°F).
Pruning: Cut down stems of A. × *hybrida* after flowering.
Propagation of fibrous-rooted species: By DIVISION between October and March. By ROOT CUTTINGS taken between November and January; keep in a cold frame until established; plant in final positions in October.
Propagation of tuberous-rooted species: By DIVISION during late summer after top growth has died down. By SEED collected when ripe and planted in trays in a cold frame.
Pests: CATERPILLARS and CUTWORMS can attack foliage and flowers. APHIDS can infest stems and leaves, and SLUGS may attack tubers and young shoots.
Diseases: Can be susceptible to a number of VIRUS DISEASES, which result in stunted plants, yellowing and distortion of the leaves and production of small, poorly coloured flowers. CLUSTER CUP RUST can result in failure to flower and thickening and malformation of the leaves; it is seen as spore-bearing yellow cups on affected stems and leaves.

ARTEMISIA   Compositae
Wormwood
A. abrotanum (southernwood, lad's love, old man)
Height and spread: 0.6-1.2m (2-4ft)
A deciduous or semi-evergreen shrub of bushy habit with finely divided, aromatic, grey-green leaves. Dull yellow, globose flowers are borne in late summer.
CULTIVATION
Planting time: March/April.
Soil: Any well-drained garden soil but prefers light soils; can succumb to winter wet in very heavy soils.
Aspect: Full sun.
Minimum temp: −12°C (10°F).
Pruning: None needed, but occasional cutting back of straggly growth will maintain a good shape; if carried out while the growth is still soft, can be easily done with a flower-cutter.
Propagation: By taking 7.5-10cm (3-4cm) SEMI-HARDWOOD CUTTINGS with heel in August; root in a cold frame and, when established, plant out in final position the following September.
Pests: ROOT APHIDS may infest leaves.
Diseases: Foliage may be affected by RUST, seen as small brown pustules, which gradually darken, on the underside of leaves.

ARUNCUS   Rosaceae
Goat's beard
A. dioicus (syn. *A. sylvester*, *Spiraea aruncus*)
Height: 1.2-1.8m (4-6ft)
Planting distance: 60cm (2ft)
A good choice for the back of low-maintenance herbaceous borders or for growing as a specimen plant. The pale green foliage is topped by plumes, 20-25cm (8-10in) long, of creamy-white flowers in summer.
Varieties: 'Kneiffii' (ht: 60cm (2ft), a shorter variety, useful for smaller gardens).
CULTIVATION
Planting time: October to March.
Soil: Moist and loamy.
Aspect: Partial shade.
Minimum temp: −15°C (5°F).
Pruning: Cut down stems almost to ground level in October.
Propagation: By DIVISION of clumps in October.
Pests: CATERPILLARS can feed on foliage in spring.

ASTER   Compositae
Michaelmas daisy
A large, variable genus of hardy herbaceous perennials. Asters are considered by many to be easily grown, low-maintenance plants, but this is not strictly true. Many species, especially the taller ones, need to be staked and the clumps lifted and divided regularly if they are to remain vigorous. However, *A. amellus*, described below, is one of the few taller species that does not demand this attention.
A. alpinus
Height: 15cm (6in)
Spread: 30-45cm (12-18in)
A vigorous dwarf aster of spreading habit, useful for the front of the border. It has grey-green foliage and produces purple-blue flowers with orange-yellow centres from mid- to late summer.
Varieties: *A. a. albus* (white-flowered and less vigorous); 'Beechwood' (mauve-blue flowers); 'Wargrave Variety' (pink flowers, tinged with purple).
A. amellus
Height: 45-60cm (18-24in)
Planting distance: 30cm (12in)
The grey-green foliage is rough textured, and large flowers are borne on woody stems in late summer. Named varieties are most commonly grown.
Varieties: 'King George' (violet-blue flowers); 'Lady Hindlip' (rose-pink flowers); 'Nocturne' (lilac flowers); 'Rudolph Goethe' (pale mauve-blue flowers); 'Sonia' (rose-pink flowers).
A. × frikartii 'Mönch'
Height: 75cm (2ft 6in)
Planting distance: 30cm (12in)
An easy-to-grow and maintain hybrid of *A. amellus* and *A. thomsonii*. The dark green leaves and orange-centred, blue flowers are freely produced from mid-summer to autumn.
A. × thomsonii 'Nanus'
Height: 45cm (18in)
Planting distance: 30cm (12in)
A short variety that does not require staking. The grey-green leaves are hairy, and large, lavender-blue flowers are produced from mid-summer to autumn.
CULTIVATION
Planting time: October to March.
Soil: Well-drained.
Aspect: Full sun.
Minimum temp: −21°C (−6°F).
Pruning: Cut down stems almost to ground level in November.
Propagation: By DIVISION of clumps between October and March.
Pests: CATERPILLARS can feed on leaves and destroy growing tips. TARSONEMID MITES stunt or scar stems and kill or distort flowers, curtailing and even preventing flowering. SLUGS feed on young plants.

Diseases: BLACK ROOT ROT and RHIZOCTONIA can rot roots and sometimes the crown, causing discoloration of the leaves and possible dieback of the shoots.

ASTILBE   Saxifragaceae
A genus of hardy herbaceous perennials, ideal for easy-care borders if given the correct growing conditions.
A × arendsii
Height: 60-90cm (2-3ft)
Planting distance: 30-45cm (12-18in)
A garden hybrid with attractive dark green, fern-like foliage. Minute flowers are borne on 30-38cm (12-15in) long, pyramidal, feathery, plume-like heads from June to August.
Varieties: 'Bressingham Beauty' (ht: 90cm (3ft), pink flowers); 'Fanal' (ht: 60cm (2ft), deep red flowers); 'Feuer'/'Fire' (ht: 60cm (2ft), salmon-pink flowers); 'Hyazinth'/'Hyacinth' (ht: 90cm (3ft), pink flowers); 'Weisse Gloria'/'White Gloria' (ht: 60cm (2ft), white flowers).
A. × japonica
Height: 60-90cm (2-3ft)
Planting distance: 30-45cm (12-18in)
Garden hybrids that are similar to *A. × arendsii*.
Varieties: 'Deutschland' (ht: 60cm (2ft), white flowers); 'Federsee' (ht: 75cm (2ft 6in), rose-red flowers); 'Red Sentinel' (ht: 75cm (2ft 6in), brick-red flowers); 'Rheinland' (ht: 75cm (2ft 6in), pink flowers).
CULTIVATION
Planting time: October to March.
Soil: Must have permanently moist soil, preferably rich in humus; water freely during prolonged periods of drought.
Aspect: Prefers shade but will tolerate full sun if soil remains moist.
Minimum temp: −15°C (5°F).
Pruning: Cut down to ground level in late October.
Propagation: By DIVISION of clumps in March/April.

AUCUBA   Cornaceae
A genus of easily grown, unisexual, evergreen shrubs, which are suitable for container as well as garden planting.
A. japonica (spotted laurel)
Height: 1.8-3.6m (6-12ft)
Spread: 1.5-2.1m (5-7ft)
A rounded, bushy shrub with shiny, dark green leaves (although variegated forms are most usually grown). Green flowers are produced in March and April, and, if both sexes are grown, female plants bear persistent clusters of scarlet berries in the autumn (plant one male form for

Acanthus mollis

Ajuga reptans 'Atropurpurea'

Achillea 'Coronation Gold'

Ajuga reptans 'Multicolor' (syn. 'Rainbow', 'Tricolor')

Achillea millefolium 'Cerise Queen'

Alchemilla mollis

Anemone x hybrida

Aster amellus

Anemone x hybrida 'Honorine Jobert'

Astilbe x arendsii 'Fanal'

Aruncus dioicus (syn. A. Sylvester)

Astilbe x arendsii 'Hyazinth' (syn. 'Hyacinth')

every three female forms to ensure cross-fertilization). Unlike the common laurel, *A. japonica* is slow growing and is a particularly useful plant for screening.

Varieties: 'Crotonifolia' (a male plant with bright yellow variegations on the leaves); *A. j. longifolia* (available in both male and female forms, the female produces a profusion of berries, both forms have bright green leaves); 'Variegata' (syn. 'Maculata', has yellow-spotted leaves).

CULTIVATION
Planting time: September/October or March/April.
Soil: Any.
Aspect: Dense shade to full sun.
Minimum temp: −15°C (5°F).
Pruning: None necessary, but can be cut back hard in April if becoming too large.
Propagation: By 15-20cm (6-8in) HEEL CUTTINGS of lateral shoots taken in August/September; root in a cold frame for planting out in April.
Diseases: PHYSIOLOGICAL DISORDERS, usually the result of poor soil, can cause black blotches on the leaves.

AZALEA
See RHODODENDRON

BERBERIS   Berberidaceae
Barberry
A genus of prickly, easy-to-grow, deciduous and evergreen shrubs. With the exception of dwarf varieties of *B. thunbergii*, berberis should be grown individually, for if two or three are grown closely together, they can form a spiny thicket, which can be difficult to control. For this reason, although berberis is often recommended as an informal hedging plant, berberis hedges are not really suitable for the easy-care garden. Berberis resents disturbance, and transplanting is best done when small. Even then, transplanting can lead to leaf loss, but, after a while, new growth will break from the base of transplanted subjects. The species described below are all hardy evergreen shrubs, except for *B. thunbergii*, which is deciduous.
B. darwinii (Darwin's barberry)
Height and spread: 2.4-3m (8-10ft)
A shrub of bushy habit with glossy, dark green, holly-like leaves and bright yellow or orange flowers, which are produced in mid- to late spring and followed by blue berries.
B. gagnepainii lanceifolia (fernleaf berberis)
Height: 1.8m (6ft)

Spread: 1.2-1.5m (4-5ft)
A shrub of dense, bushy habit, having dark green, pointed leaves with crinkled, toothed edges. In late spring pendent yellow flowers are produced, and these are followed by black berries.
B. × stenophylla
Height: 2.4-3m (8-10ft)
Spread: 3m (10ft)
Dense, downward-arching branches are covered with dark green leaves, and, in mid- to late spring, gold yellow flowers are freely produced and followed by purple berries. Can be used as a feature plant.
B. thunbergii
Height: 1.2m (4ft)
Spread: 1.8m (6ft)
A compact shrub with small, light to mid-green leaves, which turn brilliant red before they fall in autumn. Clusters of pale yellow flowers are produced from April to June and are followed by small scarlet berries.
Varieties: *B. t. atropurpurea* (purple-red leaves throughout spring and summer); 'Rose Glow' (purple-red leaves veined with pink or white).
B. verruculosa
Height and spread: 0.9-1.2m (3-5ft)
More compact and slower growing than other berberis species. The glossy, dark green leaves have silver undersides, which make the plant particularly attractive in winter. Single or paired yellow flowers, produced in late spring, are followed by black berries.
CULTIVATION
Planting time: Deciduous species should be planted between October and March; evergreen species should be planted in September/October or March/April.
Soil: Well-drained; berberis are tolerant of thin, shallow soils.
Aspect: Deciduous species do best in full sun; evergreen species prefer shade to full sun.
Minimum temp: Deciduous species, −21°C (−6°F); evergreen species, −12°C (10°F).
Pruning: None required but subjects can be cut back to remove old growth or, if becoming too large, to maintain a pleasing shape. Prune deciduous species in February; evergreen species after flowering.
Propagation: Can be grown from SEED sown in November, but species hybridize readily and seedlings may not come true. Take 7.5-10cm (3-4in) HEEL CUTTINGS of lateral shoots in August/September.
Diseases: HONEY FUNGUS infection can cause death.

BERGENIA   Saxifragaceae
B. cordifolia
Height: 30cm (12in)
Planting distance: 30-38cm (12-15in)
A useful hardy herbaceous perennial for providing evergreen ground cover. Has rounded, mid-green leaves and produces racemes of lilac-rose, bell-shaped flowers in spring. Plants should not be disturbed unless they become overcrowded.
Varieties: 'Purpurea' (purple-pink flowers and purple tinged leaves).
CULTIVATION
Planting time: October to March.
Soil: Any.
Aspect: Partial shade to full sun.
Minimum temp: −15°C (5°F).
Pruning: Remove stems after flowering.
Propagation: By DIVISION in September/October or March.
Diseases: LEAF SPOT FUNGUS can cause brown blotches.

BRUNNERA   Boraginaceae
B. macrophylla (syn. *Anchusa myosotidiflora*) (Siberian bugloss)
Height: 30-45cm (12-18in)
Planting distance: 45cm (18in)
Sprays of sky-blue, forget-me-not-like flowers are produced in late spring. The light green foliage makes effective ground cover. This hardy herbaceous perennial is ideal for planting around the base of trees.
Varieties: 'Dawson's White' (syn. 'Variegata'; the leaves have cream edges, which are more pronounced when the plant is grown in shade).
CULTIVATION
Planting time: October to March.
Soil: Any moist garden soil.
Aspect: Prefers light shade but will tolerate full sun.
Minimum temp: −15°C (5°F).
Pruning: Remove stems after flowering. Carefully remove any non-variegated foliage of 'Dawson's White' without cutting into the root.
Propagation: By DIVISION in October or March; or by ROOT CUTTINGS in October/November, placing cuttings in a cold frame and planting out in final positions the following autumn.

BUDDLEIA   Loganiaceae
B. alternifolia
Height: 2.7m (9ft)
Spread: 1.5m (5ft)
A hardy, deciduous tree with graceful, arching stems bearing narrow, pale green leaves. Clusters of fragrant, lavender-blue flowers are produced in early summer on the previous year's growth. It is a vigorous grower and can be grown on

banks or trained into a standard tree.
Varieties: 'Argentea' (silvery leaves).
CULTIVATION
Planting time: October/November or
March/April.
Soil: Rich and loamy.
Aspect: Prefers full sun but tolerates
partial shade.
Minimum temp: −21°C (−6°F).
Pruning: None required but cut back
old shoots after flowering to maintain
neatness and vigour.
Propagation: By 10-12.5cm (4-5in)
HEEL CUTTINGS of half-ripe lateral
shoots taken in July; root in a cold
frame and pot on or put in a nursery
bed the following May. Plant out the
following October or May.
Diseases: Can be susceptible to
CUCUMBER MOSAIC VIRUS, which
causes mottling and distortion of the
leaves.

CALLUNA   Ericaceae
Heather
A genus of one hardy, evergreen
species of which there are many
named varieties.
C. vulgaris (ling, Scotch heather)
Height: 7.5-75cm (3in – 2ft 6in)
depending on variety
Planting distance: Depends on variety, but generally, smaller growing
varieties should be planted 30cm
(12in) apart and larger varieties 45-
60cm (18-24in) apart
An easily grown plant, which is
excellent for ground-cover purposes.
Looks best when planted in drifts of
at least 6 plants. Leaves and flowers
vary according to variety, and flowers
are produced between July and
November.
Varieties: 'Foxhollow Wanderer' (ht:
15cm (6in)); 'Gold Haze' (ht: 60cm
(2ft), yellow leaves and white flowers); 'Joan Sparkes' (ht: 23cm (9in),
purple flowers); 'Peter Sparkes' (ht:
30-45in (12-18in), pink flowers).
CULTIVATION
Planting time: March/April/May or
October/November.
Soil: Will not tolerate limy soil; needs
moist and peaty, acid soil.
Aspect: Full sun.
Minimum temp: −15°C (5°F).
Pruning: Cut back dead flowering
stems to the foliage in spring.
Propagation: By 2.5-5cm (1-2in)
CUTTINGS of side shoots, with a small
heel of old wood, taken from July to
October. Grow on in a cold frame
and plant out in position when
cuttings are approximately 7.5cm
(5in) high. Large varieties can also be
propagated by GROUND LAYERING;
sever from parent plant after a year.

Diseases: HEATHER DIE-BACK causes
a grey discoloration of the foliage and
death of the shoot.

CAMPANULA   Campanulaceae
Bellflower
C. carpatica
Height: 15-30cm (6-12in)
Spread: 30cm (12in)
A clump-forming, hardy herbaceous
perennial, which is useful for providing some ground cover at the front of
borders. The mid-green leaves are
pointed, and open bell-shaped flowers are borne in summer.
Varieties: 'Bressingham White' (ht:
10-15cm (4-6in), white flowers); 'Dit-
ton Blue' (ht: 15cm (6in), blue
flowers); 'Isobel' (ht: 23cm (9in),
violet flowers).
C. glomerata
Height: 10-60cm (4-24in)
Spread: 30-60cm (12-24in)
A suitable hardy herbaceous perennial for growing in raised beds as well
as borders, it looks its best when
grown in association with yellow- or
gold-flowering plants such as doroni-
cums. *C. glomerata* has oval, mid-
green leaves, and the leafy stems bear
dense heads of blue, bell-shaped
flowers throughout summer.
Varieties: *C. g.* var. *acaulis* (dwarf
form); 'Alba' (ht: 45cm (18in), white
flowers); *C. g.* var. *dahurica* (ht: 45-
60cm (18-24in), the most common
form in cultivation, violet flowers).
CULTIVATION
Planting time: September to April.
Soil: Well-drained.
Aspect: Full sun to partial shade.
Minimum temp: −15°C (5°F).
Pruning: After flowering, faded
stems of *C. glomerata* may be removed.
Propagation: By SEED sown in October or March/April in a cold frame.
By DIVISION and replanting in October or March/April. By 2.5-5cm
(1-2in) CUTTINGS of non-flowering
basal shoots taken in April/May.
Pests: SLUGS and SNAILS can damage
foliage. FROGHOPPERS suck sap, causing infested shoots to wilt.
Diseases: RUST, seen as orange spots
on leaves, may infect *C. carpatica*.
TOMATO SPOTTED WILD VIRUS causes
stunting of plants and wavy lines and
yellow ring spots on leaves.

CELASTRUS   Celastraceae
A genus of deciduous shrubs and
climbers, grown for their attractive
fruits.
C. orbiculatus (oriental bittersweet,
staff vine)
Height: 12.2m (40ft) or more

A hardy, strongly growing climber of
twining habit, which is particularly
useful for covering old trees, unsightly hedges or arbours, where it
needs no extra support. The mid-
green foliage turns yellow in autumn.
Insignificant flowers in summer are
followed by brown seed capsules,
which split open to reveal attractive
bright orange-yellow and red fruits.
These often persist well into winter.
If only one plant is grown, select a
self-fertile, hermaphrodite form to
ensure fruiting.
CULTIVATION
Planting time: September to March.
Soil: Well-drained but moist.
Aspect: Sunny or partially shaded
and sheltered from strong winds.
Minimum temp: −12°C (10°F).
Pruning: None necessary; remove
unwanted growths or cut main stems
to half their length to restrict size if
wished in February.
Propagation: By LAYERING year-old
growths in October, separating from
parent plant after a year.
Pests: SCALE INSECTS may infest
stems.

CHAENOMELES   Rosaceae
Flowering quince, cydonia
A genus of deciduous, spring-
flowering shrubs, which bear, in
autumn, edible fruits that can be
used to make preserves. Although
slow growing, the larger varieties
should be given adequate space if
they are to be left unpruned. Can be
grown as free-standing shrubs or
against walls, where the flowers are
seen to best advantage.
C. japonica (Maule's quince)
Height: 90cm (3ft)
Spread: 1.5-2.1m (5-7ft)
A hardy shrub of low-growing, wide-
spreading habit, with mid-green,
downy leaves. Orange-red flowers,
5cm (2in) diameter, are borne on the
previous year's growth in late spring,
and these are followed by fragrant,
bright yellow fruits.
Varieties: *C. j. alpina* (a smaller
variety with bright orange flowers).
C. speciosa (syn. *C. lagenaria*) (Japanese quince)
Height: 1.8m (6ft)
Spread: 1.2-1.6m (4-6ft)
The commonest form of chaenomeles, this hardy shrub can be grown
singly or as an informal hedging
plant. The glossy leaves are dark
green, and red flowers, up to 5cm
(2in) in diameter, are borne in
clusters from, in mild districts, as
early as January until April and
followed by green-yellow fruits.

Aucuba japonica

Aucuba japonica 'Crotonifolia'

Berberis darwinii

Berberis thunbergii atropurpurea

Bergenia cordifolia

Campanula carpatica

Campanula glomerata

Chaenomeles speciosa 'Nivalis'

Chaenomeles x superba 'Fire Dance'

Varieties: 'Aurora' (yellow-tinted, rose flowers); 'Cardinalis' (deep crimson flowers); 'Nivalis' (white flowers); 'Rubra Grandiflora' (low-spreading habit and large, deep red flowers); 'Umbilicata' (rose-pink flowers).

C. × superba

Height: 1-1.5m (3-5ft)
Spread: 1.8m (6ft)
A hardy, free-flowering hybrid form, similar to *C. speciosa*, bearing saucer-shaped flowers in spring.
Varieties: 'Fire Dance' (spreading habit and bright red flowers); 'Rowallane' (upright habit and large, semi-double, red flowers).

CULTIVATION
Planting time: October to March.
Soil: Any garden soil; chlorosis of the leaves, shown as yellowing or whitening between the veins of the leaves, may occur if soil is too alkaline.
Aspect: Full sun to light shade; may be trained against walls of any aspect.
Minimum temp: −12°C (10°F).
Pruning: None necessary, but if branches become overcrowded or if the plant is trained against a wall, prune after flowering to 3 buds on the previous season's growth.
Propagation: By 10cm (4in) HEEL CUTTINGS of lateral shoots taken after flowering. Pot on rooted cuttings and overwinter in a cold frame. By GROUND LAYERING shoots in September, separating from parent plant when rooted, usually 1-2 years later.
Diseases: FIREBLIGHT produces a progressive die-back of branches accompanied by shrivelling and browning of the flowers and leaves.

CHAMAECYPARIS

Cupressaceae
False cypress
A genus of easily grown coniferous trees, the varieties of which vary greatly in size and shape and which can, therefore, be used for a wide range of purposes depending on the variety selected.

C. lawsoniana (Lawson cypress)

A conical, columnar, hardy, evergreen tree. The tall varieties are particularly useful for large-scale planting schemes in bigger gardens. The foliage is usually dark green with grey undersides, and a profusion of dark red cones is produced.
Tall varieties: 'Allumii' (ht: 6m (20ft), sp: 1.5m (5ft), blue-grey foliage); 'Columnaris' (ht: 10m (30ft), sp: 60cm (2ft), slender, upright habit with pale grey-blue foliage); 'Erecta Viridis' (ht: 10m (30ft), sp: 1.5m (5ft), bright green foliage); 'Fletcheri' (ht: 4.6-12.2m (15-40ft), sp: 1.8-3m (6-10ft), feathery, grey-green foliage); 'Lutea' (ht: 10m (30ft), sp: 1.8m (6ft), bright golden, pendulous foliage). **Dwarf varieties:** 'Ellwoodii' (ht: 3m (10ft), sp: 60cm (2ft), slow-growing, grey-green variety that is suitable, when young, for rock gardens); 'Ellwood's Gold' (ht: 1.8m (6ft), sp: 45cm (18in), yellow-green foliage in spring and summer turns green in autumn); 'Minima' (ht and sp: 90cm (3ft), rounded, globular habit with blue-green foliage); 'Nana' (ht and sp: 1.2m (4ft), conical habit with blue-green foliage).

CULTIVATION
Planting time: October (in light soil); April (in heavy soil).
Soil: Any.
Aspect: Full sun to light shade; golden varieties keep their colour best in sunny positions.
Minimum temp: −21°C (−6°F).
Pruning: None necessary; if main stem forks, remove one shoot in spring to maintain leading shoot.
Propagation: By 10cm (4in) HEEL CUTTINGS of strong young shoots taken in May and kept in a cold frame until rooted. Pot on and plant out when mature, which can take up to 3 years.
Diseases: HONEY FUNGUS can kill trees. Take care when choosing specimens and avoid plants with abnormal yellowing of the foliage, as this may indicate untreatable root infection.

CHOISYA

Rutaceae

C. ternata (Mexican orange blossom)

Height: 1.5-1.8m (5-6ft)
Spread: 1.8-2.4m (6-8ft)
A semi-hardy evergreen shrub of rounded, bushy habit. It has trifoliate, glossy, light green leaves. In spring fragrant, white flowers, 5cm (2in) in diameter, similar in appearance to orange blossom, are borne in clusters at the end of the shoots. If the weather is favourable, a second flowering can occur in late autumn.
Varieties: 'Sundance' (slow growing, with golden foliage).

CULTIVATION
Planting time: April/May.
Soil: Well-drained.
Aspect: Although tolerant of shade, does best in a sunny position sheltered from cold winds, which can damage the foliage. In cold or exposed gardens it is best grown against a south-facing wall and protected against north and east winds.
Minimum temp: −7°C (19°F).
Pruning: None necessary, but frost-damaged shoots should be removed in spring.
Propagation: By taking 7.5cm (3in) CUTTINGS of half-ripened growth in August. Root, pot on and overwinter in a cold frame. In mild and sheltered areas young plants can be planted out in the following May; in colder areas pot on through the summer, overwinter in a cold frame and plant out in final position the following May.
Diseases: HONEY FUNGUS infection causes rapid death.

CISTUS

Cistaceae
Rock rose, sun rose
A genus of half-hardy evergreen shrubs. Most cistus in cultivation are garden hybrids, which vary in size and habit. All bear a profusion of single, rose-like flowers, which open in the morning and drop their petals in the afternoon. However, buds are produced in such abundance that continual flowering is maintained for up to 3 months. The plants are particularly effective when planted in groups.

C. × aguilari

Height and spread: 1.2-1.5m (4-5ft)
A plant of upright, bushy habit that bears white flowers in summer.
Varieties: 'Maculatus' (purple and white flowers).

C. × corbariensis

Height: 0.9-1.2m (3-4ft)
Spread: 1.8-2.7m (6-9ft)
The hardiest cistus, this is a low-growing shrub of bushy, spreading habit. White and yellow flowers are produced in early summer; the buds are tinted red.

C. × cyprius

Height: 1.8-2.4m (6-8ft)
Spread: 2.1-2.9m (7-9ft)
The dark green foliage is sticky, and white flowers with maroon centres are borne in summer.

C. × lusitanicus

Height and spread: 30-60cm (1-2ft)
A dwarf hybrid that bears white and maroon flowers in summer.
Varieties: 'Decumbens' (a more wide-spreading habit, up to 1.2m (4ft) across).

C. × purpureus

Height: 1.2-1.5m (4-5ft)
Spread: 1.2m (4ft)
A rapidly growing shrub of upright habit with grey-green foliage. Rose-pink to purple flowers with maroon markings are produced in early summer.

C. 'Silver Pink'

Height and spread: 60-90cm (2-3ft)
A hardy hybrid with silvery-pink

flowers, which are borne on erect stems well above the grey-green foliage in early to mid-summer.

CULTIVATION

Planting time: April/May

Soil: Any but do best on poor, free-draining soils.

Aspect: Full sun in a position sheltered from cold winds; frost damage can cause shoots to die back. Minimum temp: −10°C (14°F).

Pruning: None required; older plants will not tolerate cutting back but young plants may be lightly trimmed in early spring to promote bushier growth.

Propagation: By SEED sown in trays in a cold frame in spring. Pot on and overwinter in a cold frame and plant out the following May. Hybrids do not breed true from seed. By CUTTINGS, although this is a slow process. Take 7.5-10cm (3-4in) cuttings of half-ripe, non-flowering shoots with a heel in summer. Root in a cold frame. Pot on plantlets and overwinter in a cold frame. Pot on and keep outside throughout the next season, overwinter again in a cold frame before finally planting out in permanent positions the following spring.

CLEMATIS   Ranunculaceae

A useful climbing plant for the easy-care garden. The modern hybrids require far less attention than the older, wild species. The species and varieties listed below are hardy, deciduous, largely maintenance free and self-clinging. However, if grown against a wall, they will need some support, such as a trellis.

C. alpina (syn. *Atragene alpina*)

Height and spread: 2.4m (8ft)

The dark green foliage is coarsely toothed, and cup-shaped, violet-blue flowers are borne in spring.

Varieties: *C. alpina sibirica* (white flowers).

C. flammula

Height: 4.6-6m (15-20ft)

Spread: 3m (10ft)

Dense, bushy growth is produced, mainly at the top of the plant. The foliage is bright green and small, and small, fragrant, white flowers are produced in late summer to early autumn. *C. flammula* does best when the base is in shade but the crown is in full sun.

C. macropetala

Height and spread: 1.8-2.4m (6-8ft)

A vigorous, slender-stemmed climber of bushy habit, particularly suitable for growing over a low, sunny wall. The foliage is dark green, and semi-double, bell-shaped flowers

are produced in early summer.

Varieties: 'Maidwell Hall' (deep blue flowers); 'Markham's Pink' (rose-pink flowers).

C. montana

Height: 10m (30ft)

Spread: 6m (20ft)

An easy-to-cultivate but extremely vigorous climber, which produces a mass of tangled, woody stems; it can quickly mask a wall, even in winter. The foliage is dark green, and large clusters of pure white flowers are produced in late spring.

Varieties: 'Elizabeth' (pink flowers); *C. m. rubens* (bronze-green foliage with pale pink flowers); *C. m. wilsonii* (large, fragrant, white flowers, borne in mid-summer).

C. tangutica

Height: 4.6m (15ft)

Spread: 3m (10ft)

A slender, vigorous species with grey-green foliage. Rich yellow, lantern-shaped flowers are produced from August to October, followed by fine, silvery seed heads. Seen at its best when allowed to ramble freely over large banks, it is also a useful climber for covering low walls.

CULTIVATION

Planting time: October to May.

Soil: Any, but thrives in slightly alkaline soil.

Aspect: An open position, but preferably with the base of the stem and the roots shaded from strong sun. (Shade can be provided by planting low-growing shrubs near to the base of the clematis.)

Minimum temp: −29°C (−20°F).

Pruning: None necessary, unless grown in positions where the spread needs to be restricted; then, old, weak growth should be completely cut out and remaining stems cut down to one-third of their original length in February/March for summer- and autumn-flowering species or immediately after flowering for spring-flowering species.

Propagation: By 10-12.5cm (4-5in) long stem CUTTINGS with at least two buds taken in July and kept in a cold frame. When rooted, pot on and overwinter in a cold frame. Pot on throughout the next season and plant out in permanent position from October. By SEED sown in pots during October. Overwinter in a cold frame; germination usually occurs by spring. Pot on and plant out in final positions in October. Plants can be LAYERED in March and severed from the parent plant about a year later.

Pests: SLUGS may eat young shoots. APHIDS can infest growing tips. EAR-

WIGS can feed on leaves and petals.

Diseases: CLEMATIS WILT can cause shoots to wilt and die back to the base of the plant. New growth is, however, usually produced next spring. White powdery coating of the leaves, sometimes also the flowers, is caused by POWDERY MILDEW. VIRUS DISEASE causes distortion of the flowers and yellow mottling of the leaves.

COLCHICUM   Liliaceae

Autumn crocus

A genus of hardy, mainly autumn-flowering, crocus-like plants. For best effect, colchicums should be planted in groups of at least six. They are useful for providing autumn colour in shrub borders, and they also naturalize well in grass. Wherever planted, however, the leaves must be allowed to die back naturally, which can look untidy.

C. speciosum

Height: 25cm (10in)

Spread: 23cm (9in)

Mauve, trumpet-shaped flowers are produced in autumn from the centre of a large rosette of leaves, which develop in spring.

Varieties: 'Album' (white flowers); 'Atrorubens' (purplish flowers).

There are also a number of excellent garden hybrids, including 'Autumn Queen' (violet-purple flowers); 'The Giant' (rose-pink and white flowers); 'Waterlily' (purple flowers).

CULTIVATION

Planting time: August/September; plant corms 7.5-10cm (3-4in) deep.

Soil: Well-drained.

Aspect: Full sun or partial shade.

Pruning: None

Propagation: By DIVISION of corms; lift in June/July, separate offsets and replant immediately.

Pests: SLUGS may feed on corms and leaves.

CORNUS   Cornaceae

Dogwood

C. alba (red-barked dogwood)

Height and spread: 3m (10ft)

A hardy deciduous shrub of upright habit, which bears insignificant yellow-white flowers in early summer. These are followed by white berries. The mid-green leaves have grey undersides and turn an attractive orange-red in autumn. The stems of the current season's growth are coloured brilliant red in winter.

Varieties: 'Elegantissima' (white-margined and mottled leaves); 'Sibirica' (syn. 'Westonbirt', shiny red stems); 'Spaethii' (yellow-edged,

Chamaecyparis lawsoniana 'Pottenii'

Choisya ternata

Chamaecyparis lawsoniana 'Silver Threads'

Choisya ternata 'Sundance'

Clematis montana

Clematis montana rubens

Clematis 'Comtesse de Bouchaud'

Clematis tangutica

Cornus alba 'Elegantissima'

bright green leaves).

C. florida (flowering dogwood)
Height and spread: 6-7.6m (20-25ft)
In late sping this hardy, deciduous, small tree produces tiny flowers surrounded by attractive, large, white, petal-like bracts. Strawberry-like fruits follow. The dark green foliage turns red and gold in late summer.
Varieties: *C. f. rubra* (pink and white bracts).
CULTIVATION
Planting time: September/October/November or March/April.
Soil: Moist; *C. florida* prefers non-alkaline soil.
Aspect: Full sun to light shade.
Minimum temp: $-23°C$ $(-9°F)$.
Pruning: *C. florida* requires no pruning. To produce the best coloured stems, *C. alba* should be cut back hard to a few inches above ground level in early spring every 1-2 years.
Propagation: By GROUND LAYERING long shoots in September; sever from parent plant when rooted (usually by the following October with *C. alba*, although layers of *C. florida* will often require another year). *C. alba* can also be propagated in November by removing and replanting any rooted SUCKERS.

COTONEASTER   Rosaceae

A genus of hardy evergreen and deciduous shrubs, the deciduous species often giving good autumn colours and bearing brightly coloured fruits. Some evergreen species can be used for hedges and screening, and low-growing, creeping forms are useful for ground cover.

C. congestus
Height: 15cm (6in)
Spread: 1.5m (5ft)
A hardy, low-growing, creeping shrub that is useful for ground cover. It can be used where other types would become too broad and form attractive mounds of tightly packed branches bearing evergreen, blue-green foliage. Small pink flowers are borne in summer, and these are followed by bright red berries in autumn.

C. dammeri
Height: 5-7.5cm (2-3in)
Spread: 1.5-1.8m (5-6ft)
A vigorous, hardy, carpet-forming, prostrate shrub, which is useful for ground cover, especially on inaccessible banks or bare ground beneath tall shrubs or trees. If used for ground cover, plant subjects at least 1m (3ft) apart. The dark green leaves are glossy, and white flowers pro-

duced in summer are followed by red berries.

C. horizontalis
Height: 60cm (2ft)
Spread: 1.8m (6ft) or more
A wide-spreading, hardy, deciduous shrub, the low-growing branches forming an attractive, fishbone-like network. It is a useful ground-cover subject that can be planted to good effect to hide unsightly areas such as rocky banks or manhole covers. Planting distance for ground-cover purposes is about 1.5m (5ft). The glossy, dark green leaves turn red in autumn before falling, and small pink flowers are produced in summer and followed by thickly clustered, bright red berries. It can be especially attractive planted against a shady wall, where it can reach a height of 2.4m (8ft).
Varieties: 'Variegatus' (small, cream-variegated, pink-tinged leaves).

C. lacteus
Height: 3.6m (12ft)
Spread: 3m (10ft)
A good hedging or screening hardy evergreen shrub with a mound-like habit. The leathery, dark green leaves have grey undersides, and creamy-white flowers are produced in summer; these are followed by clusters of red berries, which last until winter. For hedging purposes young plants should be 60-90cm (2-3ft) apart; for screening, they should be 1.5-1.8m (5-6ft) apart.
CULTIVATION
Planting time: October to February.
Soil: Any.
Aspect: Sunny.
Minimum temp: $-15°C$ $(5°F)$.
Pruning: None necessary.
Propagation: Although propagation by SEED is possible, results are variable, named varieties not breeding true to type. Propagation of cultivars should be by vegetative means only. Branches can be LAYERED in autumn and severed from the parent plant after a year. Alternatively, take 7.5-10cm (3-4in) HEEL CUTTINGS of ripened stems of evergreen species in September or of semi-ripened stems of deciduous species in July/August. Overwinter in a cold frame and pot on before planting out in final positions 1-2 years later.
Pests: Sticky or sooty deposits on stems and leaves in summer are caused by APHIDS or SCALE INSECTS.
Diseases: FIREBLIGHT causes leaves to brown and shrivel and flowers to blacken, resulting in a progressive die-back of the branches. HONEY FUNGUS causes rapid death. SILVER

LEAF gives leaves a silvery tinge and causes shoots to die back.

CRATAEGUS   Rosaceae

Hawthorn, ornamental thorn
A genus of very tough and hardy deciduous shrubs, which are generally tolerant of the poor soil, pollution and strong or cold winds that would make small trees unsuitable for many gardens. However, the most commonly found species, *C. monogyna* (common hawthorn), which is extensively used for hedging, especially in country gardens, requires several clips a year, and dead wood must be rigorously cut out in winter, often when the weather is at its worst. It cannot, therefore, be recommended for the easy-care garden. The following species, however, require little or no maintenance.

C. laevigata (syn. *C. oxyacantha*) (hawthorn, may)
Height and spread: 4.6-6m (15-20ft)
This hardy, deciduous shrub has mid-green foliage and bears clusters of fragrant white flowers in spring. In autumn round red berries are produced. It is best to grow one of the named varieties, which, when planted singly, make excellent specimen trees. The red-flowering varieties may take several seasons before reaching full bloom.
Varieties: 'Paul's Scarlet (syn. 'Coccinea Plena', double, bright red flowers); 'Plena' (double, white flowers); 'Punicea' (single, scarlet flowers); 'Rosea' (single, pink flowers); 'Rosea Flore Pleno' (double, pink flowers).

C. × lavallei 'Carrierei' (syn. *C. × carrierei*)
Height: 6m (20ft)
Spread: 4.6m (15ft)
A densely branched, thornless, deciduous shrub with dark green, glossy leaves, which turn orange-brown in autumn and persist into winter. Clusters of white flowers, 5-7.5cm (2-3in) across, in summer and are followed by orange-red fruits.
CULTIVATION
Planting time: October to March.
Soil: Any; crataegus are tolerant of drought and waterlogging alike.
Aspect: Open and sunny but will tolerate shade and exposed positions.
Minimum temp: $-29°C$ $(-20°F)$.
Pruning: None necessary.
Propagation: By SEED sown in February; germination is extremely slow and may take 18 months.
Pests: CATERPILLARS may feed on the leaves.
Diseases: FIREBLIGHT causes progressive die-back of the branches, with

blackening of the flowers and withering and browning of the leaves. HONEY FUNGUS can cause rapid death. LEAF SPOT, seen as black or brown spots on the leaves, can be caused by fungal diseases. Leaves are affected by POWDERY MILDEW, which causes a white, powdery coating, and RUST, which causes red or orange swellings that also appear on fruit and young shoots in early summer.

CROCOSMIA   Iridaceae
Montbretia
A genus of semi-hardy, summer-flowering, cormous plants.
C. × crocosmiiflora (syn. *Montbretia crocosmiiflora*)
Height: 60cm (2ft)
Planting distance: 10-15cm (4-6in)
This hybrid form is hardier than the South African species and has become naturalized in many countries. The upright leaves are sword-shaped, and the trumpet-shaped flowers, ranging from yellow to red depending on variety, add welcome colour to the mixed or herbaceous border in late summer. They are excellent as cut flowers. Numerous modern hybrids are available.
Varieties: 'Bressingham Blaze' (orange-red flowers); 'Emberglow' (large orange-red flowers); 'Solfaterre'/'Solfatare' (orange-yellow flowers and bronze-tinted leaves); 'Vulcan' (orange-red flowers).
CULTIVATION
Planting time: March/April; plant corms 7.5cm (3in) deep in clumps.
Soil: Moist, sandy but well-drained.
Aspect: Sunny and sheltered; by a south-facing wall or among other herbaceous plants is ideal.
Minimum temp: 5°C (41°F).
Pruning: Remove flower stems after flowering.
Propagation: By SEED collected in autumn. Sow in pots and overwinter in a cold frame, planting out the following year. By DIVISION of clumps, lifted and replanted immediately after flowering or before growth starts in spring.

CROCUS   Iridaceae
A genus of hardy, dwarf, spring- or autumn-flowering bulbs. They are particularly well suited to growing in sink gardens or tubs as well as in borders or beneath deciduous shrubs and trees, where they should be planted in groups.
C. chrysanthus
Height: 10cm (4in)
Spread: 7.5cm (3in)
The short, linear, mid- to dark green

leaves have a central white stripe, and the species and its many forms produce golden-yellow flowers in early spring. Some of the blue and white forms sold as *C. chrysanthus* are hybrids of *C. chrysanthus* and *C. biflorus*.
Varieties: 'Advance' (pale yellow flowers streaked with mauve); 'Blue Bird' (a particularly free-flowering variety with large purple-blue and cream flowers); 'Cream Beauty' (creamy-white flowers); 'E.A. Bowles' (deep yellow flowers with bronze markings; Goldilocks' (deep yellow flowers with a deep purple throat); 'Prinses Beatrix'/'Princess Beatrice' (blue flowers with a yellow throat); 'Snowbunting' (white flowers with yellow throats); 'Zwanenburg Bronze' (dark bronze flowers outside with yellow interiors).
C. vernus
Height: 7.5-12.5cm (3-5in)
Spread: 10cm (4in) or more
A robust, spring-flowering species that can be grown in a border or naturalized in short grass provided it is not mown before the leaves die down in late spring. Mowing before this time reduces the vigour of the corms, although they can usually survive this treatment for a few years; when they do fail, they are easily replaced. If left undisturbed, they form dense flowering clumps. Many large-flowered hybrids are available.
Varieties: 'Jeanne d'Arc' (white flowers with orange stigmas); 'Pickwick' (pale lilac flowers with darker lilac stripes and purple throats); 'Purpureus Grandiflorus' (a spectacular variety with purple-blue flowers that grows well in pots and tubs); 'Vanguard' (an earlier flowering variety with grey-blue flowers outside with pale blue interiors).
CULTIVATION
Planting time: September/October; plant corms 7.5cm (3in) apart and 7.5cm (3in) deep; in light soil, plant corms up to 15cm (6in) deep so that they are less likely to be disturbed by any surface cultivation.
Soil: Well-drained.
Aspect: Any; warm, sheltered sites encourage freer, earlier flowering.
Minimum temp: −15°C (5°F).
Pruning: None necessary. Flowers should not be dead-headed and the leaves should not be tied into bunches or removed before they have yellowed and died.
Propagation: By DIVISION. Lift corms after the foliage has died and remove any offsets, which should be kept in a warm place for a few days to dry

before being replanted.
Pests: APHIDS may infest young leaves. BIRDS can damage young flowers. MICE and LEATHERJACKETS may eat corms.
Diseases: GLADIOLUS DRY ROT can cause black lesions on corms, which, if untreated, may cause the corms to shrivel and rot. GLADIOLUS SCAB infection is seen as crater-like depressions, which may have a shiny coating, on the base of the corms. PHYSIOLOGICAL DISORDERS, which are caused by a check in growth, result in crinkled or distorted leaves.

CYTISUS   Leguminosae
Broom
A genus of easily grown, largely hardy and mainly deciduous shrubs, which bear pea-like flowers. They resent root disturbance, so buy pot-grown specimens only. Their height depends on the variety, and the dwarfer forms are useful for growing on rocky banks or for providing ground cover at the front of shrub borders.
C. × beanii
Height: 30-60cm (1-2ft)
Spread: 90cm (3ft)
A hardy dwarf form with mid-green foliage that bears golden-yellow flowers in late spring on the previous year's growth.
C. × kewensis
Height: 30cm (1ft)
Spread: 1.2m (4ft) or more
A hardy dwarf form with a spreading, low-growing habit. The foliage is mid-green, and sulphur-yellow flowers appear in late spring.
C. × praecox (Warminster broom)
Height and spread: 1.5m (5ft)
A vigorous, hardy shrub with grey-green foliage borne on arching branches. Acrid-smelling, creamy-white flowers are produced in abundance in late spring.
Varieties: 'Allgold' (sulphur-yellow flowers).
CULTIVATION
Planting time: September/October or March/April.
Soil: Well-drained; cytisus thrive on poor soils. Although they tolerate lime, this often makes them shorter lived.
Aspect: Full sun.
Minimum temp: −15°C (5°F).
Pruning: None necessary.
Propagation: By SEED sown in trays in spring and placed in a cold frame. Prick out seedlings when large enough and transplant into pots, planting out in permanent positions in autumn.

Cotoneaster 'Coral Beauty'

Cotoneaster horizontalis 'Variegatus'

Crocosmia x *crocosmiiflora*

Crocus 'Pickwick'

Cytisus x *beanii*

Pests: GALL MITES can cause disfiguring growths on stems.

DIANTHUS Caryophyllaceae

A large genus of annual and perennial, mainly summer-flowering species, which include carnations and pinks. The many cultivars that are available are divided into three main groups – pinks, border carnations and perpetual-flowering carnations – and pinks are further subdivided into old-fashioned and modern hybrids. The varieties listed here are particularly suited to planting in raised beds. Perennial species are usually short lived and may require propagating and replanting every 3-4 years.

Modern pinks
Height: 23cm (9in)
Spread: 38cm (15in)
These fast-growing modern hybrids are obtained by crossing an old-fashioned pink with a perpetual-flowering carnation; this cross gave rise to D. × allwoodii, which is regarded as the parent of modern pinks. Such pinks are also sometimes known as Allwoodii hybrids. The foliage is grey-green, and fragrant, single or double, pink, red or white flowers, 2.5-5cm (1-2in) across, are produced throughout summer.
Varieties: 'Alice' (semi-double, white and maroon flowers); 'Cherryripe' (double, cherry-pink flowers); 'Daphne' (single, pink flowers with bright red eyes); 'Freckles' (double, pink flowers with red mottling); 'Prudence' (semi-double, pale pink flowers laced with crimson); 'Startler' (double, pink flowers).
D. deltoides (maiden pink)
Height: 15-23cm (6-9in)
Spread: 7.5cm (3in)
A mat-forming, evergreen plant that is suited to growing in dry walls or on banks as well as in raised beds. Crimson to white flowers, 2.5cm (1in) across, are freely produced from mid-summer to autumn. The mid-green foliage is often tinted with red or purple.
Varieties: 'Albus' (white flowers); 'Brilliant' (pink flowers); 'Flashing Light' (crimson flowers).
D. gratianopolitanus (syn. D. caesius) (Cheddar pink)
Height: 10-30cm (4-12in)
Spread: 23-60cm (9-24in)
A more easily grown and longer lived species of garden pink than other types. It has creeping stems, which can root to form a mat of grey-green foliage with an eventual spread of up to 60cm (24in). Sweetly scented pink flowers, 2.5cm (1in) across, are

produced in summer.
Varieties: 'Flore Pleno' (syn. 'Double Cheddar', double, pink flowers).
CULTIVATION
Planting time: March or September/October/November.
Soil: Alkaline to neutral and well-drained.
Aspect: Full sun.
Minimum temp: −12°C (10°F).
Pruning: Stop young plants in March/April by cutting or breaking off the top of the main shoot immediately above a joint to encourage strong side shoots.
Propagation: By SEED sown in early summer in trays or pots kept in a cold frame. By 7.5-10cm (3-4in) CUTTINGS of strong side shoots in mid-summer. By GROUND LAYERING side shoots in mid-summer. The layers can usually be severed from the parent plant after about 6 weeks; after another 4 weeks the plantlets can be lifted and re-planted into their new positions.
Pests: APHIDS can slow or even stop growth. CARNATION FLY LARVAE may attack stems and leaves, causing wilting and death of the plant if the infestation is heavy. CATERPILLARS may feed on the foliage.
Diseases: LEAF ROT causes brown or grey blotches on leaves and stems. The fungus may be visible on similarly discoloured leaf bases. LEAF SPOT causes brown or white spots, sometimes with purple margins.

DICENTRA Fumariaceae

A genus of clump-forming hardy herbaceous perennials, useful in a border. All species have pendent flowers borne on arching stems and dissected, fern-like foliage. Once established, the brittle roots should not be disturbed.
D. eximia
Height: 30-45cm (12-18in)
Spread: 30cm (12in)
The attractive foliage is grey-green, and bright pink flowers are produced from late spring to early autumn.
Varieties: D. e. alba (free-flowering, white-flowered form with green foliage).
D. formosa
Height: 30-45cm (12-18in)
Spread: 45cm (18in)
The finely cut foliage is bright green, and racemes of pink flowers appear in early summer.
Varieties: 'Adrian Bloom' (a strong variety with grey foliage and carmine flowers); 'Bountiful' (attractive seed pods appear after flowering); 'Luxuriant' (bright red flowers); 'Spring Morning' (pale pink flowers).

D. spectabilis (bleeding heart, Dutchman's trousers)
Height: 45-75cm (1ft 6in – 2ft 6in)
Spread: 45cm (18in)
Arching sprays of heart-shaped, pink and white flowers are borne above grey-green foliage in early summer. The plant dies down in mid-summer after flowering.
Varieties: D. s. alba (white flowers).
CULTIVATION
Planting time: October to March.
Soil: Rich and well-drained but moist.
Aspect: Full sun to medium shade; plant where they will be protected from strong winds and late frosts.
Minimum temp: −10°C (14°F).
Pruning: None required.
Propagation: By DIVISION of the root ball between October and March. Or by 10cm (4in) ROOT CUTTINGS taken in March and kept in a cold frame. When developed, harden off and plant out in permanent positions in October.

DODECATHEON Primulaceae
Shooting star
D. meadia
Height and spread: 30cm (12in)
The erect, leafless stems of this hardy herbaceous perennial are topped, in early summer, by cyclamen-like, pink to purple flowers with yellow anthers; the flowers are produced in clusters from a low-growing rosette of long, ovate, light green leaves. If left undisturbed, plants form clumps.
CULTIVATION
Planting time: September to March.
Soil: Moist and rich in leaf mould.
Aspect: Partial shade.
Minimum temp: −15°C (5°F).
Pruning: None necessary.
Propagation: By DIVISION of established plants in autumn.

ECHINOPS Compositae
Globe thistle
A group of hardy, summer-flowering perennials, grown for their spiky, globular flower-heads.
E. ritro 'Veitch's Blue'
Height: 1.2m (4ft)
Spread: 75cm (2ft 6in)
The grey-green foliage is thistle-like but not spiny. Spherical, steel-blue, lustrous flowers, 5cm (2in) across, are produced in summer. There are several taller hybrids of E. ritro, but 'Veitch's Blue' is recommended as it does not need staking.
CULTIVATION
Planting time: October to March.
Soil: Well-drained.
Aspect: Sunny.

Minimum temp: −12°C (10°F).
Pruning: Cut stems to ground level in autumn.
Propagation: By DIVISION of roots between October and March. By ROOT CUTTINGS taken in late autumn/early winter and kept in a cold frame. Pot on and plant out in permanent positions the following autumn. By SEED sown outdoors in a sunny position in April. Transplant to permanent positions in autumn.

ELAEAGNUS   Elaeagnaceae
A genus of quick-growing, hardy shrubs and trees.
E. angustifolia (oleaster)
Height and spread: 3.6m (12ft)
A wide-spreading, deciduous small tree, suitable for the larger garden. The branches bear narrow, willow-like, grey-green leaves, and in early summer small, fragrant, creamy-yellow flowers appear, followed by amber-coloured, edible fruits.
E. pungens
Height and spread: 2.4-3.6m (8-12ft)
A vigorous and spreading evergreen shrub, which is useful for informal hedging, when the planting distance should be 60-90cm (2-3ft). It makes a good windbreak in exposed gardens. The ovate leaves are glossy green with white undersides. Silvery flowers produced in late autumn and are followed by small, red or orange fruits.
Varieties: 'Maculata' (leaves splashed with gold; slower growing than the species but it affords less protection against the wind and if used for hedging the planting distance should be 45-60cm (1ft 6in – 2ft)).
CULTIVATION
Planting time: Deciduous species, October/November/December; evergreen species, April or September.
Soil: Any; elaeagnus are tolerant of shallow, chalky land.
Aspect: Deciduous species, full sun; evergreen species, full sun or partial shade.
Minimum temp: −25°C (−13°F).
Pruning: No regular pruning necessary, but if used for hedging, the top one-third of all growth should be removed after planting to promote bushy growth. Any low lateral growth of *E. angustifolia* may be removed from the main stem to produce a good tree-like shape if desired. If it becomes too large, *E. pungens* may need to be cut back every fourth year in April or September.
Propagation: By 7.5-10cm (3-4in) CUTTINGS of evergreen species taken in September. Pot on rooted cuttings the following spring and plant out in permanent positions in October.
Diseases: LEAF SPOT infection causes brown blotches on the leaves.

EPIMEDIUM   Berberidaceae
A genus of hardy, semi-evergreen or evergreen perennials. Although relatively slow growing, once established they provide good ground cover, especially in shade where other ground-cover subjects may not thrive.
E. perralderianum
Height: 30cm (12in)
Spread: 45cm (18in)
This hardy evergreen is probably the best of the epimediums for ground cover. The leaves are bright green, marked with red in summer and turning bronze in winter. Sprays of small yellow flowers are produced in early summer.
E. pinnatum
Height and spread: 30cm (12in)
The mid-green, evergreen leaves become tinted with red in autumn, and bright yellow flowers with red nectar glands are produced from late spring to early summer.
Varieties: *E. p.* subsp. *colchicum* (a more free-flowering form with larger flowers).
E. × *youngianum*
Height: 15-30cm (6-12in)
Spread: 20cm (8in)
The semi-evergreen leaves are mid-green with red-brown markings that become orange-red in autumn. The plant will remain evergreen if given a cool, shady position. Pink flowers are produced in late spring.
Varieties: 'Niveum' (white flowers).
CULTIVATION
Planting time: September to March.
Soil: Moist and sandy; if soil tends to dry out, give a top-dressing of peat or leaf mould in spring.
Aspect: Partial shade; will grow under trees if soil does not become too dry.
Minimum temp: −12°C (10°F).
Pruning: None necessary; if wished, old foliage may be removed in spring to prevent its obscuring new growth.
Propagation: By DIVISION of the rhizomatous roots between September and March. By sowing ripe SEED in mid-summer in a cold frame; pot on and plant out in permanent positions the following spring.

EREMURUS   Liliaceae
Foxtail lily, king's spear
E. × *isabellinus*
Height: 1.5m (5ft)
Spread: 60cm (2ft)
This hardy herbaceous perennial produces showy, 60-90cm (2-3ft) long, spikes of white, yellow, pink or copper-orange flowers in mid-summer, which rise above the mid-green, strap-like foliage.
Varieties: Shelford Hybrids and several named cultivars are available.
CULTIVATION
Planting time: September/October; plant crowns 15cm (6in) below soil level.
Soil: Well-drained and loamy.
Aspect: Sunny but not exposed to early morning sun.
Minimum temp: −12°C (10°F).
Pruning: Cut down stems after flowering.
Propagation: By DIVISION in autumn.

ERICA   Ericaceae
Heath, heather
A large genus of evergreen shrubs and sub-shrubs. Most ericas are good ground-cover subjects, and all but the most vigorous varieties are suitable for growing in raised beds. When using ericas for ground cover, resist the temptation to plant them too close together to achieve quick coverage, especially the strongly growing varieties, which should be planted 75cm (2ft 6in) apart, while more compact, bushy forms should be planted 45cm (1ft 6in) apart. Not only will this give a more pleasing 'hummocky' effect when the plants are established, but it will also reduce the competition between subjects, which can impair the quality of the flowers and shorten the plants' lives. Ericas look best when planted in drifts of at least six plants.
E. carnea (syn. *E. herbacea*) (winter heath, alpine heath)
Height: up to 30cm (12in)
Spread: 60cm (2ft)
A winter-flowering, hardy, evergreen shrub, which makes good ground cover. The leaves are light green, bronze or dull yellow, and pink or white flowers are produced from November to May.
Varieties: 'Carnea' (compact form with pink flowers produced from early spring); 'King George' (compact form with rose-pink flowers); 'Praecox Rubra' (prostrate form with rich pink flowers produced from mid-winter); 'Springwood Pink' and 'Springwood White' (vigorous growers with pink and white flowers respectively).
E. erigena (syn. *E. mediterranea*)
Height: 0.9-3.6m (3-12ft)
Spread: up to 1.2m (4ft)

Dianthus gratianopolitanus (syn. *D. caesius*, Cheddar pink)

Dicentra formosa alba

Dianthus deltoides 'Flashing Light'

Dicentra spectabilis alba

Echinops ritro

Elaeagnus pungens 'Maculata'

Epimedium perralderianum

A semi-hardy evergreen shrub that produces purple or pink flowers in winter; these often last until early summer. The mid-green leaves are arranged in whorls on woody stems.
Varieties: 'Alba' (ht: 90cm (3ft), white flowers); 'Superba' (ht: 3m (10ft), sp: 0.9-1.2m (3-4ft), a form with pink flowers that is suitable for hedging); 'W.T. Rackliff' (ht: 90cm (3ft), a form bearing white flowers in late spring, whose neat, compact habit makes it ideal for raised-bed cultivation).
E. vagans (Cornish heath)
Height and spread: up to 1.2m (4ft)
A vigorous, hardy, evergreen shrub with mid-green foliage and pink or purple flowers, borne in mid-summer; these turn an attractive brown in winter.
Varieties: 'Grandiflora' (vigorous grower); 'Lyonesse' (white flowers); 'Mrs D.F. Maxwell' (a reliable form, suitable for raised beds, producing thick clusters of cerise-pink flowers on long spikes from mid-summer to late autumn).
CULTIVATION
Planting time: March to May or October/November.
Soil: Although most ericas prefer peaty and acid soil, *E. carnea* and *E. erigena* grow well on chalky soils, and *E. vagans* tolerates some alkalinity.
Aspect: Full sun.
Minimum temp: −15°C (5°F); *E. erigena*, −1°C (30°F).
Pruning: Dead flower stems of summer-flowering ericas should be clipped back close to the foliage in spring. Winter- and spring-flowering ericas should be cut back after flowering. Trimming encourages dense and compact growth and is particularly important with taller or more vigorous varieties, such as *E. vagans* 'Grandiflora', which can become leggy and loose if left.
Propagation: By 5cm (2in) CUTTINGS of young side shoots taken between July and October. When rooted, grow on in pots and plant out in final positions when plants are about 7.5cm (3in) high. Alternatively, larger plants can be propagated by GROUND LAYERING in spring; sever layers from parent plant after about a year and transplant.
Diseases: HEATHER DIE-BACK and greying of the leaves is caused by a fungal infection.

ERIGERON   Compositae
Fleabane
E. speciosus
Height: 45-60cm (18-24in)

Planting distance: 30cm (12in)
The species plant has been superseded by the many hybrids that are now available for garden cultivation. These are hardy, easily grown, low-maintenance plants that are useful for herbaceous borders, although, if grown in exposed positions, they may need staking. The daisy-like flowers have numerous narrow petals and are borne on leafy stems in summer.
Varieties: 'Dunkelste Aller'/'Darkest of All' (violet-blue flowers); 'Felicity' (light pink flowers); 'Foerster's Liebling' (semi-double, pink flowers); 'Gaiety' (pink flowers); 'Prosperity' (semi-double, blue flowers); 'Quakeress' (mauve-pink flowers).
CULTIVATION
Planting time: October to March.
Soil: Moist but well-drained.
Aspect: Full sun.
Minimum temp: −15°C (5°F)
Pruning: Dead-head faded flowers to encourage a second flowering. Cut stems to ground level in autummn.
Propagation: By DIVISION of roots between October and March.

ERYNGIUM   Umbelliferae
Sea holly
E. planum
Height: 60cm (2ft)
Spread: 45cm (18in)
A hardy herbaceous perennial whose foliage forms rosettes of thistle-like leaves from which branching stems rise. These bear teasel-like heads of globular, deep blue flowers in mid-summer. A good plant for raised beds.
CULTIVATION
Planting time: October to March.
Soil: Well-drained.
Aspect: Full sun.
Minimum temp: −15°C (5°F).
Pruning: After flowering cut stems almost to ground level.
Propagation: By ROOT CUTTINGS taken during February. Keep under glass until young leaves are well developed and plant out in final positions between October and March.

EUONYMUS   Celastraceae
A group of easily grown deciduous trees and large shrubs and evergreen shrubs, some of which are valuable ground-cover subjects. They are useful plants for the shrub border but have the disadvantages that they can be a winter host for blackfly (which may later infect broad beans) and that they produce poisonous fruits.
E. europaeus (spindle tree)

Height: 1.8-3m (6-10ft)
Spread: 1.2-3m (4-10ft)
A hardy deciduous shrub or small tree with ovate, mid-green leaves, which, in autumn, turn pink-red. A profusion of rose-red capsules are produced from late summer, and these open to reveal orange seeds.
Varieties: 'Albus' (white seed capsules); 'Red Cascade' (brilliant red fruits with yellow seeds).
E. fortunei var. *radicans*
Height: 4.6m (15ft)
Spread: 1.2-1.8m (4-6ft)
A semi-hardy, creeping or climbing, evergreen shrub that tends to be prostrate when young. The leaves are dark green and glossy, and insignificant, greenish-white flowers are followed by the fruits, which consist of pink capsules enclosing orange seeds. *E. fortunei* var. *radicans* and its cultivars are good climbers or ground-cover subjects.
Varieties: 'Carrierei' (ht: 90cm (3ft), sp: 1.8m (6ft) or more, spreading, bushy habit); 'Coloratus' (an excellent ground-cover subject, leaves turn reddish-purple in winter); 'Minimus' (prostrate form); 'Silver Queen' (ht and sp: 1.8m (6ft) when grown as a climber, ht: 30cm (12in), sp: 1.2m (4ft) when grown as ground cover, has wide, silver-edged leaves and, when grown as ground cover, forms a steadily spreading mat of trailing stems).
CULTIVATION
Planting time: Deciduous forms, October to March; evergreen forms, September/October or April/May.
Soil: Any.
Aspect: Full sun to partial shade; evergreen forms can tolerate deep shade but are less hardy (especially variegated varieties) and should be given a sheltered position.
Minimum temp: Deciduous forms, −21°C (−6°F); evergreen forms, −7°C (19°F).
Pruning: None required.
Propagation: By LAYERING shoots; separate from parent when rooted, usually after 1-2 years.
Pests: APHIDS can infest foliage and shoots.
Diseases: HONEY FUNGUS can cause rapid death. LEAF SPOT, caused by a variety of fungi, shows as irregular brown spots.

EUPHORBIA   Euphorbiaceae
Milkweed, spurge
A genus of plants ranging from annuals to evergreen sub-shrubs. The perennial species spread by sending out underground rhizomes.

Some euphorbias, notably *E. cyparissias*, are vigorous spreaders and cannot be recommended for any but the largest gardens. The species listed below, however, are less rampant and are not difficult to curb if they outgrow their allotted space.

E. amygdaloides var. *robbiae*
Height: 45cm (18in)
Spread: 30-45cm (12-18in)
A steadily spreading, hardy, evergreen perennial. It has glossy, dark green leaves and bears greenish-yellow bracts in summer. A useful ground-cover subject, it thrives in shade and tolerates heavy, clay soils.

E. griffithii
Height: 75cm (2ft 6in)
Spread: 45cm (1ft 6in)
A non-spreading, hardy perennial with attractive, narrow, mid-green leaves, which have pale pink midribs. Large, rounded heads of bright red bracts in early summer.
Varieties: 'Fireglow' (orange-red bracts).

E. polychroma (syn. *E. epithymoides*)
Height: 45cm (1ft 6in)
Spread: 60cm (2ft)
An easily grown, hardy, evergreen shrub. It is a slowly spreading plant, which bears bright green leaves and large heads of clear yellow bracts in late spring and early summer.
CULTIVATION
Planting time: September to April.
Soil: Well-drained; *E. amygdaloides* var. *robbiae* tolerates heavy soils.
Aspect: Sun to partial shade.
Minimum temp: −12°C (10°F).
Pruning: Cut faded flowers stems to ground level to promote bushy growth.
Propagation: By DIVISION of clumps between September and April.
Diseases: GREY MOULD can infect frost- or wind-damaged shoots, which causes futher die-back.

GALANTHUS   Amaryllidaceae
Snowdrop
G. nivalis (common snowdrop)
Height: 7.5-20cm (3-8in)
Planting distance: 7.5-15cm (3-6in)
An early flowering, hardy, bulbous perennial with flat, strap-like leaves and a single, white, drooping, bell-shaped flower, produced from January onwards. Snowdrops are not inhibited by competition and can be grown among other plants provided they receive sufficient light in early spring. They do well in wooded settings or in grass under trees.
Varieties: 'Flore Pleno' (elegant double flowers).
There are also many excellent garden

hybrids available including: 'Atkinsii' (a robust grower with long, graceful flowers); 'S. Arnott' (beautifully scented, large flowers).
CULTIVATION
Planting time: September/October; plant bulbs 10cm (4in) deep.
Soil: Moist; do best in heavy loam.
Aspect: Light shade.
Minimum temp: −23°C (−9°F).
Pruning: None.
Propagation: By DIVISION and immediate replanting of mature clumps just after flowering.
Pests: STEM and BULB EELWORMS discolour, rot and kill bulbs. NARCISSUS FLY MAGGOTS tunnel into and kill the growing points of bulbs.
Diseases: GREY MOULD infection shows as grey fungal growths on the stems and leaves. Black resting bodies occur on the bulbs, which decay.

GAULTHERIA   Ericaceae
G. procumbens (partridge berry, wintergreen, checkerberry)
Height: 7.5-15cm (3-6in)
Spread: 90cm (3ft) or more
A hardy, evergreen, flowering shrub that provides useful ground cover by forming a dense, low-growing mat of slowly spreading, glossy, dark green leaves. A shade-tolerant, acid-soil lover, this is an ideal shrub for growing beneath azaleas, rhododendrons or other lime-hating subjects. Tiny, bell-shaped pink or white flowers are produced in mid-summer and are followed by bright scarlet berries.

G. shallon (shallon)
Height and spread: 1.2-1.8m (4-6ft)
A vigorously growing, hardy, evergreen shrub, which spreads by suckers to form wide thickets. A useful subject if bold ground cover is required or to clothe the space beneath tall trees. It has dark to mid-green leaves, and pink or white flowers, borne in early summer, are followed by purple-black berries.
CULTIVATION
Planting time: September/October or April/May.
Soil: Moist and acid.
Aspect: Partial shade.
Minimum temp: −12°C (10°F).
Pruning: None required; *G. shallon* may be cut back hard in spring.
Propagation: By detaching and replanting SUCKERS of *G. shallon* in autumn. By 5-7.5cm (2-3in) HEEL CUTTINGS of lateral shoots taken in late summer. Root in pots under glass and pot on, planting in final positions next autumn.

GENISTA   Leguminosae
Broom
A genus of generally hardy, deciduous or almost leafless shrubs, some of which make fine feature plants while other species are excellent for ground cover.

G. aetnensis (Mount Etna broom)
Height: 4.6-6m (15-20ft)
Spread: 4.6-5.4m (15-18ft)
A tall-growing, semi-hardy, deciduous species with a loose, open habit, suitable for the larger garden. It bears few mid-green leaves on light green, spineless, pendulous branches. Golden-yellow flowers are freely produced in mid-summer. Newly planted specimens may need staking until they are established.

G. hispanica (Spanish górse)
Height: 0.6-1.2m (2-4ft)
Spread: 2.4m (8m)
A much-branched, semi-hardy, deciduous shrub that forms neat, dense, ground-covering hummocks of spiny, deep green growths with narrow, deep green leaves. In summer golden-yellow flowers are borne in profuse clusters. When grown in groups or as a barrier, subjects should be planted 75cm (2ft 6in) apart to provide quick covering.

G. lydia
Height: 60-90cm (2-3ft)
Spread: 1.8m (6ft)
A hardy, dwarf species that forms a mass of arching or prostrate, almost spineless, grey-green branches, which bear linear, grey-green leaves and provide excellent ground cover. Bright yellow flowers are produced in early summer.
CULTIVATION
Planting time: October to April.
Soil: Poor and well-drained; do not feed or mulch.
Aspect: Full sun; *G. aetnensis* and *G. hispanica* should be grown in positions sheltered from severe frosts and cold winds.
Minimum temp: *G. aetnensis* and *G. hispanica*, −7°C (19°F); *G. lydia*, −21°C (−6°F).
Pruning: No regular pruning required; after flowering pinch out the growing tips of shoots on young plants to enourage bushier growth.
Propagation: By 5-10cm (2-4in) HEEL CUTTINGS of lateral growth taken in summer. Root in pots under glass, pot on in spring and plant out in final positions between October and April.

GERANIUM   Geraniaceae
Cranesbill
A large genus of hardy and half-hardy herbaceous perennials, the

Euonymus fortunei var. *radicans* 'Silver Queen'

Euphorbia griffithii 'Fireglow'

Euphorbia polychroma

Euonymus fortunei var. *radicans* 'Sunspot'

Galanthus nivalis

Gaultheria procumbens

Gaultheria shallon

Genista lydia

Genista aetnensis

Geranium macrorrhizum

species of which vary widely in size and habit. The lower growing species make good ground-cover plants. The true geraniums should not be confused with the less hardy pelargoniums, which are popularly known as 'geraniums'.

G. macrorrhizum
Height: 30-38cm (12-15in)
Spread: 45cm (18in)
This often under-rated, hardy, long-lived perennial makes excellent ground cover. It forms dense, slowly spreading mounds of aromatic, mid-green foliage, which assumes bright colours in autumn. The upright stems, often bearing young leaves, persist in winter. Pale pink flowers appear in early summer, faded flowers being hidden by new foliage.
Varieties: *G. m. album* (white flowers); 'Ingwersen's Variety' (rose-pink flowers).

G. renardii
Height: 23cm (9in)
Spread: 30cm (12in)
A hardy, clump-forming ground coverer, this perennial has attractively veined and downy, grey-green leaves. White flowers, veined with purple, appear in early summer.

G. × riversleianum 'Russell Prichard'
Height: 23cm (9in)
Spread: 90cm (3ft)
A hardy hybrid that provides good, semi-evergreen ground cover. Dense mounds of grey-green foliage have trailing flower stems that bear a profusion of cup-shaped, magenta flowers in summer and early autumn.
CULTIVATION
Planting time: September to March.
Soil: Well-drained.
Aspect: Full sun to partial shade.
Minimum temp: −12°C (10°F).
Pruning: None.
Propagation: By DIVISION and replanting of clumps between September and March.
Pests: SLUGS can feed on young plants.

GEUM   Rosaceae
Avens
A genus of hardy, summer-flowering perennials.

G. chiloense
Height: 45-60cm (18-24in)
Spread: 30-45cm (12-18in)
The species has been superseded by the many garden varieties that are now available. These have mid-green foliage and produce long-lasting, bowl-shaped flowers on slender stems throughout summer. If grown in exposed situations, they may need the support of twiggy sticks.

Varieties: 'Fire Opal' (semi-double, flame-coloured flowers); 'Lady Stratheden' (syn. 'Goldball', double, bright yellow flowers); 'Mrs Bradshaw' (semi-double, scarlet flowers).
CULTIVATION
Planting time: September to March.
Soil: Rich.
Aspect: Full sun to partial shade.
Minimum temp: −15°C (5°F).
Pruning: Cut stems almost to ground level after flowering.
Propagation: By DIVISION of clumps in March/April.

HEBE   Scrophulariaceae
A genus of evergreen shrubs grown for their attractive flowers and foliage. The dwarf species make good ground-cover shrubs or are suitable for cultivation in raised beds. All the hebes are hardy, except for 'Youngii', which is half-hardy.

H. albicans
Height and spread: 60cm (2ft)
A shrub of dense, rounded habit with broad, silver-grey foliage. White flowers appear in early summer.

H. cupressoides
Height: 0.9-1.5m (3-5ft)
Spread: 0.6-1.2m (2-4ft)
The tiny, grey-green foliage is conifer-like, and short spikes of pale blue flowers are borne on mature plants in early summer.

H. 'Edinensis'
Height and spread: 30-45cm (12-18in)
A dwarf, hummock-forming shrub, which looks particularly attractive when grown on its own. The foliage is bright green, and white flowers are occasionally produced in summer.

H. 'Great Orme'
Height: 1.2-1.5m (4-5ft)
Spread: 0.9-1.2m (3-4ft)
A bushy shrub of upright habit with dark green foliage. Pinkish-purple flowers are borne on erect, 10cm (4in) long spikes in early summer. 'Great Orme' makes an attractive feature plant in the border.

H. pinguifolia 'Pagei' (disc-leaved hebe)
Height: 15-23cm (6-9in)
Spread: 90cm (3ft)
A dwarf, bushy species with glaucous, oval leaves. Spikes of white flowers are produced in early summer. When planted 45cm (18in) apart, 'Pagei' forms a dense, low-growing mat over the ground; it is suitable for raised-bed cultivation.

H. 'Youngii' (syn. 'Carl Teschner')
Height: 15-30cm (6-12in)
Spread: 30cm (12in) or more
This dwarf variety has a dense,

spreading habit. The small leaves are grey-green, and purple-blue flowers are borne on 2.5cm (1in) spikes in early summer. It is a good subject for ground cover or for raised beds.
CULTIVATION
Planting time: September/October or April/May.
Soil: Well-drained.
Aspect: Full sun; 'Youngii' will require a warm, sheltered position if grown in cold or exposed districts.
Minimum temp: −7°C (19°F).
Pruning: No regular pruning necessary; however, if shrubs become 'leggy', all, except *H. cupressoides*, can be cut back hard in spring.
Propagation: By 5-10cm (2-4in) CUTTINGS of non-flowering growths taken in summer. Keep in a cold frame, pot on the following spring and keep outside. Plant out in permanent positions in autumn.
Diseases: DOWNY MILDEW attack, usually in winter, causes pale blotches of grey mould on leaves. HONEY FUNGUS can cause rapid death. LEAF SPOT produces white spots with brown margins.

HEDERA   Araliaceae
Ivy

H. helix (common English ivy)
Height: 15m (50ft)
Spread: indefinite
The species plant of this hardy, evergreen climber is such a vigorous grower and spreader that it cannot be recommended for even the largest of gardens. However, numerous cultivars have been developed, and, although many of these are for indoor cultivation, several are suitable for outdoor planting. Although still quite vigorous, these are less rampant and less likely to climb than the species plant. They may, therefore, be used as ground cover for large areas or for training on a wall or trellis.
Varieties: 'Buttercup' (syn. 'Russell's Gold', a self-clinging form with light green leaves that turn rich yellow in full sun); 'Conglomerata' (clustered ivy, ht and sp: 90cm (3ft), a bushy, small-leaved form); 'Hibernica' (Irish ivy, a good ground-cover subject for shady situations); 'Sagittifolia' (the dark green foliage looks good against a light-coloured wall, but does not grow well as ground cover).
CULTIVATION
Planting time: September to March.
Soil: Any.
Aspect: Full sun to dark shade; golden-leaved or variegated forms have better colour if grown in full sun.

Minimum temp: −21°C (−6°F).
Pruning: Ivies may need an annual clip in early spring to check growth.
Propagation: By taking 15cm (6in) CUTTINGS of ripe growth in late autumn; plant in sandy soil in a sheltered position outdoors.
Pests: SCALE INSECTS may infest the undersides of leaves, making them sooty and sticky. BRYOBIA MITES cause fine mottling of the upper surface of the leaves.
Diseases: LEAF SPOT is seen as brown spots that become white with purple-brown margins.

HELLEBORUS Ranunculaceae
A genus of hardy, winter- and spring-flowering, evergreen and deciduous perennials. They are good plants for borders or for raised beds. The plants described are, with the exception of *H. orientalis*, evergreen.
H. foetidus (stinking hellebore)
Height and spread: 45-60cm (1ft 6in – 2ft)
This clump-forming perennial has dark green, glossy, deeply cut foliage and produces yellow-green flowers, often with purple edges, in early spring.
H. niger (Christmas rose)
Height and spread: 30-45cm (1ft – 1ft 6in)
The dark green, leathery leaves have 7-9 lobes, and saucer-shaped, white flowers, 5cm (2in) across, with golden anthers, are produced from late winter to early spring. In cold districts opening blooms may need some protection from frosts.
Varieties: 'Potter's Wheel' (shorter form – ht: 30cm (12in) – with glossier foliage and large, white flowers, 12.5cm (5in) across, produced in early spring).
H. orientalis (Lenten rose)
Height and spread: 45cm (1ft 6in)
In mild districts this plant is evergreen. It has broad, dark green leaves and usually produces saucer-shaped, crimson-flecked, cream flowers, although there are many named varieties available in shades of purple, crimson, pink or white. If left undisturbed, the plants form clumps.
CULTIVATION
Planting time: October.
Soil: Well-drained but moist.
Aspect: Partial shade; *H. foetidus* prefers a particularly shady site.
Minimum temp: −12°C (10°F).
Pruning: None.
Propagation: By DIVISION of roots in spring.
Diseases: LEAF SPOT causes black

blotches on leaves, which then shrivel and die.

HEMEROCALLIS Liliaceae
Day lily
A genus of clump-forming, hardy, herbaceous perennials with strap-like, pale green foliage. In summer a succession of lily-like, trumpet-shaped flowers are produced, and although individual blooms last only a day, they are borne in such profusion that they give an impressive continuous display. Once planted, do not disturb.
Garden hybrids
Height: 75-90cm (2ft 6in – 3ft)
Planting distance: 45cm (18in)
Large flowers, 12.5-17.5cm (5-7in) in diameter, are produced in summer.
Varieties: 'Black Magic' (deep mahogany flowers); 'Bonanza' (orange flowers with maroon centres); 'Cartwheels' (bright yellow flowers); 'Hornby Castle' (brick-red flowers); 'Morocco Red' (maroon flowers with yellow throats); 'Pink Damask' (pink flowers with yellow throats); 'Pink Prelude' (pink flowers).
CULTIVATION
Planting time: October to April.
Soil: Any.
Aspect: Full sun to light shade.
Minium temp: −15°C (5°F).
Pruning: Cut stems almost to ground level after flowering.
Propagation: By DIVISION between October and April.

HEUCHERA Saxifragaceae
Alum root
H. sanguinea (coral flowers)
Height: 30-45cm (12-18in)
Planting distance: 45cm (18in)
This clump-forming, hardy, evergreen perennial is useful for providing year-round ground cover, especially beneath deciduous trees. It has dark green foliage and produces 15-23cm (6-9in) long panicles of small, bright red flowers on slender stems in summer and early autumn.
Several hybrids are available that are more suitable for garden cultivation than the species as they are more attractive and taller – 45-60cm (1ft 6in – 2ft). They are available in a range of colours.
Varieties: 'Bressingham Blaze' (red flowers); 'Pearl Drops' (white flowers); 'Pretty Polly' (rose-pink flowers); 'Red Spangles' (deep red flowers); 'Scintillation' (pink flowers with red tips).
CULTIVATION
Planting time: October to April.
Soil: Light and well-drained;

heucheras do not thrive on heavy clay.
Aspect: Partial shade.
Minimum temp: −15°C (5°F).
Pruning: Remove old stems after flowering.
Propagation: By DIVISION between October and April; if crowns of old plants rise above soil level, it may be necessary either to lift, divide and replant them in spring or to apply an organic mulch to cover the crowns.
Diseases: LEAFY GALL causes shoots to split at ground level.

HOSTA Funckiaceae
Funkia, plantain lily
An invaluable hardy herbaceous perennial plant for the easy-care garden. Hostas have an architectural bearing, forming large clumps of attractive foliage with nodding, trumpet-like flowers on erect stems. Although hostas die back in winter, they are excellent ground-cover plants and, once established, need no attention. There are many excellent species and cultivars available, some of which are described below.
H. fortunei
Height: 60-90cm (2-3ft)
Planting distance: 45cm (18in)
The grey-green foliage is boldly veined, and lilac-coloured flowers are borne in summer.
Varieties: 'Albopicta' (ht: 45-60cm (18-24in)); *H. f.* var. *aurea* (yellow-green foliage); 'Aureo-marginata' (gold-margined foliage).
H. montana (syn. *H. elata*)
Height: 90cm (3ft)
Planting distance: 45cm (18in)
A robust species with dark green foliage and white to pale blue flowers, borne in summer.
H. sieboldiana
Height and planting distance: 60cm (2ft)
The strongly veined, glossy foliage is mid-green; purple-tinged, off-white flowers are produced in late summer.
Varieties: *H. s.* var. *elegans* (syn. *H. glauca*, lilac-coloured flowers produced in mid-summer).
H. sieboldii (syn. *H. albomarginata*)
Height and planting distance: 38-45cm (15-18in)
The mid-green leaves have white margins, and lilac-coloured flowers are borne in mid-summer.
H. undulata
Height and planting distance: 60cm (2ft)
The wavy, mid-green leaves have white or silvery markings. Lilac-coloured flowers are borne in mid-summer.

Geum 'Lady Stratheden'

Hedera helix 'Buttercup'

Hebe pinguifolia' 'Pagei'

Helleborus orientalis

Hebe pinguifolia

Hemerocallis 'Pink Damask'

Heuchera sanguinea

Hosta sieboldiana var. *elegans*

Hosta fortunei 'Albopicta'

Hosta undulata 'Albo-marginata'

Varieties: *H. u.* 'Albo-marginata' (syn. 'Thomas Hogg', variegated mid-green leaves with cream fringes and lavender-blue flowers); *H. u. undulata* (syn. 'Medio-variegata', light green leaves with yellow variegations in the centres and mauve flowers borne in 30cm (12in) spikes).

CULTIVATION
Planting time: October to March.
Soil: Rich, well-drained but moisture-retentive.
Aspect: Prefer partial shade but can be grown in sun if soil is moist.
Minimum temp: −12°C (10°F).
Pruning: None necessary.
Propagation: By DIVISION of crowns at the start of growth in spring.
Pests: SLUGS feed on young and mature foliage.

HYDRANGEA Hydrangeaceae
H. macrophylla (common hydrangea)
Height and spread: 1.2-2.4m (4-8ft)
A semi-hardy deciduous shrub of rounded habit with light green, glossy leaves with toothed edges. Pink or blue flowers are borne in large heads, 15cm (6in) across, in summer and early autumn. The flower colour depends on the soil type: blue varieties may become pink or purple on alkaline soils, while pink varieties may become blue or purple on acid or neutral soils. The many named varieties are divided into two groups – **hortensias,** which have rounded heads, 12.5-20cm (5-8in) across, of sterile single or double florets, and **lacecaps,** which have flattened heads, 10-15cm (5-6in) across, of fertile inner florets surrounded by sterile florets.
Varieties: *H. m.* var. *serrata* (lacecap, smaller variety – ht and sp: 0.9-1.5m (3-5ft) – mid-green leaves turn purple in autumn, white or pink flowers are surrounded by sterile blue florets); 'Altona' (hortensia, cherry-pink or blue flowers); 'Blue Wave' (lacecap, vigorous grower with pink or blue flowers); 'Kluis Superba' (hortensia, compact habit, rose-red or deep blue flowers); 'Madame Emile Mouillère' (hortensia, tender variety, pink-tinted, white flowers); 'Mariesii' (lacecap, pink or blue flowers); 'Westfalen' (hortensia, deep crimson red or purple-blue flowers); 'White Wave' (lacecap, large white flowers).
H. petiolaris (syn. *H. tiliifolia*) (Japanese climbing hydrangea)
Height: 15m (50ft) or more
A vigorous, self-clinging, hardy, deciduous climbing shrub, which is particularly well suited for growing on a north-facing wall or as a

screening plant. It has mid-green foliage and produces large heads of white to greenish-white flowers in early summer.

CULTIVATION
Planting time: October/November or March/April.
Soil: Loamy and moisture-retentive; if blue varieties do not produce blue flowers, the soil is too alkaline and should be dressed with peat and sequestrene (chelated iron) or aluminium sulphate added annually. Pink varieties may need dressing with ground limestone to maintain their colour if grown on acid soils.
Aspect: Full sun to partial shade in a sheltered position – e.g., against a wall or beneath a tall tree – and shaded from early morning sun that, after spring night frosts, may damage young growth.
Minimum temp: *H. macrophylla*, −7°C (19°F); *H. petiolaris*, −23°C (−9°F).
Pruning: No regular pruning necessary; *H. macrophylla* can be dead-headed after flowering or in spring, and 2- or 3-year-old shoots can be cut back to ground level to promote new growth in spring.
Propagation: By 10-15cm (4-6in) CUTTINGS of non-flowering shoots of *H. macrophylla* in late summer or 7.5cm (3in) CUTTINGS of side-shoots of *H. petiolaris* taken in early summer. Root cuttings, pot on and overwinter in a cold frame. Grow on and plant in final positions in autumn.
Pests: APHIDS may attack stems and foliage.
Diseases: CHLOROSIS (a yellowing of the leaves between the veins) may be caused by too alkaline soil. HONEY FUNGUS can cause rapid death.

HYPERICUM Hypericaceae
St John's wort
A genus of herbaceous perennial sub-shrubs and shrubs, of which possibly the best known member is *H. calycinum* (rose of Sharon or Aaron's beard), a carpet-forming sub-shrub, which is often recommended and used as ground cover. It is, however, extremely invasive and difficult to control, spreading rapidly by means of stolons, and it is, therefore, best avoided in all but the largest of gardens.
H. 'Hidcote'
Height and spread: 1.2m (4ft)
Dark green, oval leaves surround large, golden-yellow flowers, which are borne in profusion from mid-summer to early autumn.

H. × *moserianum* 'Tricolor'
Height: 30-75cm (1ft – 2ft 6in)
Spread: 0.9-1.2m (3-4ft)
A hardy, low-spreading, deciduous bushy hybrid with attractive green and white variegated leaves with red margins. Clusters of small yellow flowers are borne from mid-summer to autumn. It is an excellent ground-cover subject and a useful substitute for the more vigorous and invasive *H. calycinum*.
H. olympicum
Height: 23-30cm (9-12in)
Spread: 60cm (2ft)
A hardy, deciduous shrubby plant with grey-green foliage. Masses of golden-yellow flowers are produced in mid-summer.
Varieties: *H. o. uniflorum* 'Citrinum' (lemon-yellow flowers).
H. patulum
Height and spread: 1.2m (4ft)
A hardy, evergreen or semi-evergreen, rounded shrub with deep green leaves and golden-yellow flowers, which are borne in late summer.
Varieties: *H. p. forrestii* (syn. *H. forrestii*, bowl-shaped flowers).

CULTIVATION
Planting time: October to April; *H. olympicum* is best planted in spring.
Soil: Well-drained.
Aspect: Full sun.
Minimum temp: −15°C (5°F).
Pruning: Shorten previous year's growth of *H. patulum* to a few buds of the old wood in spring.
Propagation: By 5cm (2in) CUTTINGS of soft basal growth of smaller species in late spring or 10cm (4in) HEEL CUTTINGS of non-flowering lateral shoots in late summer. Root under glass and pot on, planting out in final positions in spring.
Diseases: RUST infection causes orange-yellow, later brown, spore-bearing pustules on the leaves.

IBERIS Cruciferae
Candytuft
I. sempervirens
Height: 23-30cm (9-12in)
Spread: 45-60cm (18-24in)
A hardy, evergreen, spreading sub-shrub with narrow, dark green leaves. It bears 2.5-5cm (1-2in) wide heads of white flowers in early summer.
Varieties: 'Schneeflocke'/'Snowflake' (ht: 15-23cm (6-9in), mat-forming); 'Weisser Zwerg'/'Little Gem' (ht: 10cm (4in), sp: 15-23cm (6-9in), small, neat, erect habit, which is suitable for raised beds).
CULTIVATION
Planting time: September to March.

Soil: Well-drained.
Aspect: Sunny.
Minimum temp: −12°C (10°F).
Pruning: Dead-heading extends the flowering season.
Propagation: By 5cm (2in) CUTTINGS of non-flowering shoots in summer. Root, pot on and overwinter in a cold frame. Plant out in spring.

ILEX
Holly   Aquifoliaceae

A genus of deciduous or evergreen trees and shrubs that bear brightly coloured berries if both male and female plants are grown together. Holly is useful for growing as a specimen tree or in a hedge, but large plants resent root disturbance and transplant badly, so small, container-grown plants only should be bought. Newly planted variegated varieties of *I. aquifolium* will require frequent watering during dry spells and, if planted in cold, exposed positions, winter protection until well established. When used for hedging, young plants should be spaced at intervals of 60cm (2ft) in late spring. Pinch out growing tops the following spring to promote bushy growth.
I. aquifolium (English holly, common holly)
Height: 5.4-7.6m (18-25ft)
Spread: 2.4-3.6m (8-12ft)
A hardy, slow-growing, evergreen tree with glossy, dark green, leathery leaves, which bear sharp spines on their margins. If grown close to a male plant, female trees bear bright red berries in autumn and winter. Its slow-growing nature makes it an ideal evergreen hedging plant.
Varieties: 'Angustifolia' (ht: 3.6-6m (12-20ft), sp: 1.8-3m (6-10ft), female tree of conical habit); 'Argentea Marginata' (syn. 'Argentea Variegata', silver-margined foliage); 'Argentea Marginata Pendula' ('Perry's weeping silver, ht: 2.4-3.6m (8-12ft), sp: 3-4.6m (10-15ft), female tree of weeping habit, with silver-edged leaves and red berries); 'Aurea Marginata' (ht: 4.6-5.4m (15-18ft), sp: 2.4-3m (8-10ft), male and female trees with gold-margined leaves); 'Golden Queen' (syn. 'Aurea-regina', ht: 3-5.4m (10-18ft), sp: 1.8-3m (6-10ft), despite the name, a male tree of columnar habit with golden-edged leaves); 'Handsworth New Silver' (ht: 3-4.6m (10-15ft), sp: 1.5-2.4m (5-8ft), female tree with red berries and silver-margined leaves); 'Silver Queen' (syn. 'Silver King', ht: 3-5.4m (10-18ft), sp: 1.8-3m (6-10ft), a male tree with silver-edged leaves).

I. crenata (Japanese holly, box-leaved holly)
Height and spread: 4.6m (15ft)
A densely branched, hardy, evergreen shrub with mid-green, serrated leaves that, unlike those of *I. aquifolium*, have no spines. Female plants produce small black berries in autumn and winter. It is an ideal slow-growing shrub for a low hedge.
Varieties: 'Convexa' (syn. 'Bullata', ht: 0.9-1.2m (3-4ft), sp: 60-90cm (2-3ft). a small, compact shrub, particularly suitable for dwarf hedging); 'Golden Gem' (ht: 30-60cm (1-2ft), sp: 0.6-1.2m (2-4ft), golden leaves in summer turn yellow-green in autumn, does not bear berries).
CULTIVATION
Planting time: September to May.
Soil: Moist.
Aspect: Full sun to medium shade; variegated varieties have better leaf colour if grown in sunny positions.
Minimum temp: −15°C (5°F).
Pruning: By 5-7.5cm (2-3in) HEEL CUTTINGS of ripened growth in summer. Root and overwinter under glass, potting on and planting out the following summer. By LAYERING shoots in autumn, separating from parent plant 2 years later.
Pests: Unsightly blotches on leaves can be caused by the maggots of HOLLY LEAF MINERS.
Diseases: HONEY FUNGUS can cause the rapid death of trees. White- or brown-margined grey spots on leaves can be caused by LEAF SPOT.

JUNIPERUS
Juniper   Cupressaceae

A genus of very hardy, evergreen, coniferous trees and shrubs that are tolerant of poor, thin soils and of drought. Prostrate junipers are ideal ground cover for dry banks or shady spots near trees or large shrubs.
J. chinensis (Chinese juniper)
Height: 15m (50ft) as a tree, 1-4.6m (3-15ft) as a shrub
Spread: 1.8-3m (6-10ft) as a tree, 3-4.6m (10-15ft)
A juniper with attractive peeling bark and aromatic, dark green leaves. There are several named varieties that form dense, symmetrical cones, which can be used as striking feature plants that require no clippping. Many cultivars listed under *J. chinensis* are forms of *J. × media*.
Varieties: 'Aurea' (ht: 6m (20ft), sp: 1.8m (6ft), irregularly conical habit with yellowish-green foliage); 'Kaizuka' (ht: 4.6m (15ft), sp: 3-4.6m (10-15ft), an irregular, sprawling habit with rich green foliage);

'Pyramidalis' (ht: 10m (30ft), sp: 1.8m (6ft), dense columnar habit with blue-green foliage); 'Stricta' (ht: 4.6m (15ft); sp: 1.8m (6ft), conical habit with blue-green leaves).
J. communis (common juniper)
Height: 7.6m (25ft)
Spread: 1.8m (6ft)
A slow-growing bush or small tree with grey-green foliage, striped white above. Dwarf varieties are good subjects for troughs or raised beds as well as for borders.
Varieties: 'Compressa' (ht: 60cm (2ft), sp: 20cm (8in), dwarf, erect, very slow-growing form with a narrow, conical habit, which is ideal for rock gardens or raised beds and looks particularly attractive planted in groups of 3-5 plants); 'Depressa Aurea' (ht: 60cm (2ft), slow-growing variety of wide-spreading, almost prostrate habit, with summer foliage golden, turning bronze in winter, needs full sun; 'Hornibrookii' (ht: 30cm (1ft), sp: 1.8m (6ft), prostrate, wide-spreading habit).
J. horizontalis (creeping juniper, prostrate juniper)
Height: 60cm (2ft)
Spread: 1.8m (6ft) or more
A mat-forming, ground-hugging species that is useful for ground cover. The long branches, which bear aromatic, blue-green leaves, rest on the soil's surface and often root. There are many named varieties in a wide range of colours.
Varieties: 'Douglasii' (blue-green foliage turns purple in autumn); 'Wiltonii' (syn. 'Glauca', bright blue foliage, which thickens with age).
J. × media
A group of conical conifers, suitable for ground cover or, in a small garden, as specimen plants. Some forms of *J. × media* are listed under *J. chinensis*.
Varieties: 'Blaauw' (ht: 1.2m (4ft), sp: 1.8m (6ft), a strongly growing shrub with blue-green foliage); 'Old Gold' (ht: 90cm (3ft), sp: 1.5m (5ft), semi-prostrate form with golden-bronze foliage); 'Pfitzeriana' (ht: 1.5-1.8m (5-6ft), sp: 4.6m (15ft), wide-spreading, semi-prostrate habit with grey-green leaves); 'Pfitzeriana Aurea' (ht: 1.2-1.5m (4-5ft), sp: 3m (10ft), a flatter habit than 'Pfitzeriana' with golden foliage).
J. virginiana (pencil cedar)
Height: 15-20m (50-70ft)
Spread: 6-7.6m (20-25ft)
A slow-growing conical species with aromatic, pale green foliage.
Varieties: 'Burkii' (ht: 3.6m (12ft), sp: 1.5m (5ft), blue-grey foliage turns

Hydrangea macrophylla

Hydrangea macrophylla

Hypericum 'Hidcote'

Hypericum x *moserianum* 'Tricolor'

Iberis sempervirens

Ilex aquifolium 'Golden Queen'

Juniperus communis 'Compressa'

Ilex aquifolium 'Silver Queen'

Juniperus x *media* 'Pfitzeriana Aurea'

Juniperus x *media* 'Blaauw'

purplish in winter); 'Glauca' (silver cedar, ht: 6m (20ft), sp: 1.2m (4ft), very erect, columnar habit); 'Grey Owl' (ht: 1.2m (4ft), sp: 4.6m (15ft), semi-prostrate habit with feathery, bluish-grey foliage).

CULTIVATION
Planting time: April.
Soil: Well-drained.
Aspect: Full sun to light shade; coloured varieties look best in sunny aspects.
Minimum temp: −29°C (−20°F).
Pruning: None required.
Propagation: by 5-10cm (2-4cm) HEEL CUTTINGS of lateral shoots taken in autumn. Root under glass and pot on until ready for planting out.
Pests: SCALE INSECTS can infest stems and leaves. CATERPILLARS of the juniper webber moth feed on leaves and spin them together.
Diseases: RUST infection causes gelatinous masses of yellow-orange spores to appear on foliage and stems.

KNIPHOFIA   Liliaceae
Torch lily, red-hot poker
A group of hardy herbacous perennials that, when planted in groups, make a striking focal point in a border. There are many named varieties available in a range of sizes, colours and flowering periods. All have smooth flower stems, which rise from clumps of grass-like foliage and bear long, tubular flowers. In heavy soils or in wet or cold districts, protect young crowns from winter frost by applying an insulating mulch. Leaves of mature crowns should be tied together at the beginning of winter to protect the crowns from wetness and frost.
Dwarf varieties (ht: 50cm (20in)): *K. triangularis* (syn. *K. galpinii*, orange-red flower spikes borne in late summer. **Medium varieties** (ht: 60-90cm (2-3ft), planting distance: 60cm (2ft)): 'Alcazar' (orange flowers in early summer); 'Bees Sunset' (flame-orange flowers in early summer); 'Bressingham Torch' (orange-yellow flowers in autumn); 'Burnt Orange' (orange flowers from brown buds in autumn); 'Cool Lemon' (lemon-yellow flowers in autumn): 'Gold Else' (yellow flowers in summer); 'Modesta' (white flowers tipped with rose-red in summer). **Tall varieties** (ht: 0.9-1.5m (3-5ft), planting distance: 60cm (2ft)): 'Bees Lemon' (yellow flowers in mid-summer); 'Maid of Orleans' (ivory-cream flowers in mid-summer); 'Royal Standard' (red and yellow flowers in mid-

summer); 'Samuel's Sensation' (ht: 1.5-1.8m (5-6ft), bright red flowers in mid-summer); 'Springtime' (yellow flowers tipped with red in summer).

CULTIVATION
Planting time: September/October or April.
Soil: Well-drained.
Aspect: Full sun.
Minimum temp: −5°C (23°F).
Pruning: Remove faded flower stems near the base to extend the flowering season.
Propagation: By DIVISION of established plants in spring.
Pests: THRIPS can infest plants, discolouring and distorting flowers and leaves.

LAMIUM   Labiatae
Deadnettle
A group of easily grown annuals and perennials, most of which are semi-evergreen. *L. galeobdolon* (syn. *Lamiastrum galeobdolon*, *Galeobdolon luteum*) – yellow archangel – and its varieties are often used for ground cover, but all, except *L. g.* 'Silver Carpet', are such vigorous and invasive spreaders that they cannot be recommended for the average garden. All lamiums, once introduced, can be difficult to eradicate, as any pieces of root left in the soil will grow again. The species described here, although spreading, is less vigorous and is suitable for covering large areas.
L. maculatum
Height: 15-30cm (6-12in)
Planting distance: 30-60cm (1-2ft)
The grey-green leaves, which have a silver-coloured stripe down the centre, form a weed-suppressing carpet. Pink-purple flowers are produced in early summer. The plant spreads steadily by means of rooting prostrate growths. It can be grown to effect around the base of trees.
Varieties: 'Album' (white flowers); 'Aureum' (golden foliage that needs a sheltered site); 'Beacon Silver' (strong silver markings on foliage); 'Roseum' (pink flowers); 'White Nancy' (a white-flowered form of 'Beacon Silver').
CULTIVATION
Planting time: October to March.
Soil: Any.
Aspect: Medium shade.
Minimum temp: −21°C (−6°F).
Pruning: Shear ground cover after flowering to maintain densely growing foliage.
Propagation: By DIVISION of roots in autumn or spring.

LAVANDULA   Labiatae
Lavender
L. angustifolia (syn. *L. officinalis*, *L. spica*) (old English lavender)
Height: 45-90cm (1ft 6in – 3ft)
Spread: 0.9-1.2m (3-4ft)
A hardy, evergreen shrub with bushy stems that bear silver-grey leaves. Spikes of grey-blue flowers are produced in mid-summer to early autumn. Both the leaves and flowers are aromatic and can be used for making potpourri. A useful plant for edging paths, as a low-growing hedge (when the planting distance should be 23-30cm (9-12in)), or for the borders. Lavender is fairly short lived and may need replacing every 5-6 years.
Varieties: 'Hidcote' (ht: 45cm (1ft 6in), sp: 45-60cm (1ft 6in – 2ft), a compact form with dense spikes of deep violet flowers); 'Munstead' (ht and sp: 60cm (2ft), grey-green foliage and blue flowers).
CULTIVATION
Planting time: September to March.
Soil: Well-drained.
Aspect: Full sun.
Minimum temp: −12°C (10°F).
Pruning: Plants benefit from the removal of dead flower stems and a light trimming in late summer. 'Leggy' plants should be cut back hard in spring to promote bushy growth.
Propagation: By 15-23cm (6-9in) CUTTINGS in early autumn; insert immediately in final positions.
Pests: FROGHOPPERS can infest stems producing cuckoo spit.
Diseases: FROST DAMAGE can cause shoots to die back, leading to GREY MOULD, which shows as grey fungal growth on dead shoots. GREY MOULD can also prematurely wilt or brown flowers during prolonged periods of wet weather. HONEY FUNGUS causes rapid death. LEAF SPOT shows as small spots. SCAB causes shoots to wilt and die back, which may lead to death of entire plant.

LONICERA   Caprifoliaceae
Honeysuckle
A genus of vigorous, usually deciduous, climbing shrubs. Rather than being clipped and trained, climbing species look best when left to climb naturally over archways, pergolas, walls or fences up trees or through hedges. Some species make useful hedging or ground-cover shrubs.
L. × americana (syn. *L. grata*)
Height: 10m (30ft)
A vigorous, free-flowering, deciduous and woody-stemmed clim-

ber. It bears fragrant white flowers flushed with purple-red, which turn yellow as they age, from late spring to summer.

L. nitida
Height and spread: 1.5-1.8m (5-6ft)
A useful shade-tolerant shrub, which makes a fine evergreen hedge (plant subjects 23-30cm (9-12in) apart), although it will require annual pruning. It has dark green foliage and produces insignificant yellow-green flowers in late spring; these are followed by violet-coloured fruit.
Varieties: 'Baggesen's Gold' (golden foliage, needs full sun).

L. periclymenum (common honeysuckle, woodbine)
Height: 4.6-6m (15-20ft)
The foliage is dark green, and trumpet-shaped, purplish-red and yellow flowers are borne in late summer, followed by red berries. Many improved varieties have been developed, and these are the more usual forms for garden cultivation, providing a longer and more continuous display of flowers.
Varieties: 'Belgica' (bushy habit with flowers borne in early summer); 'Serotina' (flowers in late summer).

L. pileata
Height: 60-90cm (2-3ft)
Spread: 1.2-1.8m (4-6ft)
A hardy, semi-evergreen shrub. Its low-growing, spreading habit makes it an ideal ground-cover shrub, and it can also be grown in heavily shaded positions, such as under trees. It has pale to mid-green foliage and produces insignificant, whitish flowers followed by violet-coloured berries.

CULTIVATION
Planting time: September to April.
Soil: Fertile and well-drained but moist.
Aspect: Full sun to medium shade; climbing varieties do best in light shade.
Minimum temp: −12°C (10°F).
Pruning: Remove any unwanted stems or old wood of climbers after flowering. Cut back young hedging plants by half after planting and pinch out the growing tips 2-3 times in the first summer to promote bushy growth. Clip hedges in late spring or early autumn.
Propagation: By LAYERING branches in late summer or early autumn, separating from the parent plant after a year. By 10cm (4in) stem CUTTINGS taken in summer and rooted in 10cm (4in) pots. Plunge the pots in a temporary bed outside and grow on for a year before planting out.
Pests: APHIDS may infest and distort

young shoots and flower trusses producing a sticky and sooty deposit on the leaves.
Diseases: LEAF SPOT causes small green or larger brown spots. PHYSIOLOGICAL DISORDERS resulting from unsuitable growing conditions can show as a yellowing or blackening of the leaves and possible DIEBACK of the shoots. POWDERY MILDEW causes a powdery white deposit on the leaves. SILVER LEAF can cause die-back of shoots, which bear silver-tinged leaves.

LUPINUS   Leguminosae
Lupin
A genus of annual, herbaceous perennial and sub-shrubby plants. The herbaceous perennials are excellent for planting in groups.
L. polyphyllus
Height: 0.9-1.2m (3-4ft)
Planting distance: 60cm (2ft)
The true species, *L. polyphyllus*, is rarely grown, the named varieties being much more popular. Many of these are **Russell hybrids**, which, at 0.9-1.2m (3-4ft), are suitable for the centre or back of the border. However, Russell hybrids do not always come true from seed, but there are many other strains of perennial lupins avilable. These are accommodating, quick-growing plants, which tolerate shade and atmospheric pollution well. The foliage is mid-green, and tall, stately spires of pea-like flowers are borne in a wide range of colours (mixed and single) depending on variety in summer; a second flowering is possible in early autumn if the first flush of blooms is removed when it fades. Perennial lupins will need to be replaced every 3-5 years.
Varieties: 'Chandelier' (flowers in shades of yellow); 'Guardsman' (orange-red flowers); 'Lulu' (dwarf variety, ht: 60cm (2ft), in a range of flower colours); 'Mrs Micklethwaite' (pink and gold flowers); 'My Castle' (brick red flowers); 'Noble Maiden' (white flowers); 'The Chatelaine' (pink and salmon-pink flowers); 'The Governor' (blue and white flowers); 'The Page' (carmine-red flowers); 'Thundercloud' (violet flowers).

CULTIVATION
Planting time: October to March.
Soil: Moist and acid to neutral. Plants live longer on light soils; over-rich soil encourages soft, spindly stems, which require staking when the flowers are produced.
Aspect: Full sun to partial shade.
Minimum temp: −15°C (5°F).

Pruning: Remove faded flower spikes to prevent self-seeding and to encourage a second flowering. Cut stems to ground level in autumn.
Propagation: Because some named varieties do not come true from seed, propagate by 7.5cm (3in) CUTTINGS of new shoots, preferably with some root attached, in spring. Root in a cold frame and pot on, planting out the following autumn.
Pests: APHIDS can infest young leaves and stems.
Diseases: CROWN ROT and ROOT ROT cause blackening and rotting of the crown and and roots, resulting in the wilting or die-back of the top growth. HONEY FUNGUS can cause rapid death. POWDERY MILDEW shows as a white, powdery deposit on the leaves. Yellow mottling or yellow and/or brown striping or blotching of the leaves and, occasionally, stems can be caused by a number of VIRUS DISEASES, the leaves of infected plants sometimes also becoming distorted or curling upwards.

LYSIMACHIA   Primulaceae
Loosestrife
A genus of herbaceous perennials and a few sub-shrubs. All of the plants listed are easily grown and carpet-forming and are suitable for planting in borders or for covering unsightly banks. Take are care when siting lysimachias, as they can be invasive. If the spread becomes too great, lift, divide and replant clumps every 3 years or so.
L. nummularia (creeping Jenny, moneywort)
Height: 2.5-5cm (1-2in)
Spread: 60cm (2ft) or more
A vigorous, hardy, prostrate plant that forms a carpet of creeping stems bearing rounded, mid-green leaves, which provide excellent ground cover. Bright yellow, cup-shaped flowers are produced in summer. It is a useful ground-cover subject when allowed to wander through shrub beds.
Varieties: 'Aurea' (slightly less vigorous form with yellow leaves).
L. punctata (garden loosestrife)
Height: 60-90m (2-3ft)
Planting distance: 45cm (18in)
A long-lived, spreading and hardy plant with mid-green leaves. Whorls of bright yellow, cup-shaped flowers are borne in spikes in summer. It adapts well to a wide variety of conditions and tolerates shade well; it is therefore useful for situations where little else will grow. When grown among less-competitive

Khiphofia 'Royal Standard'

Lamium maculatum 'Roseum'

Lavandula

Lonicera nitida 'Baggesen's Gold'

Lupinus 'Chandelier'

Lysimachia punctata 'Goldilocks'

plants, its invasive nature enables it to take over.

CULTIVATION
Planting time: October to April.
Soil: Moist or even boggy.
Aspect: Full sun to mid-shade.
Minimum temp: −15°C (5°F).
Pruning: Cut stems almost to ground level in autumn.
Propagation: By DIVISION of clumps between October and March.

MAHONIA   Berberidaceae

M. aquifolium (Oregon grape)
Height: 0.9-1.2m (3-4ft)
Spread:1.5m (5ft)
A hardy, slowly spreading shrub that is tolerant of shade and wind. It is useful as evergreen ground cover, when subjects should be planted 60cm (2ft) apart, especially under trees or in difficult corners. *M. aquifolium* spreads slowly by producing suckers, but it is not rampant. It is ideally suited for growing as a low hedge in a narrow, double-walled, raised bed. The leaves are composed of glossy, dark green, holly-like leaflets, which look well in sun or shade. Numerous clusters of fragrant, rich yellow flowers are produced in spring, followed by bunches of blue-black berries. In autumn the foliage is tinted with purple-bronze.
Varieties: 'Atropurpurea' (strongly coloured red-purple foliage in autumn and winter); 'Undulata' (a good ground-cover subject with glossy, wavy-edged foliage).
M. × media 'Charity'
Height: 2.4m (8ft)
Spread: 1.8m (6ft)
A medium sized hardy, evergreen shrub with a more erect habit than *M. aquifolium*. The foliage consists of narrow, dark green leaflets, and fragrant, deep yellow flowers are produced in 23-30cm (9-12in) long racemes in winter and early spring.

CULTIVATION
Planting time: September/October or April/May.
Soil: Any.
Aspect: Sun or partial shade; 'Charity' does better in partial shade.
Minimum temp: −12°C (10°F).
Pruning: None necessary. Unwanted or straggly growth may be cut back after flowering; this encourages *M. aquifolium* to form an even denser and more bushy ground cover.
Propagation: By removing and replanting rooted SUCKERS of *M. aquifolium*. Also by 7.5-10cm (3-4in) tip CUTTINGS of shoots taken from all species in late autumn. Root in a propagating case with bottom heat,

potting on when rooted for over-wintering in a cold frame. Pot on for a further year and plant out in final positions in late spring
Diseases: LEAF SPOT produces brown spots dotted with pin-point black fruiting bodies on leaves. POWDERY MILDEW is seen as a light grey or white powdery coating on leaves. RUST causes orange-red spotting of the upper leaf surface and powdery brown spores on the underside.

MUSCARI   Liliaceae

Grape hyacinth
A genus of bulbous, spring-flowering, clump-forming plants, useful for the edges of beds or borders.
M. armeniacum
Height: 15-20cm (6-8in)
Spread: 15cm (6in)
A hardy plant that forms a clump of mid-green, grass-like foliage and produces small spires of densely packed, deep blue flowers that are edged with paler blue or white. Grape hyacinths look best when planted in groups.
Varieties: 'Blue Spike' (a double form with larger spires of bright blue flowers): 'Cantab' (pale blue flowers).

CULTIVATION
Planting time: August to November; plant bulbs 7.5cm (3in) deep and 7.5-10cm (3-4in) apart.
Soil: Well-drained.
Aspect: Full sun or semi-shade.
Minimum temp: −12°C (10°F).
Pruning: None.
Propagation: By DIVISION of clumps.
Diseases: SMUT can infect the anthers and ovaries producing masses of soot-like spores.

NARCISSUS   Amaryllidaceae

A large genus of bulbous plants, which includes the daffodil, the most commonly grown of all the spring-flowering bulbs. Narcissi will grow almost anywhere – in containers, beds and borders, interplanted among shrubs, under trees or naturalized in grass or low-growing ground cover. The dwarfer species and varieties are also ideal for cultivation in raised beds. All members of the genus are easy to grow and maintain and are suitable for the easy-care garden. The choice of variety will depend on personal taste and requirements.

CULTIVATION
Planting time: August/September; plant bulbs 10-17.5cm (4-7in) deep (approximately three times the depth of the bulb).
Soil: Well-drained.

Aspect: Full sun to partial shade.
Minimum temp: −15°C (5°F).
Pruning: Dead-head faded flowers. Allow the foliage to die down naturally before cutting to ground level. 'Tidying' the leaves by knotting them together reduces the vigour of the plants and should be avoided.
Propagation: Remove OFFSETS from bulbs and replant. Flowers will be produced after 1-2 years.
Pests: STEM and BULB EELWORMS can invade bulbs and discolour the bulb tissue. In severe cases there is a discoloration of the stems, leaves and flowers, which can lead to the death of the whole plant. TARSONEMID MITES attack discolours and distorts the bulbs, stems and leaves and can check growth. NARCISSUS FLY MAGGOTS tunnel into, and feed on, bulbs, reducing the vigour of the plant, which may not flower. SLUGS may feed on bulbs.
Diseases: Several VIRUS DISEASES can cause yellow mottling or striping of the leaves and a decline in vigour and flowering. NARCISSUS FIRE causes brown spotting and rotting of the flowers and decay of the leaves. GREY MOULD can develop on infected tissues.

NEPETA   Labiatae

A genus containing both annual and herbaceous perennial species, one of which, *N. hederacea* (syn. *Glechoma hederacea*, *N. glechoma*, ground ivy), can be particularly invasive and should be avoided. The species described below is easily grown and is useful for herbaceous borders or spreading over the tops of walls.
N. × faassenii (syn. *N. mussinii*) (catmint)
Height: 30-45cm (12-18in)
Spread: 38cm (15in)
A low-growing, mat-forming hardy perennial that provides an effective ground cover. It has aromatic, grey-green foliage and produces upright, 15cm (6in) long spikes of lavender-blue flowers in summer.
Varieties: *N. × f. superba* (ht: 60-90cm (2-3ft), lavender-blue flowers and may need staking in exposed situations).
N. 'Six Hill Giant'
Height: 60cm (2ft)
A tall-growing, vigorous form.

CULTIVATION
Planting time: October to March.
Soil: Well-drained.
Aspect: Full sun.
Minimum temp: −21°C (−6°F).
Pruning: Remove faded flower spikes to encourage further flower-

ing. Cut down previous season's growth when new shoots appear in spring.

Propagation: By DIVISION of clumps in spring.

Diseases: POWDERY MILDEW causes a white coating on the leaves.

OLEARIA
Compositae
Daisy bush

A group of evergreen shrubs and trees, the taller species of which can be used for hedging. All are tolerant of sea winds and salt spray.

O. × haastii
Height: 1.8m (6ft)
Spread: 1.8-2.4m (6-8ft)

The hardiest of the olearias, *O. × haastii* may be used for hedging as well as being grown as a specimen plant. It tolerates polluted air and so is an ideal subject for town gardens. The glossy, mid-green leaves have silver or grey undersides, and a profusion of white, daisy-like flowers, borne in clusters, appears in summer.

O. × scilloniensis
Height and spread: 1.5-1.8m (5-6ft)

A semi-hardy shrub of rounded, compact habit. It has tough, leathery, grey-green leaves with white felted undersides, which complement the clusters of bright white, daisy-like flowers that are borne in such abundance in early summer that they all but hide the foliage. It is a useful and attractive windscreen for mild seaside districts.

CULTIVATION
Planting time: October of March/April.
Soil: Well-drained and loamy.
Aspect: Prefers a sunny, sheltered spot but will tolerate partial shade.
Minimum temp: *O. × haastii*, −15°C (5°F); *O. × scilloniensis*, −7°C (19°F).
Pruning: No regular pruning required. Remove dead or frost-damaged wood in spring, and if hedges become straggly after several years, shrubs can be cut back to the old wood.
Propagation: By 10cm (4in) CUTTINGS of half-ripe lateral growth in summer. Root, pot on and overwinter under glass. Plant out in final positions the following autumn.

OSMANTHUS
Oleaceae

A genus of evergreen trees and shrubs, grown mainly for their fragrant flowers.

Osmanthus delavayi (syn. *Siphonosmanthus delavayi*)
Height and spread: 2.4-3m (8-10ft)

A hardy, slow-growing and graceful shrub with small, dark green leaves. Fragrant white flowers are borne in clusters in spring.

CULTIVATION
Planting time: October to March.
Soil: Well-drained.
Aspect: Sunny or partially shaded and sheltered from cold winds.
Minimum temp: −12°C (10°F).
Pruning: None necessary.
Propagation: By LAYERING branches for separation from parent plant when well rooted after 1-2 years.

PAEONIA
Paeoniaceae
Peony

A group of hardy herbaceous or shrubby perennials, grown for their attractive foliage and flowers. The shrubby tree peonies with double blooms may require staking, so it is best to choose semi-double- or single-flowering types. Herbaceous peonies resent disturbance and are slow to become established, often taking several years to flower.

P. lactiflora (syn. *P. albiflora*)
Height and planting distance: 60cm (2ft)

The species plant of this hardy herbaceous perennial is now seldom grown having been replaced by the many garden varieties that have been developed. These have dark to mid-green leaves, and the taller varieties may need supporting with twiggy sticks if they are planted in exposed situations.

Double-flowered varieties: 'Albert Crousse' (fragrant pink flowers with deep red centres); 'Mme Calot' (fragrant pink-shading-to-white flowers); 'President Franklin D. Roosevelt' (deep red flowers); 'Sarah Bernhardt' (pink flowers); 'Shirley Temple' (white flowers flushed with pink). **Semi-double-flowered varieties:** 'Auguste Dessert' (carmine-red flowers). **Single-flowered varieties:** 'Sir Edward Elgar' (rich crimson flowers tinged with chocolate brown); 'White Wings' (white flowers). **Anemone-form varieties:** 'Bowl of Beauty' (pale carmine-pink outer petals with creamy-white central petaloids); 'Pink Delight' (blush-pink flowers).

P. lutea (tree peony)
Height and spread: 12.-1.5m (4-5ft)

A slow-growing, hardy, deciduous shrub with large, deeply cut, pale green leaves. Large, fragrant, bright yellow, single and saucer-shaped flowers are borne in mid-summer.

Varieties: 'L'Espérance (semi-double, primrose-yellow and deep red flowers); *P. l.* var. *ludlowii* (a

taller growing − to 2.4m (8ft) − and more robust form with large, golden-yellow flowers).

P. mlokosewitschii
Height and spread: 75cm (2ft 6in)

A hardy herbaceous perennial that flowers in late spring, bearing large, single, clear yellow flowers, which are followed by attractive seed pods. The foliage is initially bronze-pink, but darkens with age through pale and mid-grey-green, eventually turning orange-yellow in autumn.

P. suffruticosa (moutan)
Height and spread: 1.8m (6ft)

A hardy, large-flowered species of tree peony with mid-green leaves. It bears single, white flowers, 15cm (6in) across, which are marked with purple shading to pink at the base of the petals.

Varieties (all semi-double): 'Duchess of Kent' (bright pink flowers); 'King George V' (red flowers flecked with white); 'Mrs William Kelway' (white flowers).

CULTIVATION
Planting time: September to March; the crowns of herbaceous perennials should be planted no more than 2.5m (1in) deep or they may fail to flower.
Soil: Moist but well-drained.
Aspect: Sun or partial shade and not exposed to early morning sun.
Minimum temp: −12°C (10°F).
Pruning: Cut out dead wood of shrubby forms in spring. Dead-head herbaceous peonies as the flowers fade and cut the foliage almost to ground level in autumn.
Propagation: The branches of shrubby forms can be LAYERED in spring for separation from the parent plant 2 years later. Buy named varieties of herbaceous peonies from nurseries as they do not breed true from seed and, because they resent root disturbance, dividing clumps, although possible, is not recommended.
Pests: Crowns may be eaten by SWIFT MOTH CATERPILLARS.
Diseases: HONEY FUNGUS can cause the rapid death of shrubby forms. LEAF SPOT shows as brown and grey spots with purple edges on the leaves and sometimes the stems. PEONY WILT causes the bases of some shoots to turn brown and die, while other shoots bear leaves with brown patches. VIRUS DISEASE shows as yellow patches, rings or mottling on the leaves.

PAPAVER
Papaveraceae
Poppy

A genus of annual, biennial and

Mahonia x *media* 'Charity'

Narcissus 'Arbar'

Muscari 'Heavenly Blue'

Narcissus 'Double Event'

Narcissus 'Actaea'

Narcissus 'Golden Ducat'

Narcissus 'Kingscourt'

Olearia x *haastii*

Narcissus 'Polindra'

Olearia x *scilloniensis*

Narcissus 'Tudor Minstrel'

Paeonia lactiflora 'Felix Crousse'

perennial plants. The annual species, especially *P. somniferum* (opium poppy), are prolific self-seeders and, therefore, although welcome in some gardens, can take several years to eradicate once they are established.

P. orientale (oriental poppy)
Height: 30-90cm (2-3ft)
Planting distance: 60cm (2ft)
A clump-forming, hardy perennial species, with coarse, hairy and deeply cut leaves. It produces scarlet flowers, 10cm (4in) in diameter, often with black markings at the base of the petals, in early summer. Although the ample foliage and generally self-supporting stems make them a good choice for low-attention herbaceous borders, they can look untidy after flowering and are, therefore, best given a mid-border position.
Varieties: 'Goliath' (deep red flowers); 'King George' (frilled, scarlet flowers); 'Marcus Perry' (orange-scarlet flowers); 'Mrs Perry' (large, salmon-pink flowers); 'Perry's White' (white flowers tinged with blush).
CULTIVATION
Planting time: October or March/April.
Soil: Well-drained.
Aspect: Full sun.
Minimum temp: −15°C (5°F).
Pruning: Dead-head after flowering.
Propagation: By DIVISION in spring.
Diseases: DOWNY MILDEW infection causes yellow blotches on leaves and grey fungal growths to develop on the undersides.

PARTHENOCISSUS   Vitaceae
A group of vigorous, self-clinging, deciduous climbers, widely grown for their brilliant autumn leaf colour. All the species described below can be grown over pergolas, against walls and fences or up rough-barked trees without the need for additional support. *P. quinquefolia* and *P. tricuspidata* can be planted to provide rampant ground cover and are especially useful for cascading down otherwise difficult-to-plant banks.
P. henryana (syn. *Vitis henryana*) (Chinese virginia creeper)
Height: 10m (30ft)
A vigorous, shade-tolerant climber, capable of covering a large wall if new growths are pinched out to encourage branching. The leaves consist of 3 or 5 velvety green leaflets, each with white and purple variegations on the midrib and main veins. These become more pronounced when the leaves turn warm red in autumn, especially when the plant is grown

against a shady wall or protected from full sun.
P. quinquefolia (syn. *Vitis quinquefolia*) (five-leaved ivy, virginia creeper)
Height: 15m (50ft) or more
A climber of vigorous, branching habit, which is at its best when grown up high walls or to the tops of lofty trees. If used to cover low walls or fences, it may require attention to keep the growth within bounds. The leaves consist of 5 leaflets, bright green in summer and turning brilliant orange and scarlet in autumn. Inconspicuous yellowish-green flowers are produced in early summer, and these are followed by tiny, blue-black berries.
P. tricuspidata (syn. *Ampelopsis veitchii*) (Japanese ivy, Boston ivy)
Height: 15m (50ft) or more
A rapidly growing climber of branching habit, which is ideal for growing up flat surfaces. It is unsurpassed for its spectacular autumn colour. The large, coarse leaves, usually 3-lobed, are dark green in summer and turn brilliant red and crimson in autumn. Tiny yellowish-green flowers are produced in small clusters in early summer, and, in hot seasons, these may be followed by small, dark blue fruits.
Varieties: 'Beverley Brook' (a smaller leaved variety, ideal for gardens where space is limited); 'Veitchii' (red-purple autumn leaf colour).
CULTIVATION
Planting time: November to March; support with twiggy sticks until the plant becomes self-clinging.
Soil: Rich and loamy.
Aspect: *P. quinquefolia* and *P. tricuspidata*, any aspect; *P. henryana* should be given a sheltered site.
Minimum temp: −12°C (10°F).
Pruning: None necessary. Pinch out growing shoots of newly planted specimens to encourage a bushy habit; any overcrowded or unwanted stems of mature plants can be removed in summer.
Propagation: By 25-30cm (10-12in) HARDWOOD CUTTINGS taken in late autumn. Insert these to about half their length directly into the ground in a sheltered position outdoors. Long shoots may be LAYERED in late autumn for separation from the parent plant about a year later.
Pests: SCALE INSECTS can infest stems, producing a sticky, sooty deposit. WEEVILS can feed on the stems below the soil. APHIDS can infest new growths.
Diseases: HONEY FUNGUS can kill the whole plant.

PERNETTYA   Ericaceae
A genus of evergreen shrubs grown for their attractive fruits.
P. mucronata
Height and spread: 0.9-1.2m (3-4ft)
An attractive, hardy shrub of dense, low-growing habit. Small, glossy, stiff and sharply pointed, dark green leaves are borne on wiry, often red, erect stems. Tiny white flowers appear in spring and are followed by clusters of white, pink, red or purple berries, which last throughout winter. Because the species is unisexual, male and female plants must be grown together to ensure fruiting. Its dense habit makes it useful for ground cover in borders and, if there is room for 2 plants, in raised beds.
Varieties: 'Alba' (white berries); 'Bell's Seedling' (dark red berries); 'Lilacina' (lilac-coloured berries); 'Rosea' (pink berries); 'Sea Shell' (pink berries); 'Thymifolia' (ht: 30cm (12in), sp: 60-90cm (2-3ft), a reliable male form).
CULTIVATION
Planting time: September to March.
Soil: Lime-free, moist and peaty.
Aspect: Will tolerate some shade but full sun will ensure denser, more compact shrubs and plentiful berries.
Minimum temp: −15°C (5°F).
Pruning: No regular pruning necessary; if shrubs become too leggy, cut back hard to old wood in early spring to encourage bushy growth.
Propagation: By 5cm (2in) CUTTINGS in autumn; root in a cold frame and pot on. Plant in final position 1-2 years later.

PHILADELPHUS
Philadelphaceae
A genus of easily grown, fragrant, flowering, deciduous shrubs. They have a deserved reputation as 'grow anywhere' plants, being tolerant of poor, dry soils, atmospheric pollution and salt spray.
P. coronarius (mock orange)
Height and spread: 1.8-2.4m (6-8ft)
A dense, bushy shrub, particularly suited to dry soils. It has mid-green, prominently veined leaves and produces fragrant, white, cup-shaped flowers in summer.
Varieties: 'Aureus' (young leaves are bright golden-yellow turning green-yellow as they age, colouring best in shade or semi-shade).
P. microphyllus
Height and spread: 1.2m (4ft)
A compact shrub of neat habit. The small, pointed leaves are dark green above, silvery-grey below, and fragrant white flowers are borne singly or

in groups of two or three. Although hardy, it needs a warm sunny position to flower well.

P. 'Sybille'
Height: 1.8m (6ft)
Spread: 2.1m (7ft)
Sea-green leaves are borne on arching branches, and the white flowers have purple marks at the base.

P. 'Virginal'
Height: 3.6m (12ft)
Spread: 3m (10ft)
An upright shrub that bears large clusters of pendent, double, white flowers in summer.

CULTIVATION
Planting time: October to March.
Soil: Well-drained.
Aspect: Full sun or semi-shade, except *P. coronarius*, which prefers partial shade.
Minimum temp: −15°C (5°F).
Pruning: After flowering thin out some old flowering stems to prevent overcrowding, taking care to retain some young shoots for flowering the following year.
Propagation: By 30cm (12in) HARD-WOOD CUTTINGS in autumn inserted in a sheltered outdoor bed. Replant in final positions the following year.
Diseases: LEAF SPOT causes dark-edged yellow blotches.

PHLOX
Polemoniaceae
A genus of herbaceous perennials, shrubs, sub-shrubs and annuals. The most common phlox in garden cultivation are the cultivars of *P. panicu-lata*, but although these are attractive and easily grown plants, they can require staking and an annual mulch.

P. subulata (moss phlox)
Height: 5-10cm (2-4in)
Spread: 45cm (18in)
This hardy, evergreen sub-shrub is the easiest of all the dwarf species of phlox to grow. Spreading mats of mid-green foliage bear masses of small, pink to purple flowers in late spring and early summer. It is a useful mat-forming plant for the front of borders or for a raised bed.
Varieties: 'Apple Blossom' (pale pink flowers); 'Bonita' (light purple-blue flowers); 'Star Glow' (bright red flowers); 'Temiskaming' (carmine-red flowers).
CULTIVATION
Planting time: September to March.
Soil: Any.
Aspect: Full sun.
Minimum temp: −15°C (5°F).
Pruning: Growth is improved if plants are trimmed after flowering. This can be simply done with a pair of scissors.

Propagation: By 5cm (2in) CUTTINGS of basal shoots taken in summer. Root in a cold frame. When rooted, pot on for planting out in late spring.
Diseases: LEAF SPOT causes brown spotting. POWDERY MILDEW causes a white powdery coating on the leaves.

PHORMIUM
Agavaceae
New Zealand flax
A genus of two half-hardy, evergreen perennials, grown mainly for their foliage and architectural impact. They make impressive feature plants, but need protection from frost.

P. tenax
Height: 3m (10ft)
Planting distance: 1.2m (4ft)
Because it is hardier than the other species, *P. cookianum* (which is also shorter – 1.8m (6ft) – with narrower, more arching leaves), *P. tenax* is probably the better of the two for border cultivation. It forms striking clumps of leathery, slightly arching, deep green, strap-shaped leaves, which can be up to 2.7m (9ft) long. Red flowers, borne on long, branched panicles, appear from mid-summer to early autumn.
Varieties: *P. t. purpureum* (bronze-purple leaves); 'Variegatum' (green and yellow striped leaves).
CULTIVATION
Planting time: April/May.
Soil: Moist but well-drained.
Aspect: Full sun. In colder areas protect plants from winter frost with a covering of straw or bracken.
Minimum temp: −7°C (19°F).
Pruning: Remove dead flower stems in autumn.
Propagation: By DIVISION of clumps in spring; make sure that each piece has at least 4 leaves and replant immediately in final positions.

POLYGONUM
Polygonaceae
Knotweed
A varied genus containing both weeds (willowherbs, knotgrass and bistort belong to this group) and useful garden species. Apart from the vigorous climber *P. baldschuanicum*, the garden varieties most often found in garden cultivation provide valu-able ground cover. They are all quite vigorous growers and need ample space or to have their spread checked from time to time.

P. affine
Height: 15-30cm (6-12in)
Planting distance: 45cm (18in)
The species plant of this hardy, semi-evergreen perennial has been super-seded by several summer-flowering garden varieties, which provide use-

ful ground cover. However, if the soil becomes impoverished after a few years, the centres of the crowns tend to die down; plants should be lifted and divided and the soil fed before replanting.
Varieties: 'Darjeeling Red' (a rapidly spreading, mat-forming variety with narrow, dark green leaves, which turn russet-brown in winter, and 15cm (6in) long spikes of close-set, red flowers); 'Donald Lowndes' (a more compact variety with bright green foliage, which darkens with age before turning brown in autumn and winter, and rose-red flower spikes, 15-20cm (6-8in) long).

P. baldschuanicum (syn. *Fallopia baldschuanica*, *Bilderdykia aubertii*) (Russian vine, mile-a-minute plant)
Height: 12.2m (40ft) or more
An extremely vigorous, hardy, de-ciduous climber, which can grow 3-4.6m (10-15ft) in a year. Where there is enough space it is a useful plant for screening on a trellis or wires or for climbing over an old tree. However, it is not a plant for small or even average-sized gardens. It bears a profusion of 45cm (18in) long pani-cles of pale pink or white flowers in late summer.

P. bistorta 'Superbum' (bistort)
Height: 75-90cm (2ft 6in – 3ft)
Planting distance: 60cm (2ft)
This spreading, mat-forming hardy herbaceous perennial is a useful variety for herbaceous borders. It has pale green leaves and produces 15cm (6in) long spikes of clear pink flowers in early summer, sometimes followed by a second flowering in autumn.

P. campanulatum
Height: 90cm (3ft)
Planting distance: 60cm (2ft)
A bushier, finer and less vigorously spreading species than either *P. affine* or *P. bistorta*, this hardy, herbaceous perennial has dense, mid-green foliage and produce heads of pink flowers, 7.5cm (3in) wide, from mid-summer to early autumn.
Varieties: *P. c. album* (suitable for damp, shaded sites, it produces clusters of tiny, white, bell-shaped flowers).

P. vaccinifolium
Height: 15cm (6in)
Spread: 30-90cm (1-3ft)
This hardy evergreen perennial forms a close carpet of shiny foliage and produces a clump of 10cm (4in) long rose-red flower spikes in late summer. It is ideal for trailing over walls or covering rocky slopes. .
CULTIVATION
Planting time: October to March.

Parthenocissus henryana

Pernettya mucronata 'Pink Pearl'

Phlox subulata 'Apple Blossom'

Parthenocissus tricuspidata 'Lowii'

Phormium 'Maori Chief'

Phormium tenax purpureum

Phormium x hybrids

Phormium tenax 'Variegatum'

Soil: Any.
Aspect: Full sun to partial shade; *P. campanulatum* prefers light shade.
Minimum temp: −15°C (5°F).
Pruning: Cut flowering stems of herbaceous forms to ground level in late autumn.
Propagation: All, except *P. baldschuanicum*, can be propagated by DIVISION of clumps in spring. Propagate *P. baldschuanicum* by taking 25cm (10in) long HARDWOOD CUTTINGS in autumn and inserting directly into the soil in the final growing positions.
Pests: Young growth of *P. baldschuanicum* may become infested with APHIDS.

POTENTILLA   Rosaceae
A genus of many species of hardy annuals, perennials, deciduous shrubs and sub-shrubs, of which the most useful to the easy-care gardener are the 'grow anywhere' shrubby types. These flower continuously throughout the summer and make excellent spreading bushes that require practically no attention. They are suited to growing on sunny banks as well as in borders, and the prostrate, sub-shrubby varieties provide valuable ground cover.
P. fructicosa
Height: 90cm (3ft)
Spread: 1.5m (5ft)
A hardy, deciduous shrub of compact habit. The leaves are mid-green, and buttercup-yellow flowers, 2.5cm (1in) wide, are produced throughout summer. The many hybrid varieties, with their range of flower colour and longer flowering seasons, have superseded the species plant in garden cultivation.
Varieties: 'Elizabeth' (ht: 90cm (3ft), sp: 1.5m (5ft), dense, bushy habit and large, bright yellow flowers produced from late spring to mid-autumn); 'Gold Drop'/'Gold Kugel' (syn. 'Farreri', ht: 1.2m (4ft), sp: 90cm (3ft), bright yellow flowers); 'Katherine Dykes' (ht: 1.2m (4ft), sp: 1.5m (5ft), primrose-yellow flowers); 'Manchu' (syn. 'Mandschurica', ht: 30cm (12in), sp: 90cm (3ft), mat-forming with silver-grey foliage, purple stems and pure white flowers).
CULTIVATION
Planting time: October to March.
Soil: Well-drained.
Aspect: Full sun.
Minimum temp: −29°C (−20°F).
Pruning: After flowering remove the tips of dead flowering shoots. More vigorous and bushier growth can be encouraged by cutting weak or old

stems to ground level.
Propagation: By 7.5cm (3in) HEEL CUTTINGS of half-ripe lateral shoots in autumn. Keep in a cold frame and plant out in spring.

PRUNUS   Rosaceae
A genus of hardy, easily grown and mainly deciduous trees and shrubs, which includes the peach, almond and flowering plums and cherries. Peach and almond are very susceptible to diseases that cause unsightly leaf curl, and they are, therefore, best avoided. Newly planted trees may need staking in exposed or windy sites until they are established.
P. × blireana (ornamental plum)
Height: 4.6-5.4m (15-18ft)
Spread: 3.6-5.4m (12-18ft)
A small deciduous tree with metallic, coppery-purple foliage. Double, rose-pink flowers are borne on slender branches in spring.
P. cerasifera (cherry plum, myrobalan)
Height and spread: 6-10m (20-30ft)
A deciduous tree with mid-green leaves and white flowers, borne in early spring.
Varieties: 'Nigra' (deep purple leaves, red when young, and pink flowers in early to mid-spring); 'Pissardii' (syn. 'Atropurpurea', red foliage, turning darker with age, and pale pink flowers, borne from early to mid-spring, and followed by plum-like red fruits).
P. subhirtella (higan cherry, rosebud cherry)
Height and spread: 6-7.6m (20-25ft)
A quickly growing ornamental cherry with slender, mid-green leaves. Clusters of pale pink flowers are produced in profusion in spring.
Varieties: 'Autumnalis' (semi-double, fragrant, white flowers appear in mild winters); 'Autumnalis Rosea' (semi-double, rose-pink flowers produced in mild winters); 'Pendula' (ht: 1.5-2.4m (5-8ft) or more, sp: 4.6m (15ft), bears pale pink flowers on drooping branches in spring); 'Pendula Rubra' (deep reddish-pink flowers).
CULTIVATION
Planting time: October/early November; do not plant too deeply.
Soil: Well-drained and preferably containing some lime.
Aspect: Full sun.
Minimum temp: −23°C (−9°F).
Pruning: No regular pruning necessary but unwanted or damaged shoots may be cut out in late summer. The central leader of *P. subhirtella* 'Pendula' can be trained to

the desired height before the tree is allowed to weep.
Propagation: Branches of *P. cerasifera* can be LAYERED in spring for separation from parent plant after 2 years. Increasing other named varieties by vegetative means (layering or cuttings) is difficult, and, as they do not breed true from seed, it is better to buy new subjects.
Pests: APHIDS may infest foliage and young shoots. CATERPILLARS may feed on shoots. Bullfinches may eat shoots.
Diseases: BACTERIAL CANKER can infect branches, usually in summer, causing brown spotting on the leaves, which eventually become holed. This is accompanied by gum exuding from cankers developing on the branches, and, in the following season, the production of buds and leaves on infected branches is severely affected and the branch eventually dies back. HONEY FUNGUS can cause rapid death. SILVER LEAF is a fungal disease causing a silvering of the leaves on one or more branches, which die back. If a diseased branch is severed from the tree, a purple-brown stain will be seen on the inner tissues of the stem.

PULMONARIA   Boraginaceae
Lungwort
Pulmonarias form rapidly spreading clumps and provide valuable ground cover in shady areas.
P. angustifolia (blue cowslip)
Height and planting distance: 30cm (12in)
A hardy, clump-forming perennial with mid-green leaves and funnel-shaped, bright sky-blue flowers, sometimes tinged with pink, that are borne in spring.
Varieties (all with dark blue flowers): 'Azurea'; 'Mawson's Variety'; 'Munstead Blue'.
P. officinalis (Jerusalem cowslip, spotted dog)
Height and planting distance: 30cm (12in)
A hardy, herbaceous perennial with narrow, white-spotted, mid-green leaves. It produces clusters of tubular purple-blue flowers in late spring.
CULTIVATION
Planting time: October to March.
Soil: Moist.
Aspect: Partial to full shade.
Minimum temp: −15°C (5°F).
Pruning: None.
Propagation: By DIVISION of roots from October to March.
Pests: SAWFLY LARVAE may feed on leaves.

PYRACANTHA — Rosaceae
Firethorn
P. rogersiana
Height and spread: 3-3.6m (10-12ft)
A robust, hardy, evergreen, flowering shrub, which is suitable for the larger garden. It has glossy, mid-green leaves and produces clusters of white flowers in summer. These are followed by bright orange-red or yellow berries. Although it is often recommended for informal hedging, its strongly growing nature makes it a poor choice for low-maintenance hedges. It will, however, make an excellent free-standing shrub, and, if supported, can be grown to effect against a wall. Unpruned plants produce more attractive displays of berries.

CULTIVATION
Planting time: October to March; plant only pot-grown specimens.
Soil: Fertile and well-drained.
Aspect: Full sun to partial shade.
Minimum temp: −15°C (5°F).
Pruning: No regular pruning necessary; remove any surplus growth from wall-grown specimens in late spring or early summer.
Propagation: By 7.5-10cm (3-4in) CUTTINGS of the current year's growth in summer. Root in a propagating frame and pot on when rooted, overwintering in a cold frame. Pot on until the following autumn when plants may be set out in final positions.
Pests: APHIDS can infest stems and leaves. SCALE INSECTS produce sticky, sooty deposits on stems.
Diseases: FIREBLIGHT causes flowers to blacken and shrivel, leaves to turn brown but not drop and branches to die back. PYRACANTHA SCAB attacks berries and leaves, producing a brown coating on the berries and leaf drop.

RHODODENDRON — Ericaceae
A genus of deciduous and evergreen trees and shrubs, which is divided into two groups: large, evergreen or deciduous shubs are called **rhododendrons**, while the dwarf, small-leaved evergreen forms and smaller, deciduous shrubs are known as **azaleas.** The evergreen or Japanese azaleas have a low, spreading habit, but the hardier deciduous forms may reach 1.8m (6ft) or more in height. The 'true' garden rhododendron species are usually about 1.8m (6ft) high, but some dwarf and some very tall varieties are available. The dwarf varieties of both rhododendons and azaleas, with their acid-loving

natures, are ideal for raised-beds.
R. augustinii
Height and spread: 3-3.6m (10-12ft)
A hardy, evergreen shrub of erect habit. The foliage is dark green, and clusters of large, funnel-shaped mauve to dark blue flowers with green-spotted throats are produced in spring. Plants can be susceptible to spring frosts.
R. impeditum
Height and spread: 60cm (2ft)
A fully hardy, dwarf, evergreen shrub, which is ideal for the smaller garden or for raised beds. It forms low mounds of stems bearing small, grey-green leaves and, in spring, clusters of pale mauve to purple-blue flowers.

Kurume hybrids
A group of low-growing, evergreen azaleas, which should be given a sheltered position if grown in cold districts; the exception is 'Hinomayo', which is fully hardy and the best Kurume hybrid for general planting. All have small, glossy leaves and flower freely in late spring.
Varieties: 'Hatsugiri' (ht and sp: 60cm (2ft), compact habit and numerous crimson-purple flowers); 'Hinodegiri' (ht and sp: 1.5m (5ft), compact habit and crimson flowers); 'Hinomayo' (ht and sp: 1.5m (5ft), compact habit and clear pink flowers); 'Kirin' (ht and sp: 1.2-1.5m (4-5ft), compact habit and rose-red flowers shaded light and dark).
CULTIVATION
Planting time: September to April in mild weather.
Soil: Acid, light and well-drained. Acid soil is essential, because rhododendrons and azaleas cannot tolerate chalky or limy soils, which turn their leaves yellow.
Aspect: Partially shaded and sheltered. Do not plant too close to shallow- or surface-rooting trees such as elms or poplars or under trees with low-hanging branches.
Minimum temp: −12°C (10°F).
Pruning: No regular pruning necessary. Shrubs perform better if dead flowers are removed before they set seed. Pinch them off with a finger and thumb as secateurs may damage the shoots.
Propagation: By LAYERING young stems in summer, separating from the parent plant 2 years later.
Pests: RHODODENDRON LEAFHOPPERS are bright green with red stripes; they live on leaves in midsummer, wounding buds and allowing BUD-BLAST disease (see below) to enter. RHODODENDRON BUGS suck

sap, causing leaves to become mottled and appear 'rusty' below.
Diseases: AZALEA GALL causes red or pale green swellings, which later become coated with white, powdery spores, on the young leaves and flower buds. CHLOROSIS (yellowing of the leaves except for the veins) is caused by too alkaline conditions. HONEY FUNGUS infection, seen as discoloration and drooping of leaves (which do not fall), can cause rapid death. Purple or brown LEAF SPOT is caused by several types of fungi. RHODODENDRON BUD-BLAST infects and kills buds, which turn brown, black or silvery. RUST infection shows as discoloration of the upper surface of the leaves with orange-brown, spore-bearing pustules on the undersides. SILVER LEAF causes branches to die back and purple fruiting bodies to appear on the dead wood.

ROBINIA — Leguminosae
R. pseudoacacia (false acacia, locust tree)
Height: 15m (50ft) or more
Spread: 5.4m (18ft)
A hardy, deciduous tree, grown for its attractive shape and showy foliage, *R. pseudoacacia* makes a fine, quick-growing specimen tree. It has light green foliage and furrowed bark. Fragrant, creamy-white flowers are produced in 15cm (6in) long, pendulous sprays in summer. It is tolerant of atmospheric pollution and drought and can be grown almost anywhere except very wind-swept sites, where its brittle branches may be broken.
Varieties: 'Frisia' (golden-yellow foliage turns greenish-yellow in summer and orange-yellow in autumn).
CULTIVATION
Planting time: October to March.
Soil: Well-drained.
Aspect: Full sun to partial shade and sheltered from strong winds.
Minimum temp: −29°C (−20°F).
Pruning: None necessary. Cut out any dead or damaged wood in summer (rather than spring). Remove thorny suckers produced by mature specimens when they appear.
Propagation: Remove and replant suckers in winter.

ROSA — Rosaceae
Rose
A group of hardy, mainly deciduous shrubs grown for their flowers, which are often fragrant, and, sometimes, for their hips. Roses are divided into three categories – species, old garden and modern – and further sub-divided according to the

Polygonum affine 'Donald Lowndes'

Potentilla 'Katherine Dykes'

Prunus x *blireana*

Potentilla 'Manchu'

Pulmonaria angustifolia 'Mawson's Variety'

Pyracantha rogersiana

Robinia pseudoacacia

Pyracantha rogersiana

Rhododendron augustinii

Robinia pseudoacacia 'Frisia'

qualities of the plants within those groupings (see Chapter 8). Flowers are described as single (with 4 to 7 petals), semi-double (8-14 petals), double (15-30 petals) or fully double (more than 30 petals).

Large-flowered bush roses (Hybrid Teas)

This, the most popular class of rose for garden cultivation, is good for bedding. Recommended varieties include:

'Cheshire Life'

Height: 60-75cm (2ft – 2ft 6in)

A vigorous, robust variety of upright habit that can withstand wind and rain well. It produces faintly scented, large vermilion blooms, similar in colour to 'Super Star', but it is far more disease resistant. The semi-glossy foliage is dark green.

'Ernest H. Morse'

Height: 90cm (3ft)

A free-flowering variety with a vigorous, upright habit. It bears large, red, fragrant flowers, which are not prone to rain damage, although it should not be planted where it will be exposed to wind. The dark green foliage is semi-glossy.

'Pink Favourite'

Height: 75cm (2ft 6in)

A rose of vigorous, branching habit. It is very resistant to disease and is an excellent subject for bedding. The dark green foliage is glossy, and rose-pink blooms are borne on sturdy stems. Unfortunately, it is not fragrant.

'Polar Star' (syn. 'Tanlarpost', 'Polarstern')

Height: 1m (3ft 6in)

An upright, branching variety that is resistant to disease. White, faintly scented blooms are borne on sturdy stems. The mid-green foliage is matt.

'Precious Platinum' (syn. 'Opa Potschke')

Height: 90cm (3ft)

A vigorous, free-flowering rose of branching habit that bears slightly fragrant, fully double, deep crimson flowers in small clusters. The blooms are resistant to rain damage. The mid-green foliage is glossy.

'Simba' (syn. 'Goldsmith', 'Korbelma', 'Helmut Schmidt')

Height: 75cm (2ft 6in)

An upright, neatly growing rose, whose slightly scented, clear yellow, fully double flowers are excellent for cutting. The glossy leaves are mid-green

'Sunblest'

Height: 1m (3ft 6in)

A vigorous, disease-resistant variety of upright habit. It produces an abundance of slightly fragrant, pure yellow, medium-sized blooms on long, straight stems. The foliage is a glossy mid-green. It is tolerant of both wind and rain.

Cluster-flowered bush roses (Floribundas)

A hardy, easily grown group of roses, which require little maintenance and should be only lightly pruned. They bear flowers in clusters throughout the long flowering season and are good for bedding, while the vigorous, tall-growing varieties can be used for hedging. Recommended varieties include:

'Chinatown'

Height: 1.5m (5ft)

Spread: 1.2m (4ft)

A tall, bushy variety, which may also be classified as a modern shrub rose. It is suitable for both windy and rain-swept gardens and has good disease resistance. It produces double, fragrant, yellow blooms, 10cm (4in) across, with pink-edged petals. The foliage is mid-green.

'City of Leeds'

Height: 75cm (2ft 6in)

An easily grown, vigorous variety of upright habit. It produces rich salmon-pink, slightly fragrant flowers throughout summer. Although tolerant of wind, its petals will be damaged by heavy rain and it is only fairly resistant to disease. The small leaves are semi-evergreen.

'English Miss'

Height: 60-75cm (2ft – 2ft 6in)

A very vigorous, bushy variety. It is a free-flowering rose with good disease resistance. The fully double flowers are fragrant and blush-pink, and the leathery, dark green foliage is tinged with purple.

'Evelyn Fison' (syn. 'Irish Wonder')

Height: 75cm (2ft 6in)

A reliable variety with a vigorous, branching habit. It produces numerous, large trusses of slightly fragrant, bright scarlet blooms, which are not damaged by either strong sunlight or heavy rain. It is also disease resistant. The foliage is a glossy, dark green. This is an excellent bedding rose.

'Marlena'

Height: 45cm (1ft 6in)

A dwarf rose that is sometimes classified as a patio rose. It has a vigorous, compact, branching habit and is an excellent choice for the front of the border. It also provides some ground cover. The blooms are bright scarlet, and the glossy foliage has a bronze sheen.

'Mountbatten' (syn. 'Harmantelle')

Height: 1-1.5m (3ft 6in – 5ft)

An easily grown, vigorous variety of upright, dense habit. The foliage is semi-evergreen, and the fully double, yellow flowers are scented. It has good disease resistance and is also tolerant of wind and heavy rain. It is an outstanding rose for growing as a hedge, in borders or in large beds.

'Pink Parfait'

Height: 75cm (2ft 6in)

A bushy, vigorous rose of branching habit. Clusters of double, rain-resistant, light pink and ivory blooms are borne on slender, almost thornless stems. The glossy foliage is mid-green.

'Queen Elizabeth'

Height: 1.5m (5ft) or more

A large-flowered, disease-resistant rose that can be grown in a variety of conditions. It has slightly scented, fully double, clear pink blooms, borne on long stems with few thorns. The dark green foliage is glossy and leathery. 'Queen Elizabeth' is a vigorous grower of erect habit, and its blooms stand up well to wind and heavy rain. It is best grown in a bed of its own, where several specimens make a fine display, or as a hedge, although it can also be planted at the back of rose borders with shorter varieties in front.

Miniature bush roses (recurrent miniatures)

A class of rose of dwarf, branching habit, which are ideal for growing in raised beds and tubs as well as in borders, although miniature roses are generally more prone to disease than either large-flowered or cluster-flowered bush roses. Recommended varieties include:

'Angela Rippon' (syn. 'Ocarina', 'Ocaru')

Height: 30cm (12in)

A shrublet of compact, bushy habit, which produces fragrant, fully double, pale carmine-pink blooms.

'Darling Flame' (syn. 'Minuetto')

Height: 30cm (12in)

A healthy, bushy shrublet with dark green foliage. It produces a profusion of slightly fragrant, double flowers in orange-vermilion with a golden reverse.

'Easter Morning' (syn. 'Easter Morn')

Height: 30cm (12in)

A good disease-resistant variety that produces large, fully double, ivory-white blooms, which are not prone to rain damage.

'Fire Princess'

Height: 45cm (18in)

A bush of upright habit with glossy, dark green foliage. The fully double flowers are scarlet marked with gold, and the colour strengthens rather than fades with age.

'Hula Girl'
Height: 45cm (18in)
An easily grown, bushy rose with glossy, dark green foliage. The fully double, salmon-orange flowers are produced freely in summer and early autumn.

'New Penny' Height: 25cm (10in)
A vigorous shrublet of branching habit. The foliage is glossy, and semi-double, salmon-pink and orange flowers, which fade as they age, are produced.

'Pour Toi' (syn. 'Para Ti')
Height: 17.5-23cm (7-9in)
A shrublet of dwarf, bushy habit with glossy foliage. It produces a profusion of slightly fragrant white flowers with cream-yellow tints at the base of the petals.

'Rosina' (syn. 'Josephine Wheatcroft')
Height: 38cm (15in)
A free-flowering variety bearing as many as 10 bright yellow, double blooms on each truss.

'Sheri Anne'
Height: 30-45cm (12-18in)
An easily grown, upright variety with glossy, leathery foliage. Double, light red blooms are borne in summer and autumn. It is a good bedding subject.

Climbing roses

Although they are mainly used for growing against walls, fences or pillars, some of the more vigorous climbing roses can be used to clothe pergolas and arches instead of rambling roses, especially in those circumstances when a rambling rose's lack of resistance to disease and pruning requirements pose problems.

'Bantry Bay'
Height: 2.7-3m (9-10ft)
A repeat-flowering, fairly slow-growing variety that has good disease resistance. It can be grown against a wall but is best used for clothing pillars or fences. It has plentiful, semi-glossy, mid-green foliage and bears a profusion of large, semi-double, bright pink flowers with conspicuous yellow stamens.

'Climbing Cécile Brunner'
Height: 6m (20ft)
The climbing sport of the China rose 'Cécile Brunner' is a vigorous grower and is a useful alternative to a rambling rose for clothing large structures or for growing up trees. It produces a flush of small pink flowers in mid-summer and thereafter flowers sporadically through-

out the rest of the season.

'Climbing Etoile d'Hollande'
Height: 3-3.6m (10-12ft)
A climbing large-flowered (Hybrid Tea) rose, which is probably the best choice for clothing the walls of a house. The fragrant, double flowers are dark red and produced throughout the season.

'Compassion' (syn. 'Belle de Londres')
Height: 3-4.6m (10-15ft)
A repeat-flowering variety that is useful as a pillar rose or for growing against a wall. It bears large, sweetly scented, double flowers of salmon-apricot tinged with pink.

'Galway Bay'
Height: 2.4-3m (8-10ft)
A good, repeat-flowering, disease-resistant pillar rose. Small clusters of large, non-fading and well-formed, double, pink blooms are produced in summer and autumn.

'Mme Alfred Carrière'
Height: 4.6-6m (15-20ft)
A repeat-flowering, vigorous and shade-tolerant rose, which is particularly useful for clothing cool and shady north-facing walls. The fragrant, double flowers, creamy-white, tinged with pink, appear throughout the summer and autumn.

'Schoolgirl'
Height: 3m (10ft)
A repeat-flowering rose with fragrant, double, apricot-orange blooms. Glossy leaves are produced in abundance, but the lower ones tend to drop, and this can give the plant a rather leggy appearance.

Rambling roses

All ramblers are more prone to disease and need more attention than climbing roses. For most uses, therefore, such as growing against a wall or fence or up a pillar, it is better to choose a suitable more disease-resistant and more easily managed climber. However, if a very large structure, such as a dead tree, pergola or arch, is to be covered, a rambler can be chosen, as the thin, pliable stems make them easier plants to train than climbers.

'Albéric Barbier'
Height: 6-7.6m (20-25ft)
A robust, easily grown rose, which tolerates poor conditions and lack of sunlight. It bears a profusion of fragrant, fully double, creamy-white blooms in mid-summer. The glossy, dark green foliage persists through much of the winter.

'Crimson Shower'
Height: 3-4.6m (10-15ft)
One of the most disease-resistant

ramblers, it is a free-flowering variety, producing small, slightly scented, crimson blooms in late summer and early autumn.

'Emily Gray'
Height: 3-4.6m (10-15ft)
An almost evergreen rose that produces fragrant, fully double, butter-yellow flowers in mid-summer. It is useful for clothing pergolas or arches as it requires only light pruning and is reasonably resistant to disease.

R. filipes 'Kiftsgate'
Height: 7.6-10m (25-30ft)
A vigorous rose with a wide-spreading habit. It requires only light pruning and is suitable for covering very large structures or for growing up tall trees. It is slow to become established but will eventually produce enormous clusters of single, creamy-white flowers in late summer. These are followed by bright red hips in autumn. This is not a rose for small gardens.

'François Juranville'
Height: 6m (20ftT
A vigorous, arching rose, this variety is a good choice for growing up trees as well as for covering arches and pergolas. In early summer it produces large, fully double, fragrant flowers that are a rosy salmon-pink, which turns paler. Bronze-tinted leaves are borne on almost thornless stems.

Other recommended roses

There are so many other types of rose available from nurseries and garden centres that it is possible to select only a few for the low-maintenance garden. Some of the roses that seem to be becoming particularly prone to disease are listed in Chapter 8. This consideration apart, however, the selection of roses is a matter for personal preference and requirements.

'Blanc Double de Coubert'
Height: 1.5m (5ft) or more
Spread: 1.5m (5ft)
A repeat-flowering hybrid Rugosa of bushy habit. It is extremely resistant to disease and produces large, semi-double, fragrant, white flowers from mid-summer to autumn. Although it is often recommended for hedging, its somewhat sparse foliage, especially near the base of the bush, makes it unsuitable for this purpose.

'Candy Rose'
Height: 90cm (3ft)
Spread: 1.8m (6ft)
A repeat-flowering, disease-resistant, modern shrub rose, which is of procumbent habit and can be used for ground cover, especially beneath

Rosa 'Pour Toi' (miniature)

Rosa 'City of Leeds' (cluster-flowered bush)

Rosa 'Evelyn Fison' (cluster-flowered bush)

Rosa 'Ernest H. Morse' (large-flowered bush)

Rosa 'Queen Elizabeth' (cluster-flowered bush)

Rosa 'Pink Favourite' (large-flowered bush)

Rosa xanthina spontanea 'Canary Bird'

trees as it is tolerant of shade. It is also suitable for dwarf hedges. Clusters of semi-double, pink flowers are produced throughout summer and early autumn.

'Cécile Brunner' (syn. 'Mignon')
Height: 75cm (2ft 6in)
Spread: 60cm (2ft)
A small China rose of upright habit, which requires a sunny position. It produces clusters of slightly scented, fully double flowers of pale yellow shaded with pink throughout the season.

'Céleste' (syn. 'Celestial')
Height: 1.8m (6ft)
Spread: 1.2m (4ft)
A vigorous, spreading Alba rose, which is largely trouble free and can be used as hedging or as a tall specimen bush. It bears a profusion of fragrant, double, light pink flowers in one flush in early summer.

'Complicata'
Height: 1.8m (6ft)
Spread: 2.4m (8ft)
A Gallica rose with long, thorny, arching shoots, 'Complicata' can be used as a low climber, for covering trees or as a wide-spreading specimen shrub. It produces a flush of large, single, pink blooms with white centres in early summer.

'Fountain'
Height and spread: 1.5m (5ft)
A reliable and disease-resistant modern shrub rose of upright habit. It produces large, double, deep red blooms, either singly or in trusses throughout the season. The tall stems may be prone to snapping if 'Fountain' is planted in windy exposed situations.

'Fru Dagmar Hastrup'
Height: 1.2m (4ft) or more
Spread: 1m (3ft 6in)
A robust and disease-resistant Rugosa rose that will grow well in a wide range of soils and situations. It is repeat-flowering and produces fragrant, pink blooms throughout summer and large red hips in autumn. It is useful for borders or as a low-growing hedge.

'Golden Wings'
Height: 1m (3ft 6in)
Spread: 1.2m (4ft) or more
An excellent, disease-resistant modern shrub rose that is suitable for borders. It is repeat-flowering and produces large, single, fragrant yellow blooms from mid-summer onwards as long as the old flowers are dead-headed.

'Grouse' (syn. 'Korimro')
Height: 45cm (18in)
Spread: 2.4-3m (8-10ft)
A modern ground-cover rose with abundant glossy foliage, which makes 'Grouse' one of the most effective weed-suppressing roses. It is useful ground cover for quite large areas, covering banks or trailing over walls. Single, fragrant, blush-pink flowers are produced throughout the season.

'Paulii'
Height: 1.2m (4ft)
Spread: 4.6m (15ft)
A low-growing, thicket-forming Rugosa, which roots as it spreads. Clusters of fragrant, white blooms are produced throughout summer. It is a useful rose for providing large areas of ground cover, such as a on banks, or for covering several old tree stumps. It can also be trained as a climber.
Varieties: 'Paulii Rosea' (pink flowers).

'Rosy Cushion' (syn. 'Interall')
Height: 1m (3ft 6in)
Spread: 1.2m (4ft)
A repeat-flowering modern shrub rose of prostrate habit, which can be used as ground cover for smaller areas or in a border. It is also a good rose for hiding unsightly objects. Semi-double, pink flowers with ivory centres are produced throughout the season.

'Scabrosa'
Height: 1.5m (5ft)
Spread: 1.8m (6ft)
A Rugosa rose of spreading habit, which bears large, fragrant, magenta-pink blooms from late spring until autumn, when large, bright red hips are produced. It is a good rose for a wide hedge or as a specimen bush.

R. xanthina spontanea 'Canary Bird'
Height and spread: 1.8m (6ft)
An early-flowering species rose that is a good choice for growing in borders or as a hedge. Although the small, single, yellow flowers are produced in one flush in early summer, the fern-like foliage makes this an attractive plant even when flowering is finished. 'Canary Bird' is resistant to most pests and diseases, although die-back can be a problem, and it is tolerant of both wind and rain, making it a suitable subject for exposed gardens.

CULTIVATION
Planting time: October/November or March; roses can be planted at any time between October and March as long as the soil is workable. Prepare the ground one month before planting.
Soil: Any, although preferably slightly acid. Apart from Alba, Gallica, Rugosa and some species roses, roses need a rich, moist and free-draining soil. Poor soils should be enriched by the addition of organic or inorganic fertilizer when the bed is prepared.
Aspect: Sunny and airy, sheltered from cold and strong winds.
Minimum temp: −15°C (5°F).
Pruning: See Chapter 8.
Propagation: Species roses and their hybrids, miniature roses and those shrub roses that flower in one flush can be propagated by CUTTINGS. Take 5-10cm (2-4in) heel cuttings of miniature roses between July and October, rooting them in a cold frame and potting on into 7.5cm (3in) pots when rooted. Plunge outdoors the following spring and plant in final positions in autumn. To propagate shrub roses take 23-30cm (9-12in) cuttings of strong, non-flowering lateral shoots with a heel in late summer. Remove any buds and strip off all the leaves except for the topmost 2 or 3. Make a 15cm (6in) deep V-shaped trench in a partially shaded, sheltered position and fill the bottom 2.5cm (1in) with coarse sand to provide drainage. Dip cuttings in hormone rooting powder and place them in the sand, refilling the trench with soil. Firm in gently. Replant in final positions the following autumn.
Pests: APHIDS can infest foliage, stems and flower buds, making them sooty and sticky and reducing vigour and checking and distorting growth. Infested buds may fail to open. FROGHOPPERS, seen by cuckoo spit on the stems, can distort growth and may cause leaves of affected stems to wilt. LEAFHOPPERS cause light mottling on the upper surface of leaves.
Diseases: BLACK SPOT causes black or dark brown spots, usually with yellow edges, on the leaves, which eventually turn yellow and drop. Heavy infection can result in quite severe defoliation. CROWN GALL, a large, brown, walnut-like growth, can develop close to the base of stems. This does little harm and can be cut off in autumn and the wound treated with a proprietary protective paint. GREY MOULD can infect flower buds, which may become covered with fine, grey fungal growth, causing them to turn brown and decay. HONEY FUNGUS can cause the rapid death of the whole plant. MINERAL DEFICIENCIES can cause poor growth and discoloration of the leaves. Magnesium deficiency, seen as yellowing of the leaves between the veins, is common on sandy soils especially

after a heavy application of high potash feed. POOR GROWING CONDITIONS can cause purple spots on the leaves (distinguished from black spot as the marks are smaller, irregular and have no yellow fringe) and also DIE-BACK of shoots. Die-back can also be caused by various fungal diseases entering through dead wood, wounds or pruning cuts. POWDERY MILDEW produces a white powdery coating on leaves and buds, which become distorted. RUST causes orange swellings to be produced on stems and the undersides of leaves. The swellings eventually turn black. Severe defoliation or even death of the whole plant can result if rust is left untreated. Soil sickness (replant diseases) can cause the failure of new rose bushes planted in soil in which roses have previously been grown (usually 10 years or more). When planting new bushes in such sites, remove the old soil from a hole 60cm (2ft) across and 45cm (1ft 6in) deep and replace it with soil from another part of the garden. The old soil can safely be used for other plants.

ROSMARINUS   Labiatae
Rosemary
R. officinalis
Height: 1.5-1.8m (5-6ft)
Spread: 1.5m (5ft)
A decorative, hardy, evergreen shrub of erect or spreading habit according to the variety chosen. It has strongly aromatic mid- to grey-green leaves with white undersides. These can be used either fresh or dried for culinary flavouring. Small, mauve flowers are borne in clusters in spring and, sporadically, until early autumn.
Varieties: *R. o. albus* (syn. 'Albiflorus', white or pale blue flowers); 'Miss Jessopp's Upright' (syn. *R. o. pyramidalis*, 'Fastigiatus', dark green leaves and blue flowers).
CULTIVATION
Planting time: March/April.
Soil: Well-drained and light; does not do well on clayey soil.
Aspect: Full sun.
Minimum temp: −12°C (10°F).
Pruning: Cut out any dead wood or shorten straggly growth in spring. Hedges benefit from a light clip after flowering.
Propagation: By 15-23cm (6-9in) CUTTINGS of mature shoots in autumn or spring. Plant cuttings immediately in final growing positions.

RUDBECKIA   Compositae
Coneflower
R. fulgida (black-eyed Susan)

Height: 60-90cm (2-3ft)
Planting distance: 45-60cm (18-24in)
A bushy, hardy, herbaceous perennial of variable habit. It has mid-green foliage and bears yellow to orange flowers with purple-brown centres in summer and autumn. The true species is now seldom grown, having been superseded by named varieties. They are easily grown and maintained, although they may need staking if grown in exposed positions, and they provide long-lasting colour in the border into autumn.
Varieties: *R. f.* var. *deamii* (dark-centred, star-shaped, golden flowers); 'Goldsturm' (large, golden flowers with conical, black-brown centres).
CULTIVATION
Planting time: March/April.
Soil: Well-drained but moist.
Aspect: Full sun to partial shade.
Minimum temp: −12°C (10°F).
Pruning: Dead-head as flowers fade and cut down stems to ground level in late autumn.
Propagation: By DIVISION of the roots between October and March. Replant the stronger, more vigorous outer shoots only.
Pests: SLUGS and SNAILS can eat the flowers, stems and leaves.

SALIX   Salicaceae
Willow
A genus of hardy, deciduous trees and shrubs.
S. × boydii
Height and spread: 30cm (12in)
A dwarf, slow-growing shrub, which has silver-grey foliage and, once established, catkins in spring.
S. caprea (goat willow, pussy willow, sallow)
Height: 10m (30ft)
Spread: 7.6m (25ft)
A bushy tree or shrub with grey-green foliage. Catkins are produced throughout spring. It is better to grow the non-seeding male form, for not only are the golden catkins more attractive than the silver catkins of the female plants, but willows are insidious seeders and, if female plants are grown, self-sown seedlings will constantly need to be removed.
CULTIVATION
Planting time: October to February.
Soil: Moist.
Aspect: Sunny, although *S. × boydii* will tolerate light shade.
Minimum temp: −20°C (−4°F).
Pruning: Remove any dead wood in winter.
Propagation: By 23-38 (9-15in) HARDWOOD CUTTINGS taken between

October and March. Root in a nursery bed and replant in permanent positions a year later.
Pests: CATERPILLARS may feed on leaves. GALL MITES can distort and stunt the growth of young shoots. SAWFLY larvae cause brightly coloured, bean-shaped galls to be produced on the leaves.

SALVIA   Labiatae
S. officinalis (sage)
Height: 60cm (2ft)
Planting distance: 38cm (15in)
This hardy, evergreen, aromatic sub-shrub is a well-known culinary herb. The grey-green leaves, which can be used either fresh or dried, are borne on strong stems, which become woody. Violet-blue flowers are produced in summer.
Varieties: 'Purpurascens' (racemes of purple-blue flowers).
S. var. *superba*
Height: 60cm (2ft) or more
Planting distance: 45-60cm (18-24in)
An erect, clump-forming, hardy, herbaceous perennial with mid-green foliage. Blue-purple flowers, borne in spikes, are produced from mid-summer to early autumn.
CULTIVATION
Planting time: March/April.
Soil: Light and well-drained.
Aspect: Full sun.
Minimum temp: −12°C (10°F).
Pruning: Trim *S. officinalis* regularly to prevent plants from becoming leggy. If grown for culinary purposes, pinch off flowers as they appear to encourage leaf growth.
Propagation: *S. officinalis* may be propagated by SEED sown in trays in a cold frame in early spring or in open ground in late spring. Alternatively by 7.5cm (3in) HEEL CUTTINGS taken in autumn. Pot on when rooted and overwinter in a cold frame. Pinch out tips to encourage bushy growth and plant out in spring. *S. × superba* can be propagated by DIVISION between September and March.
Pests: CAPSID BUGS can attack young shoots of *S. officinalis*, resulting in distortion and holing of the leaves.
Diseases: *S. officinalis* can be prone to GREY MOULD, which causes die-back of young growth in damp conditions, accompanied by a light grey, fungal growth on the leaves and stems. POWDERY MILDEW causes a white powdery deposits on leaves.

SAXIFRAGA   Saxifragaceae
A genus of a wide variety of low-growing, evergreen and semi-

Rosmarinus officinalis

Salix caprea

Rudbeckia fulgida 'Goldsturm'

Salvia officinalis

Salvia officinalis 'Purpurascens'

Saxifraga x *urbium*

evergreen, hardy plants, some of which are ideal for sink gardens or raised beds.

S. burseriana
Height: 5cm (2in)
Spread: 15-30cm (6-12in)
A slow-growing, evergreen perennial, this 'cushion' saxifrage is ideal for raised-bed or sink cultivation. It forms a dense, flattened cushion of blue-grey foliage and produces white flowers, 2.5cm (1in) across, borne on red stems, in spring.
Varieties: 'Brookside' (bright yellow flowers); 'Gloria' (white flowers with red sepals); 'Major Lutea' (large yellow flowers); 'Sulphurea' (grey foliage and pale yellow flowers).

S. × urbium (London pride)
Height: 30cm (12in)
Spread: 30-45cm (12-18in)
This hybrid is sometimes sold under the name *S. umbrosa*, to which it is very similar. The mid- to dark green leaves are arranged in rosettes, which form an effective weed-suppressing carpet, from which a profusion of pink, star-shaped flowers appears in late spring and early summer.
Varieties: *S. × urbium primuloides* (a finer, dwarf form, to 15cm (6in) high, suitable for raised-bed cultivation); 'Aureopunctata' (syn. *S. umbrosa variegata, S. × urbium primuloides* 'Variegata').
CULTIVATION
Planting time: September/October or March.
Soil: Well-drained but moist, alkaline and gritty.
Aspect: *S. burseriana*, full sun; *S. × urbium*, full sun to deep shade.
Minimum temp: −20°C (−4°F).
Pruning: None.
Propagation: By DIVISION after flowering. *S. × urbium* may be made to cover a large area fairly quickly by breaking up the carpet into single rosettes, each with some root, and replanting each of these 25cm (10in) apart. The individual plants will quickly grow together to form a mat.
Pests: Roots can be attacked by ROOT APHIDS and WEEVIL GRUBS.
Diseases: RUST, appearing as reddish-brown, spore-bearing pustules, can sometimes infect plants.

SCHIZOPHRAGMA
Hydrangeaceae
A genus of hardy, deciduous climbers, which are closely related to the hydrangea. Both the species described here are self-clinging and can be grown up walls, pergolas or trees without the need to provide extra support.

S. hydrangeoides (Japanese hydrangea vine)
Height: 10-12.2m (30-40ft)
A freely growing climber with large, coarsely toothed, deep green leaves with paler undersides. Large, flat flower heads of creamy-white flowers surrounded by pale yellow bracts and 25cm (10in) across, are produced in summer.
Varieties: *S. h. roseum* (pink-flushed bracts).

S. integrifolium
Height: 10m (30ft)
A less vigorous climber than *S. hydrangeoides*, it has bright green, often straight-edged leaves with grey-green undersides. Large, flattened heads, 30cm (12in) across, of tiny white flowers surrounded by large, white bracts are produced from mid-summer to autumn.
CULTIVATION
Planting time: October/November or March/April.
Soil: Rich and moisture-retentive.
Aspect: Semi-shade.
Minimum temp: −15°C (5°F).
Pruning: Remove dead flower heads and any unwanted, damaged or dead wood in autumn.
Propagation: By LAYERING stems of mature plants in late autumn for separation from the parent plant about a year later.

SEDUM
Crassulaceae
Stonecrop
A genus of plants that can survive a good deal of neglect. Although most are not ideal weed-smotherers, some species form effective carpets, which provide a useful ground cover, especially when grown in association with spring-flowering dwarf bulbs. It is important that *S. acre* and *S. angelicum* are avoided: they spread too vigorously and are invasive, rapidly outspreading their allotted space.

S. spathulifolium
Height: 5-10cm (2-4in)
Spread: 23cm (9in) or more
A low-growing, hardy evergreen, which forms a carpet of tightly packed rosettes of grey-green leaves. In early summer yellow flowers in flattened heads, 5cm (2in) across, are produced. A shallow-rooted, slow spreader, this is in no way an invasive plant, and specimens therefore need planting quite close together – about 20cm (8in) – to obtain good cover.
Varieties: 'Cape Blanco' (syn. 'Cappa Blanca', silvery-green foliage); 'Purpureum' (purple-tinted foliage).

S. spurium
Height: 12.5cm (5in)

Spread: 30cm (12in) or more
A mat-forming, hardy, semi-evergreen perennial with mid-green foliage borne on red stems. Purplish-pink flowers are produced in flattened heads, 5-7.5cm (2-3in) across, in mid-summer. Although it is a good ground-cover subject, care must be taken about its position as it is a vigorous spreader.
Varieties: *S. s. album* (white flowers); 'Green Mantle' (red-pink flowers); 'Schorbuser Blut'/'Dragon's Blood' (deep red flowers).
CULTIVATION
Planting time: October to April.
Soil: Well-drained; sedums are resistant to drought.
Aspect: Full sun.
Minimum temp: −15°C (5°F).
Pruning: Old flower stems should be left on until spring, when they can easily be removed at the base.
Propagation: By DIVISION between October and March. Even small pieces without roots will establish themselves easily.
Pests: APHIDS may feed on stems and leaves. SLUGS may eat leaves and stems, checking early growth.
Diseases: CROWN or ROOT ROT may occur if grown in too wet conditions.

SENECIO
Compositae
S. laxifolius (syn. *Brachyglotis laxifolia*)
Height: 90cm (3ft)
Spread: 1.2m (4ft)
A hardy, evergreen shrub of rounded habit, which forms a dense mound. It is a useful subject for the shrub border or for a low-growing, easily maintained, informal hedge. It has silver-grey, downy leaves, which become greener as they mature, and produces clusters of bright yellow, daisy-like flowers in late summer.
CULTIVATION
Planting time: October to April.
Soil: Well-drained.
Aspect: Prefers full sun although will tolerate light shade. In colder areas senecios should be planted in a sheltered position for, although hardy, very severe winters can damage or even kill them.
Minimum temp: −7°C (19°F).
Pruning: None necessary, although old flowering stems can be cut back to first leaf and straggly growth removed in autumn. Do not clip hedges of *S. laxifolius*.
Propagation: By 7.5-10cm (3-4in) CUTTINGS of half-ripe lateral shoots taken in autumn. Overwinter in a cold frame and pot on in spring, planting out the following autumn.

Pests: Attack by APHIDS makes foliage sticky and can check growth.

SKIMMIA   Rutaceae
S. japonica

A slow-growing, hardy, evergreen shrub of neat, compact habit. The pale green leaves are leathery, and clusters of fragrant, tiny, creamy-white flowers are borne in spring. The shrubs are unisexual, and if male and female forms are grown, the female plants produce clusters of bright red berries after flowering and these persist throughout winter.
Varieties: 'Foremanii' (syn. *S. × rogersii*, a hybrid female form with dark green leaves that bears larger clusters of flowers and berries); 'Fragrans' (a male form).
CULTIVATION
Planting time: September/October or March/April.
Soil: Well-drained.
Aspect: Full sun or partial shade; young leaves may be damaged by frosts if plants are in exposed positions.
Minimum temp: −15°C (5°F).
Pruning: None required.
Propagation: By 7.5cm (3in) HEEL CUTTINGS of half-ripe lateral growth in summer. Root and overwinter in a cold frame, planting out the following spring. Transplant to final positions 2-3 years later.
Diseases: FROST DAMAGE may cause whitening of the leaves. PHYSIOLOGICAL DISORDERS resulting from unsuitable growing conditions may show as a yellowing of the leaves and die-back of shoots.

SOLIDAGO   Compositae
Golden rod

A genus of easily grown perennials. Named varieties are more robust and better for garden cultivation than the species, which are apt to be vigorous growers and can be invasive. The varieties, although useful plants for borders, are gross feeders and can exhaust the soil of nutrients if they are not divided and replanted every few years. Smaller varieties are suitable for raised-bed cultivation.
Hybrid cultivars
Height: 0.3-2.1m (1-7ft) depending on variety.
Planting distance: 30-38cm (12-15in) for varieties up to 75cm (2ft 6in) tall; 60cm (2ft) for taller varieties.
All these hardy, herbaceous perennials produce small yellow flowers closely packed together in either terminal plumes or horizontal sprays in late summer and early autumn. All

but the tallest varieties need no staking.
Tall varieties: 'Golden Wings' (ht: 1.5m (5ft)); 'Mimosa' (ht: 1.2-1.5m (4-5ft)); 'Peter Pan' (90cm (3ft)), erect habit). **Shorter varieties:** 'Cloth of Gold' (ht: 30cm (12in)); 'Goldenmosa' (ht: 75-90cm (2ft 6in-3ft)); 'Golden Thumb' (syn 'Queenie', ht: 30cm (12in), a rounded, bushy plant); 'Lemore' (60cm (2ft)).
CULTIVATION
Planting time: October to March.
Soil: Any.
Aspect: Full sun to partial shade.
Minimum temp: −12°C (10°F).
Pruning: Cut down flowering stems in late autumn.
Propagation: By DIVISION of the rootball between October and March.
Pests: TORTIX CATERPILLARS spin leaves together and feed on them.
Diseases: POWDERY MILDEW causes white, powdery coating on leaves, stems and sometimes flowers.

STACHYS   Labiatae
S. byzantina (syn. *S. lanata, S. olympica*) (lamb's tongue, bunnies' ears)

Height: 30-45cm (12-18in)
Planting distance: 30cm (12in)
A slow-spreading, half-hardy, herbaceous perennial, which is useful for ground cover. It forms a dense mat of mid-green leaves, which are covered with silvery hairs. The foliage generally persists throughout winter, although some leaf-drop does occur. A little top-dressing may be necessary in spring, before new growth starts, to prevent bare patches. Spikes of purple flowers are produced in mid-summer, although these are of little visual value and tend to detract from the foliage; non-flowering forms tend to be most widely grown.
Varieties: 'Silver Carpet' (rarely produces flowers).
CULTIVATION
Planting time: September to April.
Soil: Well-drained.
Aspect: Full sun although stachys can be grown in partial shade if the soil does not get too damp in winter.
Minimum temp: −7°C (19°F).
Pruning: None required.
Propagation: By DIVISION of the rootball for immediate replanting between October and April.

SYMPHYTUM   Boraginaceae
Comfrey
S. grandiflorum (dwarf Russian comfrey)

Height: 20cm (8in)
Planting distance: 38cm (15in)
A rapidly spreading, hardy, semi-evergreen, herbaceous perennial, which is particularly useful for providing dense ground cover in deep shade, such as under trees and shrubs. It can be invasive, but, if it exceeds its bounds, it can be easily checked. The rough, hairy, mid-green foliage often persists through winter. Short-lived, drooping flowers are borne in early summer.
CULTIVATION
Planting time: October/November or March/April.
Soil: Any.
Aspect: Full sun to deep shade.
Minimum temp: −15°C (5°F).
Pruning: Flower stems can be cut back after flowering.
Propagation: By DIVISION of the roots in October or March.

SYRINGA   Oleaceae
Lilac

Most lilacs are large and difficult to dead-head and to maintain generally. However, the species described below is a more compact shrub that requires little maintenance.
S. meyeri 'Palibin' (syn. *S. palibiniana, S. velutina*)
Height and spread: 1.5m (5ft)
A deciduous, hardy, dense, compact, free-flowering shrub, which produces panicles of lavender-purple flowers in late spring.
CULTIVATION
Planting time: October/November.
Soil: Fertile.
Aspect: Full sun to partial shade.
Minimum temp: −21°C (−6°F).
Pruning: No regular pruning necessary. Flowers can be dead-headed if desired. Suckers should be removed as close as possible to the roots or the main stem.
Propagation: By 7.5-10cm (3-4in) HEEL CUTTINGS of half-ripe shoots in late summer. Root in a propagator, with bottom heat, and pot on, when rooted, overwintering in a cold frame. Plant out 1-2 years later.
Pests: CATERPILLARS of LILAC LEAF MINER may feed on leaves. SCALE INSECTS can infest stems, producing a 'whitewashed' look if infestation is severe.
Diseases: FROST DAMAGE causes death of flowers and die-back of shoots. The damaged tissues may then be prone to GREY MOULD, showing as greyish-brown fungal growths. HONEY FUNGUS can cause rapid death. LILAC BLIGHT causes blackening and withering of young

Sedum spathulifolium 'Purpureum'

Skimmia japonica

Senecio laxifolius

Stachys byzantina 'Silver Carpet'

Tellima grandiflora rubra

Symphytum grandiflorum

shoots and brown spotting of the leaves. MAGNESIUM DEFICIENCY causes leaves to become brittle and curved, folowed by yellowing and formation of brown blotches. Other PHYSIOLOGICAL DISORDERS resulting from poor soil conditions can cause discoloration of the foliage, premature leaf fall and die-back of the branches. SILVER LEAF causes leaves to become tinged with silver and branches to die back.

TELLIMA Saxifragaceae

A monotypic genus of semi-evergreen perennials.

T. grandiflora (false alum root, fringe-cups)
Height: 45-60cm (18-24in)
Planting distance: 45cm (18in)
A clump-forming plant that provides good, year-round ground cover. It can be particularly useful in shaded borders or wild gardens. The maple-like leaves are bright green in summer and deep, rich red in winter. Racemes of creamy-yellow flowers are produced in late spring.
Varieties: *T. g. rubra* (syn. 'Purpurea', bronze-purple leaves).
CULTIVATION
Planting time: September to March.
Soil: Any.
Aspect: Partial shade, although will grow successfully in full sun.
Minimum temp: −15°C (5°F).
Pruning: Remove old flower spikes after flowering.
Propagation: By DIVISION of clumps between September and March.

THYMUS Labiatae

Thyme
T. serpyllum
Height: 15cm (6in)
Spread: 30cm (12in)
This low- and slow-growing, hardy, evergreen perennial is an ideal carpet for planting in association with dwarf bulbs. It can also be used for clothing small areas at the front of borders or for interplanting in paving. It forms a dense mat of small, woolly, grey or green leaves, which are aromatic when brushed against or walked on. White, red or pink tubular flowers are produced in small spikes.
Varieties: *T. s. albus* (white flowers); *T. s. coccineus* (crimson flowers); 'Pink Chintz' (an abundance of pink flowers).
CULTIVATION
Planting time: October to March.
Soil: Well-drained.
Aspect: Full sun.
Minimum temp: −12°C (10°F).
Pruning: Flower heads should be

removed with shears after flowering to maintain dense, healthy growth.
Propagation: By DIVISION in March or August/September; replant immediately.

TIARELLA Saxifragaceae

T. cordifolia (foam flowers)
Height: 15-30cm (6-12in)
Spread: 60cm (2ft)
A dependable, hardy, evergreen perennial, which forms a dense mat of foliage. The pale green leaves become tinted red and bronze in autumn and winter. Erect, 15cm (6in) long spikes of white flowers are produced in spring and summer. Tiarellas are useful and beautiful ground-cover plants for any situation, but they are particularly useful for growing around the base of shrubs. They spread steadily by creeping, rooting stems, but they cannot be said to be invasive.
CULTIVATION
Planting time: October or March/April.
Soil: Moist soil that does not dry out.
Aspect: Cool and shady, although tiarellas will grow in full sun.
Minimum temp: −21°C (−6°F).
Pruning: None.
Propagation: By DIVISION in October or April.

TULIPA Liliiaceae

Tulip
A genus of mostly spring-flowering bulbs, which produce usually one goblet-shaped flower on a single stem. The numerous hybrid varieties vary greatly in size and colour, and their selection is largely a matter of personal taste and requirements. However, the species tulips have shorter stems, which make them less prone to being broken or damaged by wind. The species described below do not need to be lifted each year and, if left undisturbed will flower dependably for several years.
T. eichleri (syn. *T. undulatifolia*)
Height: 25-30cm (10-12in)
Planting distance: 10-15cm (4-6in)
A robust, early- to mid-spring-flowering plant with grey-green foliage. The deep red flowers, 10cm (4in) across, have pointed petals, often with yellow and black margins.
T. greigii
Height: 20-25cm (8-10in)
Planting distance: 15cm (6in)
The grey-green foliage is attractively streaked with purple-brown and bronze variegation. The blunt-petalled flowers are orange-red and appear in early spring.

Varieties: 'Oriental Beauty' (red flowers); 'Pandour' (red and yellow flowers); 'Red Riding Hood' (red flowers); 'Yellow Dawn' (red and yellow flowers).
T. praestans
Height: 30-45cm (12-18in)
Planting distance: 10-15cm (4-6in)
This species bears 2-5 pure red flowers, 5cm (2in) long, on each stem in early spring. The broad leaves are grey-green.
Varieties: 'Fusilier' (orange-red flowers); 'Van Tubergen's Variety' (red flowers).
CULTIVATION
Planting time: Late October/November; plant bulbs 15cm (6in) deep.
Soil: Well-drained and alkaline; if soil is acid add a dressing of ground limestone just before planting.
Aspect: Full sun.
Minimum temp: −12°C (10°F).
Pruning: Remove old leaves and stems as they die after flowering.
Propagation: By DIVISION by removal of offsets produced at the base of flower stems or growing out from mature bulbs. Lift bulbs and remove offset, storing them in a dry place until planting time. Select the larger offsets and plant 10-15cm (4-6in) deep. Small offsets will grow if planted 5cm (2in) deep, but they will take at least 3 years to flower.
Pests: SLUGS may feed on developing young plants, mainly below the soil's surface. APHIDS can infest new growth. STEM and BULB EELWORMS can cause the malformation of the leaves and stems and the bulb tissue to rot.
Diseases: GREY BULB ROT prevents the shoot getting above ground level by rotting the nose of the bulb, which becomes grey. The bulb then dies. Resting bodies are produced by the fungus, which can stay in the soil and infect other bulbs the following season. PHYSIOLOGICAL DISORDERS can be the result of poor growing conditions. BLINDNESS or shrivelling of the flowers before opening can be due to excessively dry soil. BLUE MOULD often occurs on damaged bulbs or on bulbs grown in poor conditions. TULIP FIRE causes scorching and spotting of the leaves and, possibly, the flowers, which decay and, in damp conditions, may show grey fungal growths; the bulbs then rot.

ULEX Leguminosae

A genus of almost leafless shrubs, which appear to be evergreen because of the green shoots and spines that are produced through the year.

U. europaeus 'Flore Pleno' (syn. *U. e.* 'Pleno') (gorse, furze)
Height and spread: 1.2-1.5m (4-5ft)
A compact, although quite large, shrub, which can grow well on the poorest of soils. It produces no suckers and does not spread (unlike the single-flowered common gorse). It has small leaves, which quickly drop, leaving the spiny, densely branched shoots. A profusion of scented, double, yellow flowers appears in spring. It can be used as an informal hedging shrub as well as in the border, but it resents root disturbance, so container-grown plants should be bought for planting in final positions.
CULTIVATION
Planting time: October to March.
Soil: Poor to ordinary garden soil.
Aspect: Full sun.
Minimum temp: −7°C (19°F).
Pruning: No regular pruning necessary for many years, but older plants tend to become leggy and should be cut back hard in spring.
Propagation: By SEED sown in pots in spring. Keep in a cold frame until summer and plunge outdoors, planting in final position in autumn.
Diseases: Severe FROST can cause die-back of shoots.

VERONICA   Scrophulariaceae
Speedwell
A large genus of perennials and sub-shrubs, some of which are evergreen or semi-evergreen.
V. spicata (spiked speedwell)
Height: 30-38cm (12-18in)
Planting distance: 20cm (8in)
A hardy, herbaceous, clump-forming perennial with oval, silvery-grey, hairy leaves, which are borne on erect stems. Spikes of small, mid-blue, star-shaped flowers, 15cm (6in) long, are produced in late summer.
Varieties: *V. s. incana* (clear blue flowers and lance-shaped leaves).
CULTIVATION
Planting time: October to April.
Soil: Rich, moist but free-draining.
Aspect: Full sun to partial shade.
Minimum temp: −12°C (10°F).
Pruning: Cut to ground level in late autumn.
Propagation: By DIVISION in spring.
Diseases: POWDERY MILDEW causes a grey coating on leaves, which may become disfigured.

VIBURNUM   Caprifoliaceae
A genus of evergreen and deciduous shrubs. Some are spring- or summer-flowering; some deciduous viburnums are winter-flowering on bare wood. Others produce decorative berries in autumn.
V. × bodnantense
Height: 2.1m (7ft)
Spread: 1.2m (4ft)
Fragrant, rose-tinted, white flowers are produced in clusters on bare wood in late winter and early spring. The dull green leaves are tinged with bronze when young. This is a particularly good, frost-resistant winter-flowering shrub.
Varieties: 'Dawn' (deep pink buds open to pale pink flowers, the most usual variety in garden cultivation).
V. davidii
Height: 60-90cm (2-3ft)
Spread: 1.2-1.5m (4-5ft)
A hardy, evergreen shrub with a neat, rounded habit, which is useful for ground cover. The foliage is dark green, and white flowers, borne in flat heads, are produced in summer. If both male and female shrubs are grown together, attractive turquoise fruits are produced after flowering on female plants.
V. farreri (syn. *V. fragrans*)
Height: 2.1-3m (7-10ft)
Spread: 2.4m (8ft)
A deciduous, winter-flowering species with a stiff, upright habit. Pendent clusters of sweetly scented, white flowers, tinged with pink, are borne on bare wood in late winter and early spring. The bright green foliage, which is tinged with bronze when young, develops in early spring.
Varieties: 'Candidissimum' (pure white flowers).
V. opulus (guelder rose)
Height and spread: 3.6m (12ft)
A summer-flowering, hardy, deciduous shrub, which thrives in wet conditions and can be grown on boggy land. It has an upright, bushy habit and bears dark green, maple-like leaves. Richly fragrant, white flowers are borne in flattened heads in early summer, and these are followed by translucent red berries.
Varieties: 'Compactum' (ht: 1.5-1.8m (5-6ft), bears a profusion of berries); 'Sterile' (snowball bush, produces large, rounded heads of initially green, then pure white, flowers); 'Xanthocarpum' (yellow fruits and mid-green leaves that turn yellow in autumn).
V. tinus (laurustinus)
Height and spread: 2.1-3m (7-10ft)
A hardy, evergreen, winter-flowering viburnum of thick, bushy habit, which never becomes leggy, always producing leaves at the base. Pink-budded, white flowers are borne in flat heads, and the leaves are mid- to dark green.
Varieties: 'Eve Price' (deep pink buds and white flowers, followed by blue fruits); 'French White' (white flowers); 'Variegatum' (green and cream leaves, needs a sheltered site).
CULTIVATION
Planting time: Evergreen species, September/October or March/April/May; deciduous species, October to March.
Soil: Rich and moist; *V. opulus* will tolerate boggy conditions.
Aspect: Full sun; winter-flowering viburnums should be planted where they will be protected from cold winds and where morning sun after night frost will not damage flowers or young growth.
Minimum temp: −12°C (10°F).
Pruning: No regular pruning required. If, after several years, shrubs become too large, they can be cut back in late spring. They will not then require further cutting back for some years.
Propagation: By LAYERING long shoots in September; separate from parent plant after about a year.
Pests: APHIDS may cause leaf curl. WHITEFLY can sometimes be found on the undersides of the leaves of *V. tinus*, causing the formation of black scales fringed with white wax.
Diseases: FROST DAMAGE can cause die-back of shoots; the dead wood is then prone to GREY MOULD attack, showing as grey cushions of spores. HONEY FUNGUS can cause the rapid death of the whole shrub. LEAF SPOT shows as pale or purple spots on leaves and is caused by one or more types of fungal infection. PHYSIOLOGICAL DISORDER causes flower buds to shrivel before opening.

VINCA   Apocynaceae
Periwinkle
V. major (greater periwinkle)
Height: 30-45cm (12-18in)
Spread: 1.2m (4ft) or more
A vigorous, hardy plant, *V. major* provides sure and easy ground cover for large areas. The leaves are mid- to dark green, and purple-blue flowers are produced in early summer, with occasionally a second flush in autumn. It spreads by sending out rooting stems over the soil's surface, and it is such a robust grower that it can suffocate neighbouring plants if it is not given sufficient space or kept in check. It is a rather coarse-looking plant that is best suited to wilder

Thymus serpyllum

Viburnum tinus

Veronica spicata

Viburnum tinus 'Variegatum'

Vinca minor 'Bowles Variety'

Weigela florida 'Foliis Purpureis'

Yucca filamentosa

Wisteria sinensis 'Alba'

parts of the garden.
Varieties: 'Variegata' (syn. *V. m. elegantissima*, a less vigorous variety, with pale green leaves variegated with white).
V. minor (lesser periwinkle)
Height: 5-10cm (2-4in)
Spread: 1.2m (4ft) or more
A finer, neater and less vigorous plant than *V. major*, *V. minor* provides easily controlled ground cover for both small and large areas. The small, dark green leaves are glossy, and purplish-blue flowers are produced from mid-spring to early summer and then intermittently until autumn.
CULTIVATION
Planting time: September to March.
Soil: Well-drained.
Aspect: Partial shade but will grow in full sun.
Minimum temp: −15°C (5°F).
Pruning: None.
Propagation: By DIVISION between September and April. As the trailing stems root at every node when in contact with the soil, 15cm (6in) STEM CUTTINGS taken in September or March/April will quickly root if inserted obliquely into the soil.
Diseases: RUST infection produces powdery, brown, spore-bearing pustules on the leaves of *V. major*. Stunted growth, accompanied by yellow mottling of the leaves and a white streaking of the flowers, is caused by CUCUMBER MOSAIC VIRUS.

WALDSTEINIA   Rosaceae
A genus of semi-evergreen perennials, which are ideal for ground cover.
W. ternata (syn. *W. trifolia*)
Height: 5-10cm (2-4in)
Planting distance: 30cm (12in)
Loose, spreading mats of glossy, strawberry-like, deep green foliage are produced, and, in spring and early summer, bright yellow flowers appear. A suitable subject for covering a bank, this accommodating plant spreads by means of short, rooting runners but is in no way rampant.
CULTIVATION
Planting time: Any time.
Soil: Any.
Aspect: Full sun to deep shade.
Minimum temp: −12°C (10°F).
Pruning: None.
Propagation: By DIVISION of established mats in autumn or early spring.

WEIGELA   Caprifoliaceae
A group of deciduous shrubs, which are grown mostly for their funnel-

shaped flowers.
W. florida
Height and spread: 1.8-2.4m (6-8ft)
A hardy, bushy shrub with light green, prominently veined, wrinkled leaves, which are borne on wide-spreading, arching branches. In late spring and early summer clusters of rose-pink flowers are produced.
CULTIVATION
Planting time: October to March.
Soil: Good and well-drained but not prone to drying out.
Aspect: Full sun to partial shade.
Minimum temp: −15°C (5°F).
Pruning: None necessary. Old stems may be cut to ground level after flowering if wished.
Propagation: By 25-30cm (10-12in) CUTTINGS in autumn of strong shoots of the current season's growth. Insert in a nursery bed and replant in final positions a year later.

WISTERIA   Leguminosae
A group of hardy, deciduous climbers, grown for their very attractive flowers. Their twining habit makes wisterias particularly suitable for growing up arches, pergolas, trees and the like, but they can also be grown against a fence or wall if additional support is provided.
W. floribunda (Japanese wisteria)
Height: 10m (30ft)
Although it is a vigorous grower, this is the best wisteria for growing up house walls. The light green leaves consist of 12-19 leaflets, and drooping, 30cm (12in) long trails of fragrant, violet-coloured flowers are produced in early summer.
W. sinensis (syn. *W. chinensis*) (Chinese wisteria)
Height: 30m (100ft)
Although this is the most popular wisteria, it can be unsuitable for house walls as its rampant growth can block gutters and invade roofs. The leaves consist of 11 dark green leaflets, and 23cm (9in) long, pendent racemes of fragrant, mauve flowers are produced in early summer.
CULTIVATION
Planting time: October to March.
Soil: Moist, rich loam; wisterias will grow in almost any soil, except very alkaline grounds.
Aspect: Any, but south- or west-facing aspects that are exposed to early morning sun should be avoided as the rapid thawing of late spring frosts can damage flower buds.
Minimum temp: −15°C (5°F).
Pruning: In early spring cut back all the previous season's growth to within 2-3 buds of the older wood. If

large specimens require further cutting back to limit their size, cut the current season's growths back to about 6 buds of the base in summer.
Propagation: LAYER stems of *W. sinensis* in late spring for separation from the parent plant after a year.
Pests: APHIDS can infest young growths. Infestation of THRIPS can damage foliage.
Diseases: BUD-DROP can be caused by too dry soil or too low night temperatures. CHLOROSIS, a yellowing or whitening of the leaf between veins, is caused by too alkaline soil conditions. HONEY FUNGUS can cause death of the whole plant. LEAF SPOT, caused by various fungi, can make foliage unsightly but seldom causes any serious defoliation.

YUCCA   Agavaceae
A genus of hardy and tender, long-lived, evergreen shrubs and small trees, which are extremely tolerant of poor, sandy soils. The stemless species have a basal rosette of long, narrow, strap-shaped leaves, which forms a large, dense mound of foliage from which a tall flower stalk emerges. Both the species described here are hardy.
Y. filamentosa (Adam's needle)
Height: 90cm (3ft)
Spread: 1.2-1.5m (4-5ft)
A basal rosette is formed of erect, stiff, mid-green leaves. Once established, after about 3 years, a 1.2-1.8m (4-6ft) tall flower stalk, bearing a plume of cup-shaped, white flowers, is produced in mid-summer.
Varieties: 'Variegata' (yellow- and cream-margined leaves).
Y. recurvifolia
Height: 0.9-1.8m (3-6ft)
Spread: 1.8-2.1m (6-7ft)
A dense rosette of narrow, arching, deep green leaves is borne on a slow-growing, woody trunk. When mature (usually when the trunk is about 90cm (3ft) tall), a 1.8m (6ft) flower stalk, bearing creamy-white, bell-shaped flowers, is produced in late summer and early autumn.
CULTIVATION
Planting time: April or October.
Soil: Free-draining.
Aspect: Full sun.
Minimum temp: −12°C (10°F).
Pruning: None necessary.
Propagation: By the removal and replanting of any rooted SUCKERS from the base of the plant in spring.
Diseases: LEAF SPOT shows as large, brown spots with grey centres.

PART 3
PESTS AND DISEASES

Although many of the plants recommended in the previous sections of this book have been selected partly for their ability to resist pests and diseases, no garden can ever be totally immune to these problems. You will, however, be an unlucky gardener if you are troubled by more than a few pests and diseases in any one season.

Controlling pests and diseases involves the use of chemicals in the garden. While most fungicides are generally harmless to man, some pesticides can be harmful to both man and animals. Wherever possible, use the less toxic pesticides, such as derris or pyrethrum, or those, like malathion, that remain active for only a short period, long enough to remove the infestation but harmless to wildlife and the possibly beneficial insects that may arrive later. It is essential, however, for safety's sake, that no matter what kind of pesticide or fungicide is used, the manufacturer's instructions are followed exactly. When using a spray, also wear protective clothing and a face shield.

Foliage pests and diseases must be controlled by spraying. Using conventional pump-action or pressure-type sprayers can be arduous and slow, as they require the mixing and transportation of large quantities of liquids. This may discourage reluctant gardeners from spraying at the first sign of attack, when often the pest or disease is most easily controlled, with the result that the spraying is left until the problem becomes acute, resulting in unnecessary damage to plants. A controlled droplet application (CDA) sprayer, however, is light and easy to use, and is far more efficient as it uses less liquid than other types of sprayer. CDA sprayers are powered by batteries and emit a very fine mist. They can usually be obtained from professional horticultural equipment suppliers, as can the special formulations of chemicals to use in them.

The best time to spray insecticides is in the early morning or late afternoon when other, possibly beneficial insects such as bees, are least active. Choose a calm, dull day. Never spray in strong sunshine, which may scorch leaves, and always stand with your back towards any wind.

PESTS

Adelgids These sap-sucking insects can infest conifers. They weaken the leaves and stems and produce a sticky honeydew, which can become a medium for mould growth. Infestation can occasionally produce galls or malformations on young growths. Colonies produce white, waxy, wool-like coverings, which can make chemical control difficult. Protect young trees by spraying with gamma-HCH or malathion in early spring.

Aphids A group of common sap-sucking pests, which includes black-fly, greenfly and blight. Infestation can produce galls on leaves and shoots, distort young growth and deposit a coating of sticky honeydew. Aphids can also transmit virus diseases. Infestation can be controlled by spraying with malathion, pirimicarb or nicotine, but systemic insecticides, such as dimethoate or formothion, are best used against aphids in protected positions, such as under curled leaves or waxy coverings. Eggs laid by overwintering aphids can be destroyed by spraying with tar oil or DNOC-petroleum.

Blackfly See Aphids.

Bryobia mites These microscopic pests can be particularly troublesome on apples, gooseberries and ivy. Infestation is indicated by a light freckling on the upper surfaces of leaves, which later turn bronze and shrivel. Overwintering eggs can be destroyed by spraying with DNOC-petroleum in winter. Spraying with dimethoate, formothion or malathion during the growing season will effectively control the mites.

Capsid bugs Capsid bugs suck the sap of young growths and inject a toxic saliva, which kills the plant tissue. Infestation causes death of growing points and buds and damage to leaves, which become ragged and distorted, and makes fruits and flowers mis-shapen and discoloured. Capsid bugs can move rapidly from plant to plant and have usually left a plant before the symptoms have become apparent. Damage prevention is difficult, but spraying deciduous hosts with DNOC-petroleum in winter can kill overwintering eggs. Summer infestations can be reduced by spraying with fenitrothion or gamma-HCH.

Carnation fly Maggots of the carnation fly cause the wilting and death of infected shoots by tunnelling into the leaves and stems. Once infestation has occurred, control is difficult, but dusting or spraying with gamma-HCH can have some effect.

Caterpillars Some species live in the soil and feed on the roots; others tunnel into stems, branches or fruit; most, however, affect only leaves. Control caterpillars feeding on exposed leaves and shoots by spraying with contact insecticides.

Cutworms These are the caterpillars of various kinds of moth, which live in the top-soil. They can attack the leaves and stems of various herbaceous plants, often eating and severing the stems at soil level. Treat the soil with gamma-HCH or bromophos. Diazinon or chlopyrifos granules will also provide some control.

Earwigs Earwigs feed by night, making ragged holes in young foliage and flower petals. Control at the first sign of damage by dusting or spraying infested plants and the soil beneath with gamma-HCH or trichlorphon. Non-chemical control can be effected by trapping earwigs in inverted flowerpots filled with straw on canes. Pick out the earwigs daily.

Froghoppers These produce masses of froth, commonly known as cuckoo spit, on the stems and leaves of some plants. They feed on sap and distort new growth. Control by spraying with malathion, gamma-HCH or nicotine.

Gall mites Gall mites feed in or on plant tissues, and infestation stimulates the production of galls on leaves and buds. Control is difficult for most of the year as they are protected from contact with chemicals, although infestations can be checked by spraying with benomyl in spring.

Greenfly See Aphids.

Holly leaf miners These tunnel into the leaves of *Ilex* (holly) causing ugly, white blotches. Although established trees suffer little, infestation can cause leaf fall and check the growth of young trees. Where necessary, control by spraying with gamma-HCH in early summer.

Leaf miner A variety of larvae of various species of moths and flies, each of which attacks a different host. They tunnel into leaves, causing a variety of symptoms, ranging from simple blotches on the leaves to long, sinuous, light-coloured tunnels. In most cases infestation does not cause extensive damage to the plant, and chemical control is generally unnecessary. However, if the infestation is particularly severe or persistent, spray with gamma-HCH or diazinon.

Leatherjackets The grubs of craneflies or harvestmen (daddy-long-legs) live in the soil and feed on the roots of plants. They are particularly troublesome in lawns, where they can cause brown patches in summer, and in newly cultivated land, where they can cause wilting and even the death of some plants. Control by watering with a solution of gamma-HCH during warm, damp weather in spring or autumn.

Lilac leaf miner These burrow into the leaves, producing disfiguring blotches from early summer onwards. Control small infestations by picking off and burning affected leaves; otherwise, spray with gamma-HCH or pirimiphos-methyl.

Narcissus fly maggots By tunnelling into bulbs, narcissus fly maggots cause death or failure to flower. Infestation can be confirmed by examining the bulbs, which will be soft and contain a short, fat maggot. There is no effective chemical control available, and infested bulbs should be destroyed.

Pine shoot moth caterpillars See Caterpillars.

Rhododendron bugs These pierce the undersides of rhododendron leaves and feed on the sap. If infestation is severe, fine mottling on the upper surfaces and a rusty-brown spotting on the undersides of the leaf occur. Mild infestations may be checked by cutting out and burning all infested branches in late spring. Control severe outbreaks by spraying with gamma-HCH or fenitrothion in late spring or early summer.

Rhododendron leafhopper A serious pest and one that is difficult to eradicate, rhododendron leafhoppers cause lesions in the buds of the plant, which may become infected with rhododendron bud-blast (q.v.). Young leafhoppers can be seen on the leaves of infested plants from late spring onwards. Reduce infestation by spraying two or three times in late summer and early autumn with gamma-HCH or fenitrothion.

Root aphids These aphids live in the soil and feed on roots, thereby checking growth. Affected plants often turn yellow and wilt. Control by drenching infested root systems with a solution of diazinon.

Root mealy bugs See Root aphids.

Sawfly larvae These caterpillars hatch from eggs laid in the plant tissues and, usually, feed on leaves. They are easily controlled by spraying with malathion or derris. However, some kinds of sawfly larvae remain inside galls or plant tissues and cannot be controlled by insecticide.

Scale insects Scale insects are often associated with houseplants or plants grown under glass. However, some species can infest trees and shrubs grown outdoors. Infestation causes the leaves to become coated with a sticky, sooty deposit, and the waxy, brown, yellow or white, scale-like insects themselves may be visible on close examination of the stems and leaves. Control by spraying with malathion or diazinon in summer, with tar oil in winter or with DNOC-petroleum during dormancy in winter or early spring.

Slugs Slug attack can cause a great deal of damage to leaves, stems, buds and flowers above ground as well as to roots, tubers, bulbs and corms below ground. Control by scattering slug baits containing methiocarb around plants, especially on warm, humid nights when slugs are most active.

Snails Snails cause similar damage to slugs but are generally less of a problem; they can be controlled with slug bait.

Stem and bulb eelworm These microscopic pests rot and distort plant tissues, causing the collapse of the whole plant. Eelworms can persist in any infested, rotting tissues in the soil for some time. Good garden hygiene, the purchase of healthy plants and the rotation of susceptible plants are the best means of preventing infestation, as there are no effective preventative chemical control methods. Infested plants should be dug up and burnt, and the site should not be replanted with susceptible hosts for at least 2-3 years.

Suckers Suckers are aphid-like pests that feed on sap and cause the distortion of young growth and deposit a sticky coating on stems, leaves and blossoms. Control by spraying with dimethoate, formothion or malathion in late spring or with tar oil or DNOC-petroleum in winter.

Swift moth caterpillars These 5cm (2in) long, white caterpillars with brown heads live in the soil and feed on the roots of many plants. They can frequently be seen when the soil is dug over. Frequent cultivation and good weed control can discourage these pests, but if plants are repeatedly attacked, work gamma-HCH dust into the soil.

Tarsonomid mites Distortion, scarring and discoloration of young plant tissue may be caused by tarsonomid mites. There are no effective chemical control measures that will completely eradicate the pests, but infestations can be limited by the application of sulphur dust or lime-sulphur sprays.

Thrips Tiny, yellow or black insects suck sap from plant tissues and cause a silvery-white mottling of affected leaves and petals. Heavy infestation can prevent normal flowering and leaf development. Thrips are easily controlled by spraying with malathion, dimethoate or BHC.

Tortrix caterpillars These caterpillars spin silken webs, which draw together the leaves, stems, fruits or flowers into a protective cover under which the caterpillars feed. Control is difficult, but a high-pressure spray of pirimiphos-methyl may help.

Weevils Both the adults and the larvae can feed on all plant tissues both below and above the ground, although the damage caused is seldom serious. Infestations can be limited by good garden hygiene alone, but the application of gamma-HCH as a dust or spray to the foliage or soil gives excellent control.

Whitefly The adults of these pests resemble tiny, white moths, but both the adults and the scale-like larvae suck sap and cause similar damage to aphids, excreting honeydew and making the plant sticky. Control by spraying with pyrethrum, BHC, bioresmethrin or pirimiphos-methyl when whiteflies are seen.

DISEASES

Azalea gall Symptoms usually appear quite some time after the initial infection. The flowers and leaves are replaced by fleshy red or pale green galls, which later become coated with a powdery, white coating of spores. Cut off and burn galls before they turn white and spray with a suitable copper-based fungicide such as Bordeaux mixture or zineb before new leaves unfurl.

Bacterial canker A canker producing disease that mainly affects plants of the *Prunus* (cherry) genus. It can be controlled by thoroughly spraying foliage from late summer to early autumn with Bordeaux mixture. As shoots are infected only in autumn and winter, infection can be prevented by pruning in summer and painting wounds with a proprietary canker paint.

Black root rot A fungal disease that causes the rotting of root and crown tissues of some plants. Infection is seen as a blackening of rotting tissues. Rotating plants can prevent the disease, and watering infected plants with a solution of captan at 3-week intervals will give limited control.

Black spot A disease of roses, black spot causes black or dark brown spotting on leaves, which eventually turn yellow and drop. In severe cases, the whole bush may become defoliated. First symptoms can appear in late spring on lightly pruned roses and as late as midsummer on roses that have been heavily pruned. Whenever possible, avoid infection by growing only the more disease-resistant varieties. To control or prevent infection spray at 2-week intervals with captan, dichlofluanid, thiophanate-methyl, triforine or maneb. As the disease overwinters on fallen leaves, these should be gathered from infected roses and burnt.

Blindness This is the failure to flower of bulbous plants such as narcissi and tulips. Container-grown specimens are particularly prone to the condition, which can be caused by excessive dryness, water-logging or excessively high temperatures.

Botrytis See Grey mould, Peony wilt or Tulip fire.

Bracket fungus Bracket fungus forms large, flattened fruiting bodies, up to 30cm (12in) across, on dead or damaged wood. The infection can spread to the living tissue causing die-back. Small diseased branches should be removed, but if the main trunk is infected, cut out the brackets and all rotting wood and apply protective paint to wounds.

Bud drop Usually caused by unsuitable cultural conditions, most often too dry soil, bud drop can be avoided by applying a mulch and by watering thoroughly during dry periods.

Canker Canker shows as swollen areas of bark or a new callousforming tissue on a wound. It can also be caused by bacterial or fungal infection.

Chlorosis Often caused by virus diseases, mineral deficiencies or growing acid-loving plants on too alkaline soil, chlorosis resulting from virus infection cannot be cured, and severely infected plants should be destroyed. Mineral deficiencies can be remedied by adding a suitable fertilizer containing trace elements. Excess alkalinity of the soil can be corrected by digging in peat or by applying acid fertilizers or sequestrene or aluminium sulphate annually.

Clematis wilt This fungus diseases causes a sudden wilting of the upper parts of the shoot. Wilted shoots never recover and should be cut back to healthy tissue. Coat wounds with a protective paint and spray new shoots with Bordeaux mixture the following spring. Infected plants are rarely killed, and new growth will often break from the base.

Cluster cup rust The formation of cup-like, spore-bearing pustules on stems and leaves is caused by rust fungus; for control, see Rust. Gooseberry cluster cup rust is caused by a different fungus. Control by removing and destroying all infected leaves and shoots and prevent re-infection by an annual spray with copper fungicide such as Bordeaux mixture before flowering.

Coral spot The fungus initially lives on dead wood, but it can eventually spread to living tissue and cause the death of branches or even the whole tree. The disease can be prevented by cutting out and burning all dead wood and painting wounds with a protective paint. Infected shoots should be pruned back to 10–15cm (4–6in) of the diseased area.

Crown rot The symptoms and control measures are as for root rot (q.v.).

Cucumber mosaic virus This is a troublesome viral disease that can be rapidly transmitted from plant to plant by aphids, pruning tools or handling diseased plants. Infected plants should be destroyed at the first sign of symptoms. Inhibit the spread of the disease by controlling aphids with a suitable spray.

Damping off Young seedlings collapse and die if they suffer from damping off. Attack is more likely if seedlings are overcrowded, kept too wet, grown on compacted soil or grown in excessively high temperatures. Water seed trays or pots with Cheshunt compound, captan or zineb.

Die-back Young shoots of trees and shrubs gradually die back along the shoot and, if this is not checked, it can cause the death of the larger branches. Although die-back can be caused by parasitic fungi, it is most often the result of physiological disorders (q.v.) caused by poor growing conditions. Cut back all infected shoots to healthy tissue and coat wounds with protective paint. If die-back is the result of fungal infection, apply a suitable fungicidal spray or improve growing conditions.

Downy mildew White tufts or downy patches, generally on the underside of leaves, appear on infected plants. The disease can be prevented by good cultural conditions. Spray infected plants with zineb.

Fireblight This bacterial disease infects trees and shrubs of the Rosaceae family, particularly of the *Rosa* (rose), *Crataegus* (hawthorn) and *Cotoneaster* genera. It is a notifiable disease in the UK and, if suspected, must be reported to the Ministry of Agriculture. Treatment consists of cutting out all diseased wood 0.6–1.2m (2–4ft) below the infected tissue.

Frost damage Damage by frost can kill young growth, produce cracks in tree trunks, distort leaves or blacken flowers and buds. Damaged growth should be cut out after the danger of frost has passed to prevent the entry of disease-causing fungi by means of dead or damaged tissue.

Gladiolus dry rot This is a disease that can cause corms to rot and spread to adjacent plants, possibly contaminating the soil. Destroy all diseased corms. Healthy corms of nearby plants should be lifted and dusted with quintozene or submerged in a solution of captan for 30 minutes. Apply quintozene to the soil and work well in before replanting.

Gladiolus scab This bacterial disease can overwinter in the soil. Dig up all diseased plants and burn them. Healthy corms should be treated as for gladiolus dry rot and replanted in a new site.

Grey bulb rot Grey bulb rot is a fungal disease that can rot plant tissue and contaminate the soil. Dig out and destroy all diseased plants and some of the surrounding soil. Work quintozene into the soil and replant susceptible bulbs in a different part of the garden.

Grey mould This fungal disease can enter through wounds or through dead or decaying tissue. Dust infected herbaceous plants with captan or spray with captan, thiram or zineb. Cut out all infected tissues of tree and shrubs, and coat wounds with a protective paint. Infected bulbs should be removed and destroyed. Dust the remainder of the clumps with quintozene and rake the fungicide into the soil before replanting. If soft fruit becomes infected, spray with dichlofluanid, captan or thiram as soon as the first flowers open. Repeat every 10 days until just before the fruits ripen.

Heather die-back A fungal disease that can be present in the soil and that attacks the root tissue of callunas, ericas and daboecia, heather die-back causes foliage to become grey. Dig up and burn diseased plants. Before refilling any gaps with new plants, dig out and change the soil. It may be possible to save some mildly infected plants by spraying them regularly with a foliar feed.

Honey fungus This highly damaging, soil-borne fungal disease produces honey-coloured toadstools. It spreads through the soil by black, root-like structures or rhizomorphs, which can penetrate healthy plant roots and then spread through the rest of the plant. Remove dead or dying plants, together with as much of the root as possible. Change or

sterilize the soil with creosote or a 2 per cent solution of formalin before replanting.

Leaf rot A disease that is particularly active in winter, leaf rot commonly affects plants of the *Dianthus* genus. To control it, remove and destroy all diseased leaves and spray the plant with a fungicide such as Bordeaux mixture, repeating the treatment as necessary.

Leaf spot Leaf spot is caused by a number of fungi and bacteria. Infection tends to occur only in plants that have become starved of nutrients and that, as a result, lack vigour. Reduce the risk of infection by careful feeding of susceptible plants in the growing season. As the disease overwinters on leaf debris, pay particular attention to good garden hygiene around infected plants. Control is by the use of fungicides such as captan, maneb, zineb and Bordeaux mixture.

Magnesium deficiency See Mineral deficiencies.

Manganese deficiency See Mineral deficiencies.

Mineral deficiencies A variety of symptoms can be caused by a deficiency of one or more of the necessary elements for healthy growth. It is often difficult to determine which nutrient – or nutrients – is lacking, but the regular application of a general fertilizer to the soil or foliar feeding in summer should restore affected plants to full health.

Magnesium deficiency shows as a discoloration of the leaves, which yellow between the veins and may, later, become tinted orange, brown or red. Light acid soils are particularly prone to this deficiency, although all soils can have the magnesium leached out by heavy rain. Symptoms may also be shown by plants that have recently been fed with high-potash fertilizers, which hinder magnesium absorption by the roots. Spray deficient plants with a solution of magnesium sulphate (Epsom salts) at a rate of 225gm (8oz) to 10 litres (2½ gallons) of water, with a little soft soap added. Magnesium sulphate dust may also be added to the soil at a rate of 25gm (1oz) to 1 sq m (1 sq yard). **Manganese deficiency** is often associated with a deficiency of iron, causing chlorosis, especially of older leaves. Spray or water affected plants with a manganese sulphate solution or with chelated iron compounds if the soil is alkaline. **Potassium deficiency**, which is measured by the amount of potash in the soil, causes stunted

growth and a dulling of the leaf colour. The leaves may eventually brown at the tips or margins or develop spots or irregular patches; they may also curve downwards. Deficient plants are also more susceptible to some fungal diseases. Apply a potassic fertilizer. See also Chlorosis.

Narcissus fire This fungal disease of narcissi causes a grey mould on the leaves and, sometimes, especially in wet seasons, the flowers to rot. Destroy all infected leaves to prevent the disease overwintering. Any plants still showing signs of infection the following spring should be lifted and destroyed. Spray remaining plants when they are about 2.5cm (1in) tall with thiram and continue the treatment at 10-day intervals until the flower buds appear.

Peony wilt (peony blight) A serious fungal disease that can kill herbaceous peonies and cause dieback of shoots of tree peonies. It is particularly troublesome in wet seasons. Infection shows as a dense grey mould forming on the stem bases of herbaceous plants or on or around the flower buds of tree peonies. This can spread to form brown blotches on leaves. Remove and destroy all infected shoots of non-herbaceous types. Herbaceous peonies should be cut back to below ground level and the crowns dusted with a copper dust. Spray plants with captan, dichlofluanid, thiram or zineb as soon as leaves appear; repeat at 2-week intervals until flower buds appear.

Physiological disorders These are the result of unsuitable or poor growing conditions with respect to water supply, light intensity, temperature, mineral salts or atmosphere, and they can be corrected only by improving growing conditions. See also Mineral deficiencies.

Potassium (potash) deficiency See Mineral deficiencies.

Powdery mildew Infection by a number of closely related fungi produces a powdery, white coating on stems and on one or both sides of the leaves, usually in spring and summer. To control, remove any diseased shoots in autumn to prevent fungi overwintering. Spray infected plants in spring and summer with dinocap (infected asters should be sprayed with a copper fungicide). Plants are more likely to become infected if they are allowed to dry out in spring and summer. Prevent infection by mulching and by watering well during any dry spells.

Pyracantha scab This fungal disease causes a brown or black coating on the leaves or berries of pyracanthas. Cut out all diseased shoots and spray the plants with captan at 2-week intervals.

Rhizoctonia A fungal disease, rhizoctonia causes a variety of symptoms depending on the type of host plant and the time of infection. Established plants that are infected can develop collar, crown, foot, root and stem rot, and the foliage becomes discoloured. The disease may also cause basal rot of bulbs. Rhizoctonia is often less serious for plants grown in good cultural conditions. Cut out all rotting and dead tissues of infected herbaceous plants and dust crowns with quintozene and dig it into the soil before replanting.

Rhododendron bud-blast Transmitted from plant to plant by rhododendron leafhoppers (q.v.), rhododendron bud-blast is a fungal disease that can enter the plant through wounds. It affects the flower buds of evergreen rhododendrons, which become discoloured, turning grey or brown in late autumn. In spring black, bristle-like structures develop. Prevent the disease by controlling the vectors.

Root rot Root rot can have many symptoms, including discoloration of leaves, early leaf fall, die-back of shoots or the complete collapse of plants. Rotting may be caused either by too dry or too wet soil or by fungal diseases such as black root rot or rhizoctonia. Usually, when symptoms become apparent, the plant will be beyond saving. However, watering with captan, Cheshunt compound or zineb may occasionally be effective.

Rust This is a fungal disease that generally causes orange, brown or black spotting of the foliage. The disease is usually systemic, spreading throughout the entire plant, and it can be difficult to control. Control methods vary according to the type of plant. Remove and burn the diseased leaves of perennial plants and spray with maneb, thirum or zineb at 2-week intervals. If rust appears regularly even after treatment, the fungus is probably systemic and the plant should be destroyed. Potassium deficiency makes vegetables more susceptible to rust infection. Apply a potassic fertilizer. Further control measures are not usually required, except any infected leaves should be destroyed in autumn to prevent the fungus overwintering. Rusts tend to become a problem for trees and shrubs only if plants are malnourished or grown in too dry conditions. Prevent infection by adequate feeding, mulching or watering. Remove infected leaves of diseased shrubs and spray at 2-week intervals with maneb, thiram or zineb (triforine can be used on roses). The disease can occasionally become systemic on roses and may appear annually on stems and leaf stalks. Destroy all diseased shoots.

Scab Seen as discoloured patches on the skins of fruits and vegetables and as dark green blotches on leaves, scab is a fungal disease. Regular spraying from early spring until midsummer with benomyl, captan, thiophanate-mehyl or thiram should control the disease. Burn all infected leaves and skins.

Silver leaf This fungus, which commonly lives on dead wood, can infect living plants by entering wounds. It causes die-back of shoots and branches and sometimes the death of the whole tree or shrub. The foliage of infected plants (except rhododendrons) takes on a silvery appearance and, in severe cases, can turn brown. Infection can be confirmed by examining a cross-section of a diseased branch. Infected tissue will have a brown or purple inner stain. If disease is found, cut back the branch to 15cm (6in) below the point where the stain ceases and coat the wood with a suitable fungicidal paint. After all diseased wood has been cut out, feeding and good general care will help to save the tree.

Smut Smut is a fungal disease that produces, annually, masses of black, sooty spores, which, when released, can spread the disease to other plants. Although it does not normally kill plants, infected specimens should be destroyed to prevent the disease spreading. Spraying healthy plants with a copper fungicide will give some protection against infection.

Tar spot This fungal disease is specific to acers. It causes black blotches on the leaves, and the fungus can overwinter on fallen leaves. Control is effected by burning all diseased leaves as they fall and by spraying small trees in spring with a copper-based fungicide or captan.

Tomato spotted wilt virus This is a viral disease that affects a wide range of plants. It is seen as mottling or as a mosaic on the leaves, which may also become distorted. Any plant showing symptoms of infection should be immediately destroyed, and the thrips (q.v.) that transmit the virus should be controlled with a suitable pesticide.

Tulip fire This serious fungal disease of tulips shows as grey mould on infected tissues, with black resting bodies developing between the outer skin and the scales of the bulb. These overwinter in the soil. The disease is more common if it is particularly cold and wet in spring. Lift and destroy all diseased plants and bulbs, apply quintozene to the soil and rake it in before replanting. Healthy plants can be protected from infection by dipping new bulbs in a solution of benomyl for 15 minutes and by spraying with thiram, dichofluanid, maneb or zineb at 10-day intervals from when the plants are 2.5–5cm (1–2in) high until flowering.

Verticillium wilt This is a soil-borne fungal disease. The fungus enters through wounds on established plants or infects the roots of young plants. Diseased plants wilt and show brown discoloration of leaves and stems. Dig up and burn any diseased herbaceous plants. If only one or two branches of shrubs are affected, these should be cut back to healthy, living tissue and the wounds coated with a fungicidal paint. Further die-back may occur, but this will seldom cause the death of a tree or shrub.

Virus diseases Viruses can cause a variety of symptoms, including colour change and distortion of the leaves, stems and flowers, stunted growth and wilting and death of tissues. There is no chemical treatment for infected plants, which should, therefore, be destroyed. Control the spread of viruses by destroying the vectors, such as aphids, eelworms, leafhoppers, thrips and mites, by spraying with a suitable insecticide. Avoid handling infected plants, pay particular care to garden hygiene and use only healthy plants for propagation.

Witches' brooms An abnormal development of many shoots growing from a single shoot, witches' brooms is most often caused by a fungus, which can also produce blistering of the leaves. Cut out all infected branches to 15cm (6in) below the broom and coat the wounds with a protective paint.

PRUNING

The specific pruning requirements of individual plants are described in its entry in Part 2. Pruning is not, however, merely a method of limiting a plant's size. It can also be used to produce new, branched growth, which can enhance the plant's appearance and increase its vigour and resistance to disease. Most woody plants will benefit if pruned, but many types will remain attractive and grow quite happily for many years without any pruning.

One task that should not be neglected, however, is the removal of dead or damaged wood. This can become diseased, and the disease can spread to living tissue and possibly result in severe damage to the whole plant. Cut out all dead wood until living tissue is reached. The cut surface of living tissue appears white; if wood looks brown, cut back even further.

PRUNING CUTS

Make pruning cuts at a bud. The cut should be angled from the side opposite the base of the bud to the top of the bud. Do not leave a snag (a short length of a branch) above the bud as this will die back and may eventually become diseased. It can also produce a cluster of short, straggly growths. If whole branches are to be removed, cut them back flush with the stem from which they have arisen.

REMOVING UNWANTED WOOD

Before pruning a tree or shrub, examine it from all sides and note any imbalances of growth. Branches can be removed or shortened to produce a more pleasing shape. Keep the centre of the plant fairly open by removing any overcrowded branches. This will increase the penetration of light and air to the centre of the plant, which will discourage the production of thin, straggly growths that are more prone to disease and to damage by severe weather than sturdier, well-ripened growth. Also remove any crossing branches that rub against each other as the chafing can cause wounds through which diseases enter.

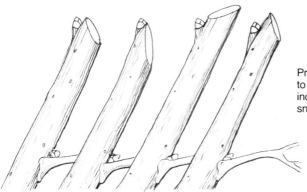

Pruning cuts, from the left: a correct cut; a cut made too close to the bud and at too acute an angle; a cut made at the incorrect angle; a cut made too far from the bud, leaving a snag, which will die back.

PROPAGATION

Home propagation is a cheap and rewarding way of increasing plant stocks. Some methods, such as division and layering, are particularly easy and need no specialist equipment whatsoever. Other methods of propagation, such as raising from seed and taking cuttings, can be more difficult and may sometimes require heated propagating cases or cold frames. However, if only a small number of plants are to be propagated in these ways, it may not be worth buying or constructing such equipment. A few plants can be raised in a simple propagator kept in a warm, light position in the house.

The specific methods by which plants may be propagated are included in the descriptions in Part 2. Generally, if there are several alternative propagation methods available for a plant, the easiest and most convenient methods are described.

DIVISION

Division is probably the simplest method of propagating crown- or clump-forming perennials and suckering shrubs. Suitable plants should be lifted during the period of dormancy and divided into separate portions, which should be immediately replanted in their new permanent positions. As well as increasing plant stocks, division also increases the vigour of overcrowded or old plants.

Small crowns may be easily divided by hand or with a small hand fork. If the crowns are large or tough, the plants may need to be levered apart by using two forks, back to back. Woody crowns – produced by such plants as lupins – and thickened underground stems – rhizomes and tubers, produced, for example, by astilbes – can be cut with a sharp knife. Make sure that each section contains some growth buds and roots. Some tuberous plants, such as dahlias, produce root tubers, which do not have growth buds. These should be cut into sections with a knife, making sure that each section contains part of the parent stem.

Bulbs and corms divide naturally and produce offset bulbs from the mature bulb. When the parent bulb is lifted, the offsets can be separated from it and replanted.

LAYERING

This is a method of vegetative propagation by which a stem or shoot of a plant is made to root into soil or compost while it is still attached to the parent plant.

Many woody, and some herbaceous, plants can be propagated in this way. Layering can be a useful means of propagation in the easy-care garden as it requires little effort. There are two methods – ground layering and air layering.

GROUND LAYERING

This system of layering consists of pulling down an outer shoot of a tree or shrub, wounding it and holding it in contact with the soil until it has rooted. Some pendulous plants layer themselves naturally when the stems touch the ground. Other plants, notably soft or hardwood shrubs, can be ground layered provided that they possess sufficiently flexible young shoots that can reach the ground without splitting or snapping.

Pull down an outer, one- or two-year-old shoot to the soil's surface and make an angled cut in the stem at the point at which it is in contact with the soil. Prevent the cut healing over by holding it open with a matchstick or twist of paper.

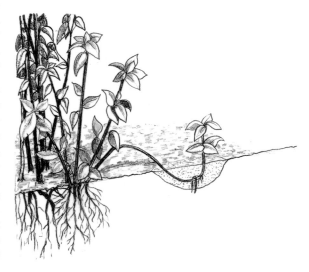

Layering involves the development of adventitious roots on a stem that is still attached to the parent plant. In spring select a shoot from the previous season's growth and make a cut or notch in the stem. Peg the shoot into nearby soil, and when the layer is well rooted, the new plant may be severed from the parent and planted out.

Apply rooting hormone to the cut to encourage quicker rooting. Hold the cut portion of the stem in contact with the soil by a wooden peg or a length of wire. Rooting should occur after 6-12 months (although some plants take longer), when the layered stem may be severed from the parent plant with secateurs and the rooted portion potted on. If the soil is particularly heavy or otherwise unsuitable for easy rooting, either apply a dressing of coarse sand and peat or sink a pot filled with suitable compost into the soil and layer the shoot directly into the pot. The entire pot can be dug up when the stem has rooted and can be detached from the parent plant.

Air Layering

If it is not possible to lower any suitable branches to ground level, air layering may be used. Select a shoot and wound it as for ground layering. In exposed siutations, where wind stress may cause a stem weakened by a cut to snap, it is better to wound the stem by removing a small sliver or circlet of bark. Make a sleeve out of a polythene bag and pack it with moistened rooting compost (a mixture, by volume, of 2 parts sphagnum moss, 1 part peat and 1 part sand). Insert the cut stem into the sleeve and fasten both ends with string. The sleeve must be airtight to prevent the compost drying out. Roots should develop in the compost after about 6

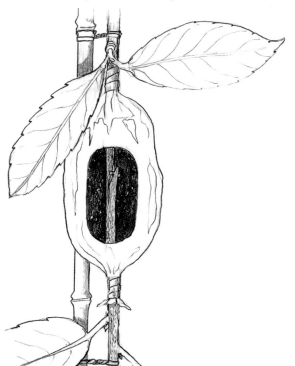

If a stem is too rigid to be ground layered, air layering may be possible. If necessary, provide extra support by tying a cane to the parent shoot above and below the sleeve so that the weakened stem does not snap in strong winds.

months, when the rooted stem can be severed from the parent plant and potted up.

Cuttings

There are many different types of cuttings, all of which have specific requirements. The type and size of cutting for individual plants is given in Part 2, but all cuttings must receive adequate light, moisture and warmth if they are to root successfully.

The rooting medium is of prime importance. Specially formulated seed and cutting compost is available from garden centres and nurseries, or, if you prefer, you can make your own. For most types of cutting a mixture of equal parts (by volume) of peat and coarse sand will be suitable. Any mixture used should be free draining yet retain sufficient moisture, allow air to permeate through it and be free of pests and diseases. Given the correct conditions, most cuttings will root readily if taken at the right time of year, but the process can be encouraged if the base of the cutting is dipped in a hormone rooting agent. These are available in powder and liquid form, but the powders have the advantage of containing fungicide to inhibit rot.

Most cuttings should be given a closed, humid environment to reduce excessive water loss from the cutting while it develops a root system. This is especially important for cuttings that still bear leaves. Cuttings taken in late spring or in summer will generally root successfully in a cold frame. However, those that need to be taken in the colder months will usually require additional heat. One of the commercially made heated propagating cases can be used for this purpose, or an unheated, portable frame placed on hot water pipes to provide some bottom heat can be equally successful. If you have not got a cold frame or propagating case, cuttings can be rooted in individual pots placed in sealed ploythene bags or in trays covered with a transparent polythene 'tent'. Place the pots or trays in a warm position either inside or outside the house according to the time of year and type of cutting. All containers should be situated in good light but out of direct sunlight, which can cause scorching.

Apart from hardwood cuttings that are planted outdoors, all cuttings will require some aftercare. When well rooted, individual cuttings should be potted up into 7.5–10cm (3–4in) pots containing a suitable compost that has a relatively low content of fertilizer. After some time, gradually expose the plants to lower temperatures and more light and air. When the roots have filled the existing pots, pot on into larger containers using a richer compost. Plant out when the cuttings are well established at the time of year recommended for the species.

HARDWOOD CUTTINGS

Although it can be rather slow, taking hardwood cuttings is a simple and reliable way of propagating some trees and shrubs. Choose healthy, well-ripened wood of the current season's growth. Take the cutting of the recommended length, trim it off immediately below a node or bud and remove any soft tip growth. Before planting, clear the soil of weeds and, if it is poor, enrich it by adding peat. The aeration and drainage of heavy soils can be improved by the addition of coarse sand. The cutting should be inserted to a depth of about half or two-thirds of its length in either a temporary bed or its permanent position if that is sheltered. Firm the cutting well in and leave it for about a year before attempting to move it.

SEMI-HARDWOOD CUTTINGS

These cuttings are of less mature wood than hardwood cuttings, and they are generally taken for the propagation of shrubs and heathers and some conifers and climbers. It may be possible to root semi-hardwood cuttings in open ground in mild and humid areas, but a cold frame usually provides a more suitable environment. Take the cuttings of partially ripened growth that is just beginning to become woody and trim them off immediately below a node. Remove the soft tip, severing the shoot above a bud. Remove the leaves from the lower half of the cutting and insert it to about one-third or half its length in a suitable compost. Keep the atmosphere around the cutting humid until it is well rooted.

SOFTWOOD CUTTINGS

Cuttings taken of soft, immature, non-woody growth can be used for many perennials and sub-shrubs. Take cuttings of firm and healthy, non-flowering growth just below a node or bud; if flowering shoots have to be used, remove the flowering tips or buds. As softwood cuttings can wilt very quickly after being taken, keep them in polythene bags to keep them fresh until they can be inserted in the growing medium. Remove a few basal leaves but keep the upper ones. Insert the cuttings to a depth of about one-third of their length in the rooting compost and keep the atmosphere around the cuttings warm and humid. When the cuttings are rooted – usually between 10 days and month later – pot up immediately using a suitable potting compost.

Root cuttings are a valuable way of increasing stocks of some herbaceous plants. This can be done most easily if the plant is lifted, but it is possible to take root cuttings from plants left in the soil. Remove the soil from near a clump of the plant so that some of the roots are exposed. Cut off a section of thick root and cut it into sections, which can be put in the open ground or in containers. Tuberous plants can be propagated by dividing the tubers, making sure that each section contains part of the parent stem. When herbaceous plants become overcrowded the crowns may be divided by placing two forks, back to back, in the clump and forcing it apart.

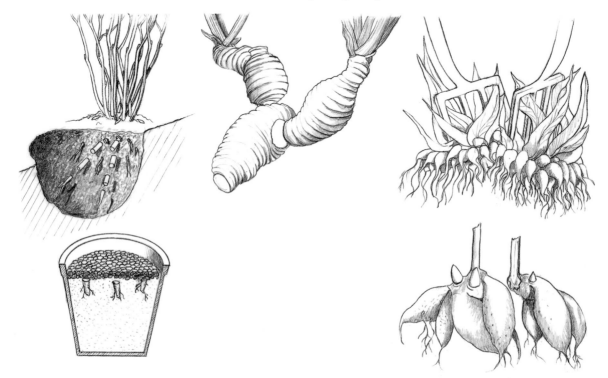

HEEL CUTTINGS

Some hardwood or semi-hardwood cuttings are easier to root if they are taken with a heel. This is a small piece of older wood from the main stem, which is left attached to the base of the cutting. Cut or pull the side-shoot from the main stem and trim off any ragged edges of the heel with a sharp knife.

BASAL CUTTINGS

Cuttings taken of non-flowering shoots at the base of the plant or just below ground level are known as basal cuttings.

ROOT CUTTINGS

Plants that have fleshy roots may be propagated, when the plants are dormant, by root cuttings. It is easier to take the cuttings if the plants are lifted, but it is possible to take root cuttings from plants left in the ground by digging a hole next to the plant to expose some roots. Cut off a section of thick root, usually about 12mm (½in) in diameter, and divide it into sections 5–15cm (2–6in) long, using a horizontal cut at the top and an angled cut at the base. Insert the cuttings in open ground or in pots or boxes containing a mixture of equal parts (by volume) of peat, coarse sand and loam, with the angled end downwards. If the roots are particularly thin – as with phlox roots, for example – lay the cuttings, which should be about 2in (5cm) long, flat on the compost. Apply a top-dressing of sand. New shoots should appear in spring.

SEED

Propagation by seed is the easiest way of raising large numbers of plants, but, unlike the vegetative methods described above, which produce plants identical to the parent, propagation by seed may produce specimens that differ widely from the parent from which the seed was taken. Commercially produced, packeted seed usually comes from true-breeding parents and the nature of the resulting plant is known. However, if you are propagating from seed collected from garden plants, you should bear in mind that some plants hybridize readily and tend not to breed true to type, and this may often result in a less attractive plant or a plant of different colour, habit or form. This process is exploited by commercial plant breeders to develop new plant strains, but for every new strain that is of value to the breeder, many hundreds may have been discarded.

Fortunately, some plants do breed true to type, and these can be successfully propagated from home-saved seed. However, it is worth noting that some types, especially slow-growing shrubs and trees can take many years to reach maturity, and while raising such plants from seed is interesting and rewarding, it is not a practicable way of stocking a garden.

Gather ripened seed-heads on a warm, dry day and place them in paper bags; seed can be prone to mould if kept for any length of time in plastic bags. Label the bags and hang them up in an airy place to dry. Generally, when stored in suitable conditions, seed will remain viable for several years, but it is better to use fresh seed whenever possible. Sowing fresh seed of known viability saves a great deal of wasted time on trying to grow old, unreliable or even dead seed.

SOWING SEED

Seeds may be grown in trays or pots of various sizes. Those made of plastic are most widely used nowadays, and they are not only easy to handle but also tend to retain moisture better than those made of clay or of wood. Rearing plants in their own individual containers, whether small pots or sectioned propagating trays, although rather wasteful of space, avoids the often fiddly task of potting on small seedlings and ensures that delicate roots will not have to be disturbed. If boxes deeper than 7.5cm (3in) or pots larger then 10cm (4in) are used, an extra layer of drainage material to a depth of 2.5cm (1in) should be added at the bottom of the containers before they are filled with compost. Crocks (broken pieces of old clay pots) are best, but, if they are not available, coarse peat or compost can be used. Fill the container to within 12mm (½in) of the rim with a suitable growing medium. Commercially produced peat-based composts often give the best results and it is possible to ensure that they are sterile and weed free; they are also light and easy to handle. The depth at which the seed is sown depends on its size. The size, type and germination time of seed varies greatly from species to species, but a general rule of thumb is that seed should be sown at a depth equal to its thickness. Scatter small seed very thinly on the compost's surface; larger seeds should be covered with compost or sand. Water the surface of the compost with a fine-mist spray of a liquid fungicide such as Cheshunt compound to prevent damping off, a fungal disease that causes seedlings to collapse. If possible, maintain a temperature of 15–18°C (59–64°F) and never allow the compost to dry out. Cover containers with a sheet of glass or of clear plastic (kept well away from the compost's surface) or moisten as often as necessary with a fine-mist sprayer. Watch for symptoms of damping off and water with a fungicide at the first signs of attack.

When seedlings are large enough to handle – usually when the first pair of leaves has fully developed – those that have not been grown in individual containers should be pricked off. Carefully lift the plantlets using a small wooden spatula. Be sure to handle them gently by the leaves only, taking care not to pinch the root or stem. Such damage to the seedling at this stage will severely check its growth. Replant seedlings in individual containers or, if trays are used, at least 2.5–5cm (1–2in) apart. Make planting holes that are large enough to accommodate the root with a blunt-pointed dibber. Insert the seedling and firm the surrounding compost carefully, using the dibber and not your fingers. Keep the pricked-off seedlings at the germination temperature for a while, then gradually expose them to more light and air before hardening them off in a cold frame or similar until they are ready to be planted out.

SOWING SEED OUTDOORS
Some hardy annual flowers and vegetables grow from seeds that can be sown directly into garden soil outdoors. The soil must, however, be fine and well-cultivated and have been enriched with a suitable fertilizer, peat, well-decayed compost or leaf-mould before sowing. Either broadcast the seeds or sow them in drills. Sow more seed than will be required. Seedlings can be thinned out later by hand, leaving only the strongest plantlets that are the recommended planting distances for the plant concerned. Germinating seed outdoors takes longer and is less reliable than using cover, and it is not suitable for perennial plants. However, annual flowers and some vegetables can be pre-germinated before planting into a prepared bed by the fluid-drilling technique. Germinate the seed on moist blotting paper in a plastic container (old food containers or sandwich boxes are ideal). Cover the container and store it in a warm, dark place (such as an airing cupboard) until a tiny embryo root has developed; this usually takes 2-4 days. The seed can then be removed from the blotting paper by washing off under a gently running tap into a fine sieve. Add the germinated seed to a bowl half-filled with already prepared, half-strength wallpaper paste (do not use paste that contains a fungicide). Fill the bowl with more wallpaper paste and stir in the seeds well. Put the mixture in a clear polythene bag with one corner cut off to make a nozzle, and the seeds can be sown into the prepared ground by squeezing the bag gently.

BIBLIOGRAPHY

Boddy, Frederick A., *Ground Cover and Other Ways to Weed Free Gardens*, David & Charles, Newton Abbot, 1974

Brickell, Christopher (editor in chief), *The Royal Horticultural Society Gardeners' Encyclopedia of Plants and Flowers*, Dorling Kindersley, London, 1989

Brookes, John, *The Small Garden*, Marshall Cavendish Books Ltd/Aura Editions, London, 1979-87

Chaplin, Mary, *Gardening for the Physically Handicapped and Elderly*, B.T. Batsford Ltd, London, 1978

Evans, Hazel, *The Patio Garden*, Windward Books, Leicester, 1985

Fretwell, Barry, *Clematis*, Collins Ltd, London, 1989

Gorer, Richard (editor), *Garden Flowers from Seed: An Illustrated Dictionary*, Webb & Bower Ltd, Exeter, 1981

Griffiths, Trevor, *The Book of Old Roses*, Mermaid Books, London, 1984

Harkness, Peter, *Modern Roses*, Century Hutchinson Ltd, London, 1987

Hay, Roy and Synge, Patrick M., *The Dictionary of Garden Plants*, Mermaid Books, London, 1986

Hessayon, D.G., *The Lawn Expert*, P.B.I. Publications, Waltham Cross, Herts, 1982

Hessayon, D.G., *The Rose Expert*, P.B.I. Publications, Waltham Cross, Herts, 1988

Loads, Fred, *Fred Loads' Gardening Tips of a Lifetime*, Hamlyn Publishing Group, Feltham, Middlesex, 1980

Massingham, Betty, *Gardening for the Handicapped*, Shire Publications Ltd, Buckingham, 1972

Mathew, Brian, *Flowering Bulbs for the Garden*, Collingridge Books Ltd, London, 1987

Mitchel, Alan, *A Field Guide to the Trees of Britain and Northern Europe*, Collins Ltd, London, 1974

Reader's Digest Encyclopedia of Garden Plants and Flowers, The Reader's Digest Association Ltd, London, 1971

Reader's Digest Illustrated Guide to Gardening, The Reader's Digest Association Ltd, London, 1975

Rose, Graham, *The Low Maintenance Garden*, Windward Books, Leicester, 1983

Saville, Diana, *The Illustrated Garden Planter*, Penguin Books Ltd, London, 1986

Stevenson, Violet, *Daily Telegraph Guide to Easier Gardens*, Collins Ltd, London, 1978

Warner, Christopher, *Climbing Roses*, Century Hutchinson Ltd, London, 1987

Wright, Michael (editor), *The Complete Book of Gardening*, Mermaid Books, 1981

INDEX

ACKNOWLEDGEMENTS

All the photographs were taken by and are copyright of Jonathon Bosley with the exception of the following: St Bridget Nursery, Old Rydon Lane, Exeter (pages 87 below right, 95 below, 99 top right, 111 below left, 127 below right, 131 below right and 143 below); Suttons Seeds Ltd, Hele Road, Torquay (pages 87 top, 99 top left, 110 below right, 114 below, 115 below, 118 centre left and 134 below); Ella Jackson (pages 2, 11, 17, 20, 24, 29 top, 42, 43, 83 top right and centre left, 91 centre right, 127 top right, 130 top left and 142 top right); Ian Wilson (pages 32, 94 below, 103 centre right, 110 centre left, below left, 114 top left and 127 below left); Steven Williams (pages 82 centre left and below left, 83 below left and below right, 91 top right, 106 top left, 110 top left, 115 top right, 126 centre left, 131 top right and 142 top left).

The author and publishers would also like to thank the staff of the County Demonstration Garden and Centre for Rural Studies, Probus, Cornwall; the staff of St Loyes College for the Disabled, Exeter, Devon; Suttons Seeds Ltd, Hele Road, Torquay, Devon; St Bridget Nursery, Old Rydon Lane, Exeter, Devon; Colin Randel for his assistance in the identification of many of the photographs; and Ralph Stobart and Malcolm Couch for preparing the line illustrations.

Also special thanks to Charles Parsons and Vic Giolitto for their invaluable help in producing the cover photograph; Mr and Mrs C. J. Langdon and Stella and David McLarin for the use of their delightful gardens and Shirley for the deckchair.

Among the many other people who have assisted with this book, special mention must be made of June Payne, Leigh Swan and Lois Trayler-Jenkins.